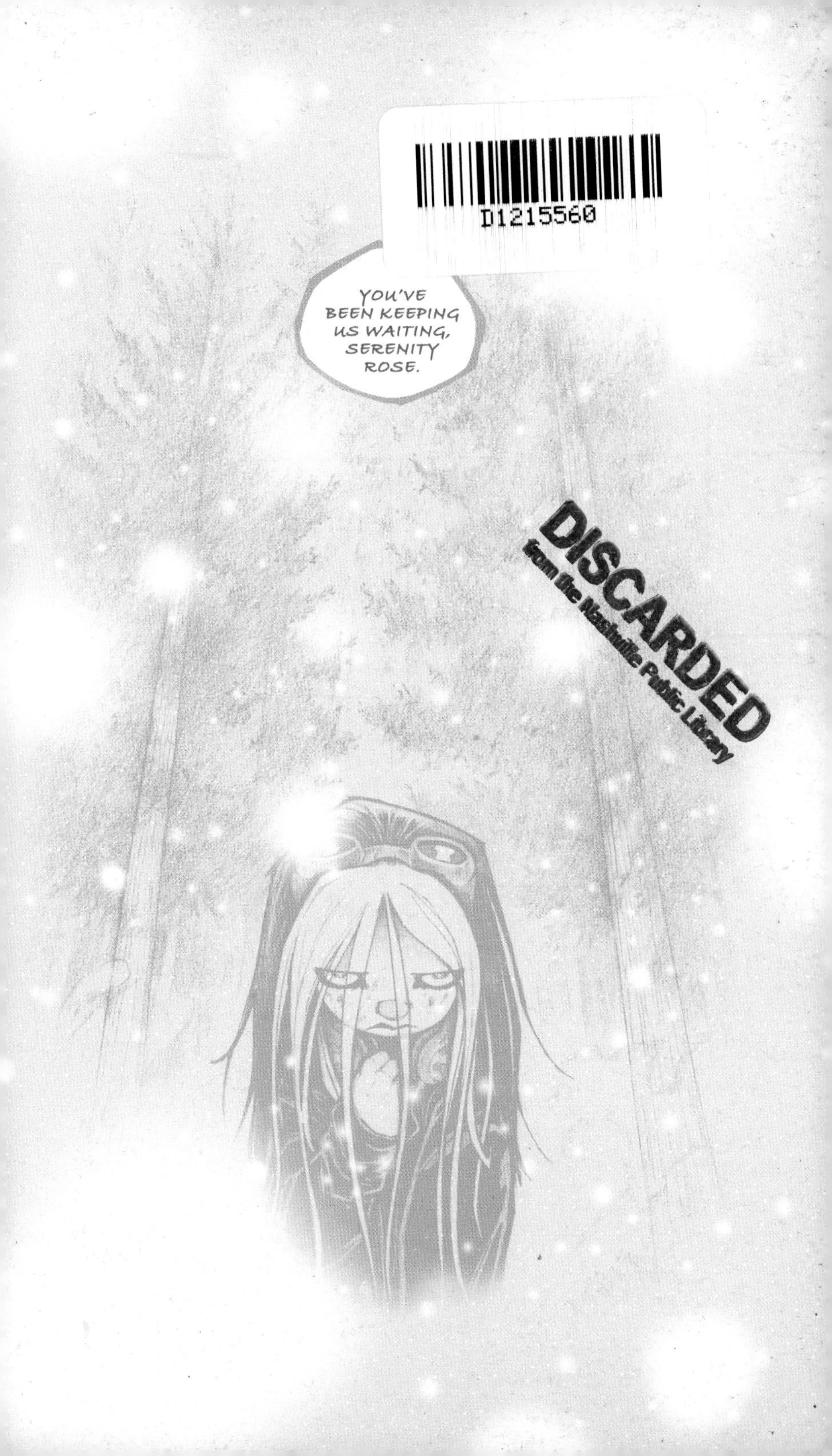
YOU'VE BEEN KEEPING US WAITING, SERENITY ROSE.

YOU KNOW I'M A PATIENT MAN.

PEOPLE LIKE US HAVE VERY LITTLE USE FOR IMPATIENCE.

...BUT, SADLY, NO AMOUNT OF PATIENCE WILL EVER STOP THE CLOCK, SO I'M AFRAID WE'RE GOING TO NEED AN ANSWER.

NOW.

SERA!

NO.

NO, I...

...THE ANSWER IS NO.

...

GOOD.

IT'S GOOD TO LISTEN TO YOUR FATHER, SERA. HE'S A FINE MAN.

BUT I WANT YOU TO REMEMBER ONE THING, SERENITY ROSE:

THIS WORLD... IS A DREAM.

AND PEOPLE LIKE US, WE ARE THE LUCID DREAMERS.

UNDERSTAND THAT, AND YOU'VE LEARNED EVERYTHING I HAVE TO TEACH.

...NOW FORGET ME.

Serenity Rose Vol. 2 "Goodbye, Crestfallen."

WRITTEN, PENCILED, AND SEMI-COLORED
BY AARON ALEXOVICH
PUBLISHED BY:
SLG PUBLISHING
PRESIDENT AND
PUBLISHER: DAN VADO
EDITOR-IN-CHIEF:
JENNIFER DE GUZMAN
SLG PUBLISHING
P. O. BOX 26427
SAN JOSE, CA 95159
FIRST PRINTING DECEMBER 2009
ISBN: 978-1-59362-181-0

SERENITY ROSE ©2009 AARON
ALEXOVICH. ALL RIGHTS RESERVED.
NO PART OF THIS PUBLICATION
MAY BE REPRODUCED WITHOUT
THE PERMISSION OF AARON
ALEXOVICH AND SLG PUBLISHING,
EXCEPT FOR PURPOSES OF REVIEW.
PRINTED IN CHINA

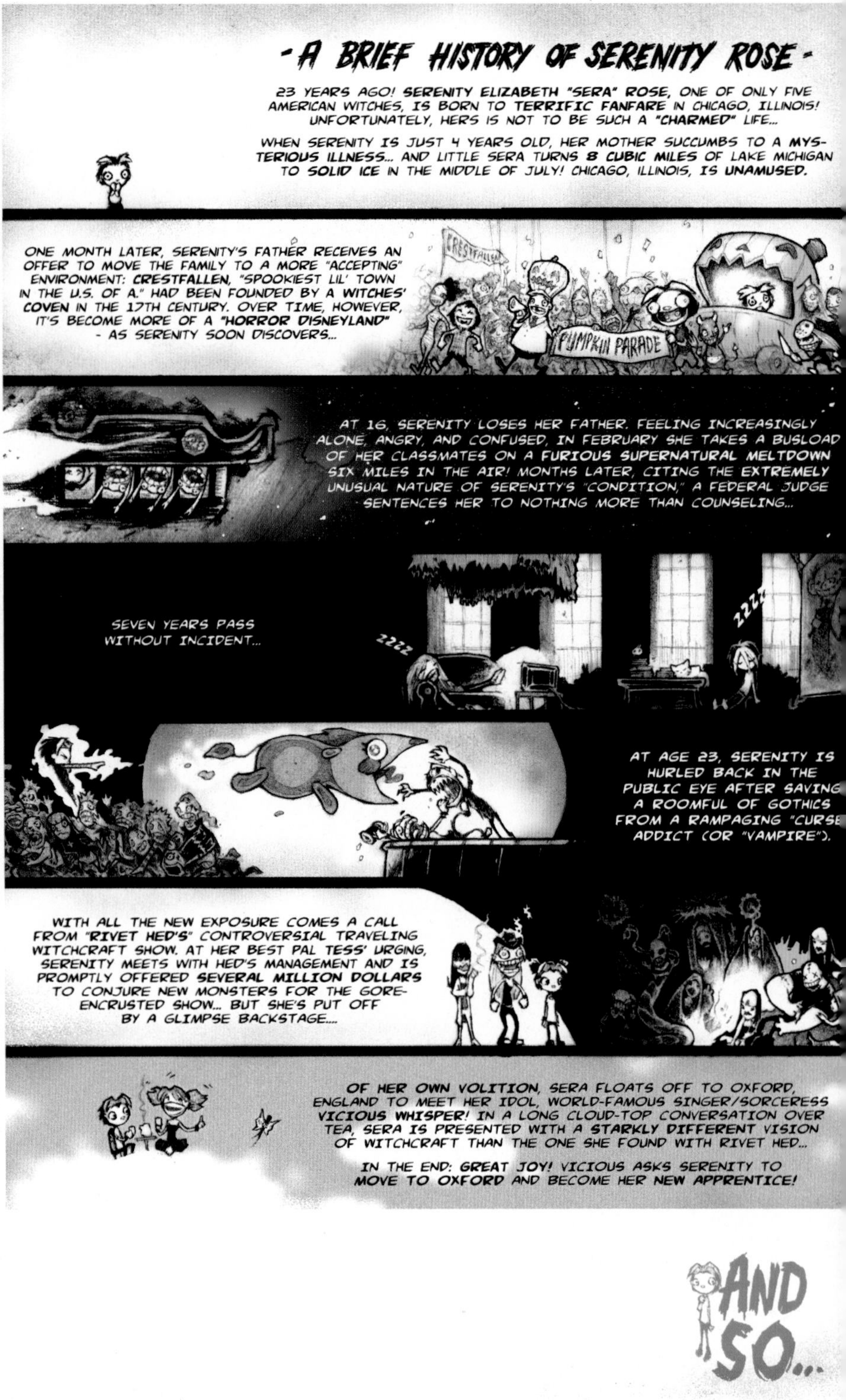
- A BRIEF HISTORY OF SERENITY ROSE -
23 YEARS AGO! SERENITY ELIZABETH "SERA" ROSE, ONE OF ONLY FIVE AMERICAN WITCHES, IS BORN TO TERRIFIC FANFARE IN CHICAGO, ILLINOIS! UNFORTUNATELY, HERS IS NOT TO BE SUCH A "CHARMED" LIFE...
WHEN SERENITY IS JUST 4 YEARS OLD, HER MOTHER SUCCUMBS TO A MYSTERIOUS ILLNESS... AND LITTLE SERA TURNS 8 CUBIC MILES OF LAKE MICHIGAN TO SOLID ICE IN THE MIDDLE OF JULY! CHICAGO, ILLINOIS, IS UNAMUSED.
ONE MONTH LATER, SERENITY'S FATHER RECEIVES AN OFFER TO MOVE THE FAMILY TO A MORE "ACCEPTING" ENVIRONMENT: CRESTFALLEN, "SPOOKIEST LIL' TOWN IN THE U.S. OF A." HAD BEEN FOUNDED BY A WITCHES' COVEN IN THE 17TH CENTURY. OVER TIME, HOWEVER, IT'S BECOME MORE OF A "HORROR DISNEYLAND" - AS SERENITY SOON DISCOVERS...
CRESTFALLEN
PUMPKIN PARADE
AT 16, SERENITY LOSES HER FATHER. FEELING INCREASINGLY ALONE, ANGRY, AND CONFUSED, IN FEBRUARY SHE TAKES A BUSLOAD OF HER CLASSMATES ON A FURIOUS SUPERNATURAL MELTDOWN SIX MILES IN THE AIR! MONTHS LATER, CITING THE EXTREMELY UNUSUAL NATURE OF SERENITY'S "CONDITION," A FEDERAL JUDGE SENTENCES HER TO NOTHING MORE THAN COUNSELING...
SEVEN YEARS PASS WITHOUT INCIDENT...
ZZZZ
ZZZZ
AT AGE 23, SERENITY IS HURLED BACK IN THE PUBLIC EYE AFTER SAVING A ROOMFUL OF GOTHICS FROM A RAMPAGING "CURSE ADDICT (OR "VAMPIRE").
WITH ALL THE NEW EXPOSURE COMES A CALL FROM "RIVET HED'S" CONTROVERSIAL TRAVELING WITCHCRAFT SHOW. AT HER BEST PAL TESS' URGING, SERENITY MEETS WITH HED'S MANAGEMENT AND IS PROMPTLY OFFERED SEVERAL MILLION DOLLARS TO CONJURE NEW MONSTERS FOR THE GORE-ENCRUSTED SHOW... BUT SHE'S PUT OFF BY A GLIMPSE BACKSTAGE....
OF HER OWN VOLITION, SERA FLOATS OFF TO OXFORD, ENGLAND TO MEET HER IDOL, WORLD-FAMOUS SINGER/SORCERESS VICIOUS WHISPER! IN A LONG CLOUD-TOP CONVERSATION OVER TEA, SERA IS PRESENTED WITH A STARKLY DIFFERENT VISION OF WITCHCRAFT THAN THE ONE SHE FOUND WITH RIVET HED...
IN THE END: GREAT JOY! VICIOUS ASKS SERENITY TO MOVE TO OXFORD AND BECOME HER NEW APPRENTICE!
AND SO...

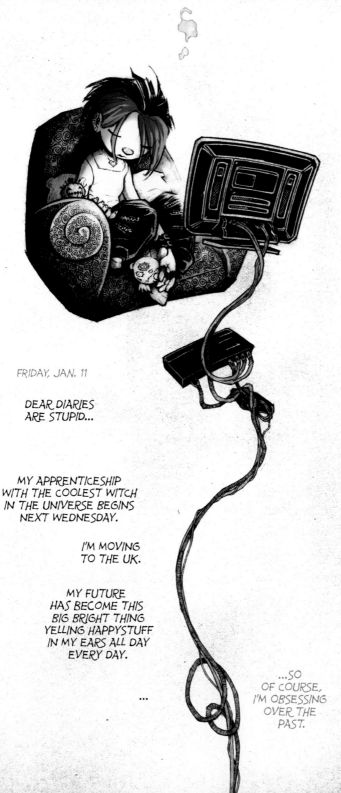

FRIDAY, JAN. 11

DEAR DIARIES
ARE STUPID...

MY APPRENTICESHIP
WITH THE COOLEST WITCH
IN THE UNIVERSE BEGINS
NEXT WEDNESDAY.

I'M MOVING
TO THE UK.

MY FUTURE
HAS BECOME THIS
BIG BRIGHT THING
YELLING HAPPYSTUFF
IN MY EARS ALL DAY
EVERY DAY.

...

...SO
OF COURSE,
I'M OBSESSING
OVER THE
PAST.

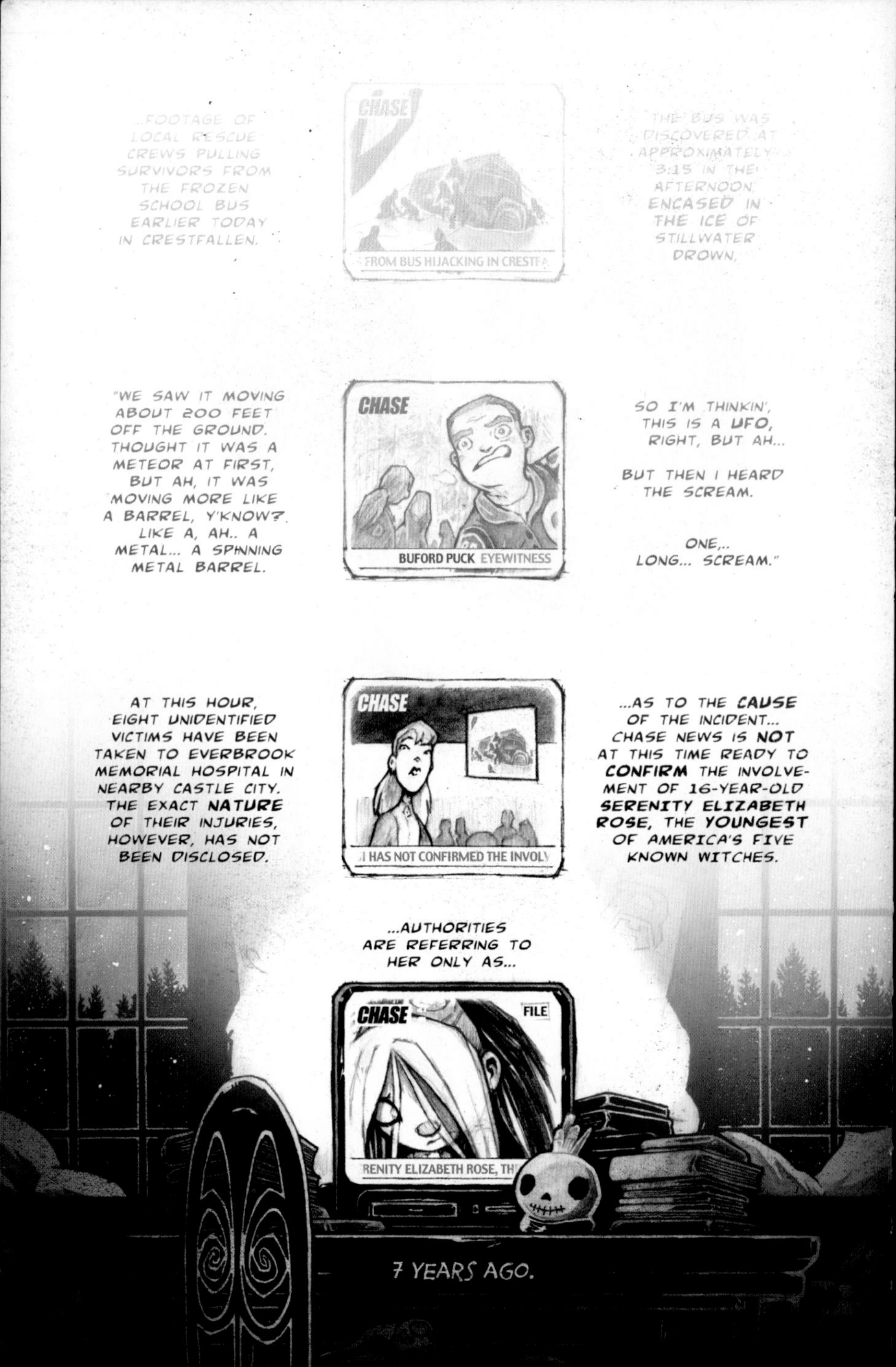
...FOOTAGE OF LOCAL RESCUE CREWS PULLING SURVIVORS FROM THE FROZEN SCHOOL BUS EARLIER TODAY IN CRESTFALLEN.
CHASE
FROM BUS HIJACKING IN CRESTFA
THE BUS WAS DISCOVERED AT APPROXIMATELY 3:15 IN THE AFTERNOON, ENCASED IN THE ICE OF STILLWATER DROWN,
"WE SAW IT MOVING ABOUT 200 FEET OFF THE GROUND. THOUGHT IT WAS A METEOR AT FIRST, BUT AH, IT WAS MOVING MORE LIKE A BARREL, Y'KNOW? LIKE A, AH.. A METAL... A SPINNING METAL BARREL.
CHASE
BUFORD PUCK EYEWITNESS
SO I'M THINKIN', THIS IS A UFO, RIGHT, BUT AH...
BUT THEN I HEARD THE SCREAM.
ONE,.. LONG... SCREAM."
AT THIS HOUR, EIGHT UNIDENTIFIED VICTIMS HAVE BEEN TAKEN TO EVERBROOK MEMORIAL HOSPITAL IN NEARBY CASTLE CITY. THE EXACT NATURE OF THEIR INJURIES, HOWEVER, HAS NOT BEEN DISCLOSED.
CHASE
I HAS NOT CONFIRMED THE INVOLV
...AS TO THE CAUSE OF THE INCIDENT... CHASE NEWS IS NOT AT THIS TIME READY TO CONFIRM THE INVOLVEMENT OF 16-YEAR-OLD SERENITY ELIZABETH ROSE, THE YOUNGEST OF AMERICA'S FIVE KNOWN WITCHES.
...AUTHORITIES ARE REFERRING TO HER ONLY AS...
CHASE
FILE
RENITY ELIZABETH ROSE, TH
7 YEARS AGO.

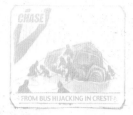

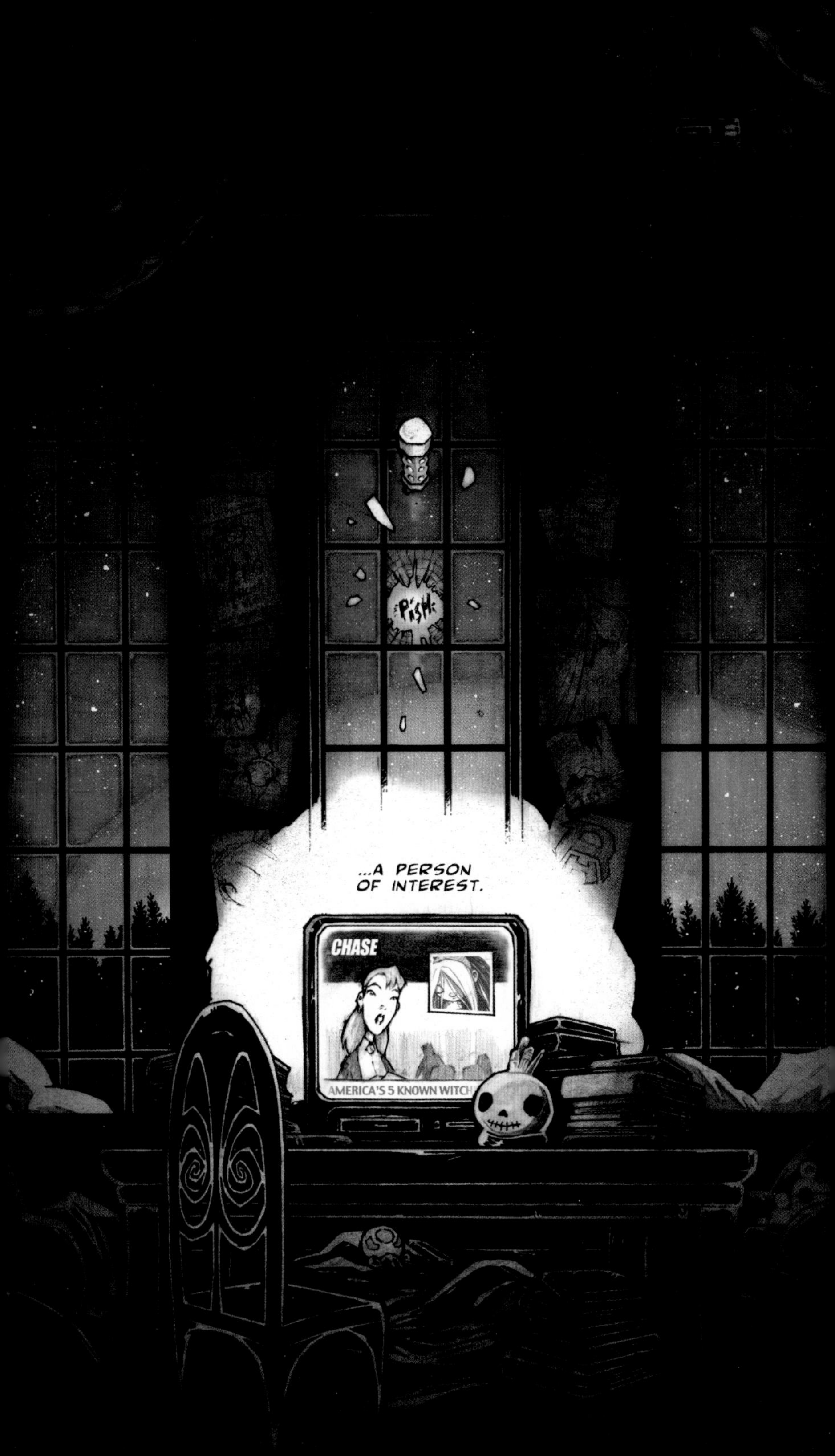

PISH!
...A PERSON OF INTEREST.
CHASE
AMERICA'S 5 KNOWN WITCH

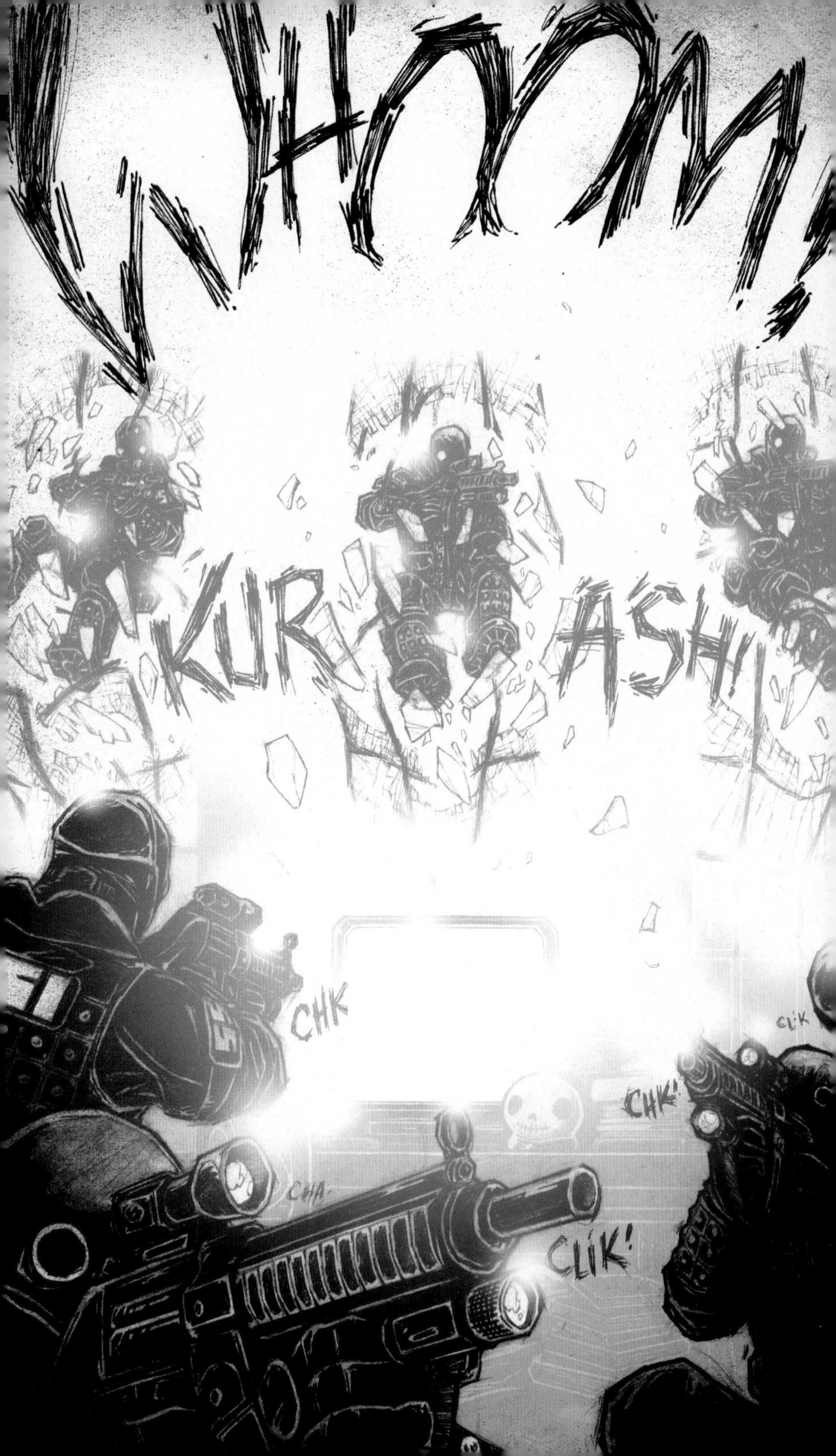
WHOOM!
KUR-ASH!
CHK
CLIK
CHK!
CHA-
CLIK!

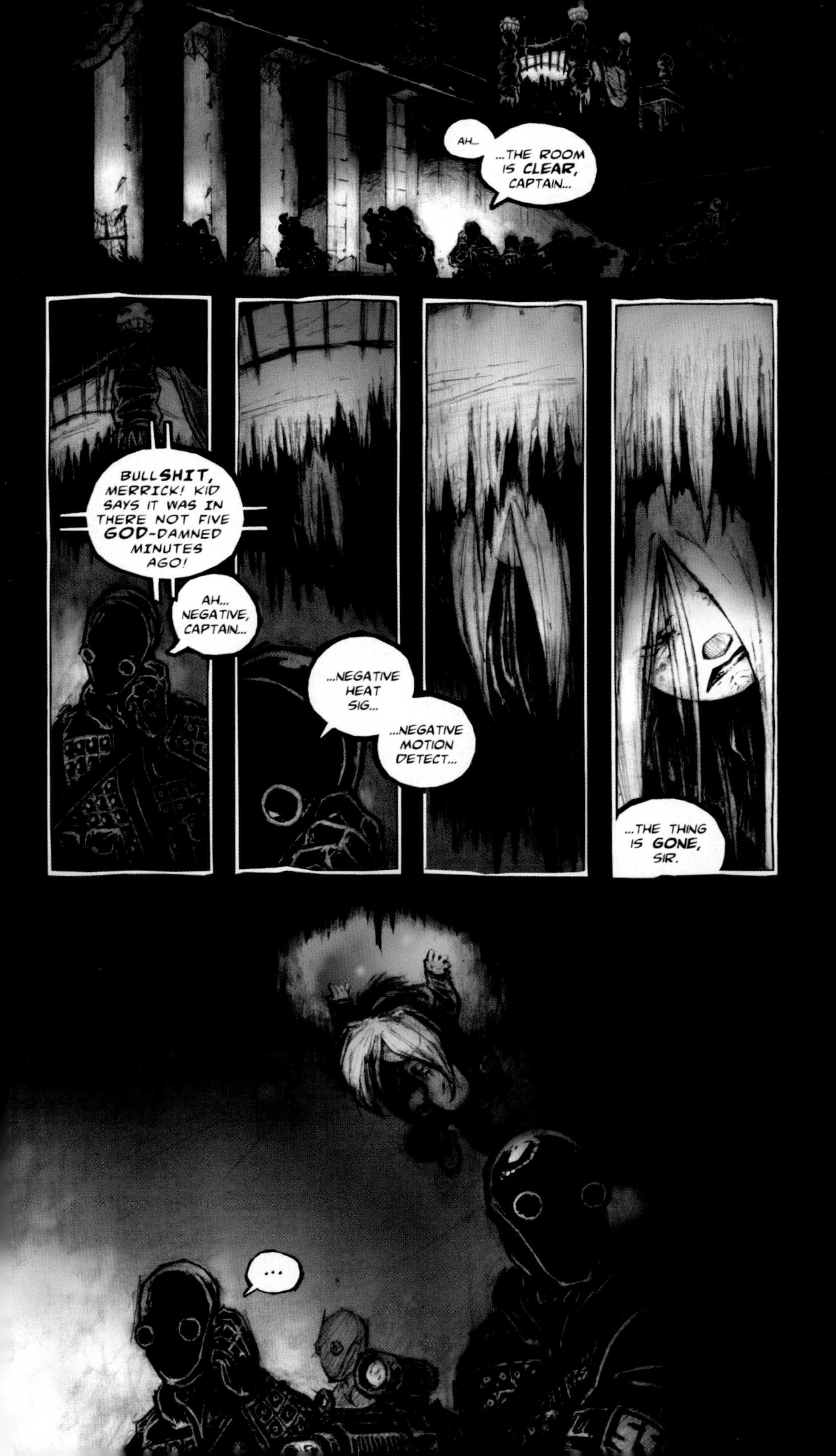
AH...
...THE ROOM IS CLEAR, CAPTAIN...
BULLSHIT, MERRICK! KID SAYS IT WAS IN THERE NOT FIVE GOD-DAMNED MINUTES AGO!
AH... NEGATIVE, CAPTAIN...
...NEGATIVE HEAT SIG...
...NEGATIVE MOTION DETECT...
...THE THING IS GONE, SIR.
...

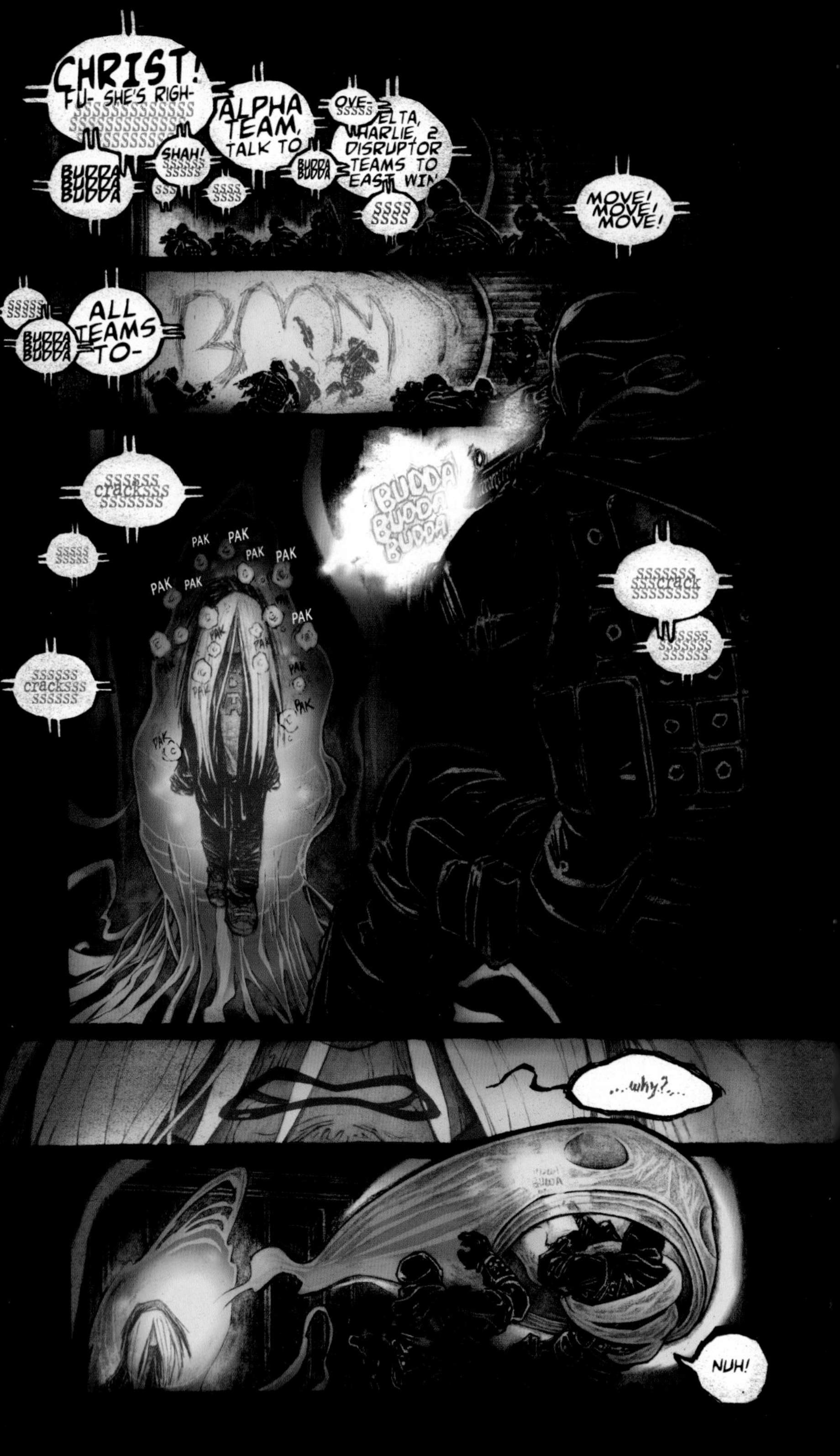
CHRIST! FU- SHE'S RIGH- SSSSSSSSSSSSS SSSSSSSSSSSSS SSSSSSSSSS
BUDDA BUDDA BUDDA
SHAH! SSSSS SSSSS
SSSS SSSS
ALPHA TEAM, TALK TO
BUDDA BUDDA
OVE- SSSSS
ELTA, HARLIE, 2 DISRUPTOR TEAMS TO EAST WIN
SSSS SSSS
MOVE! MOVE! MOVE!
SSSSS SSSSS
BUDDA BUDDA BUDDA
ALL TEAMS TO-
SSSSSS cracksss SSSSSSS
SSSSS SSSSS
BUDDA BUDDA BUDDA
PAK PAK PAK PAK PAK PAK PAK PAK PAK PAK PAK PAK
SSSSSS cracksss SSSSSS
SSSSSSS SSScrack SSSSSSSS
SSSSSS SSSSSS SSSSSS
...why?...
NUH!

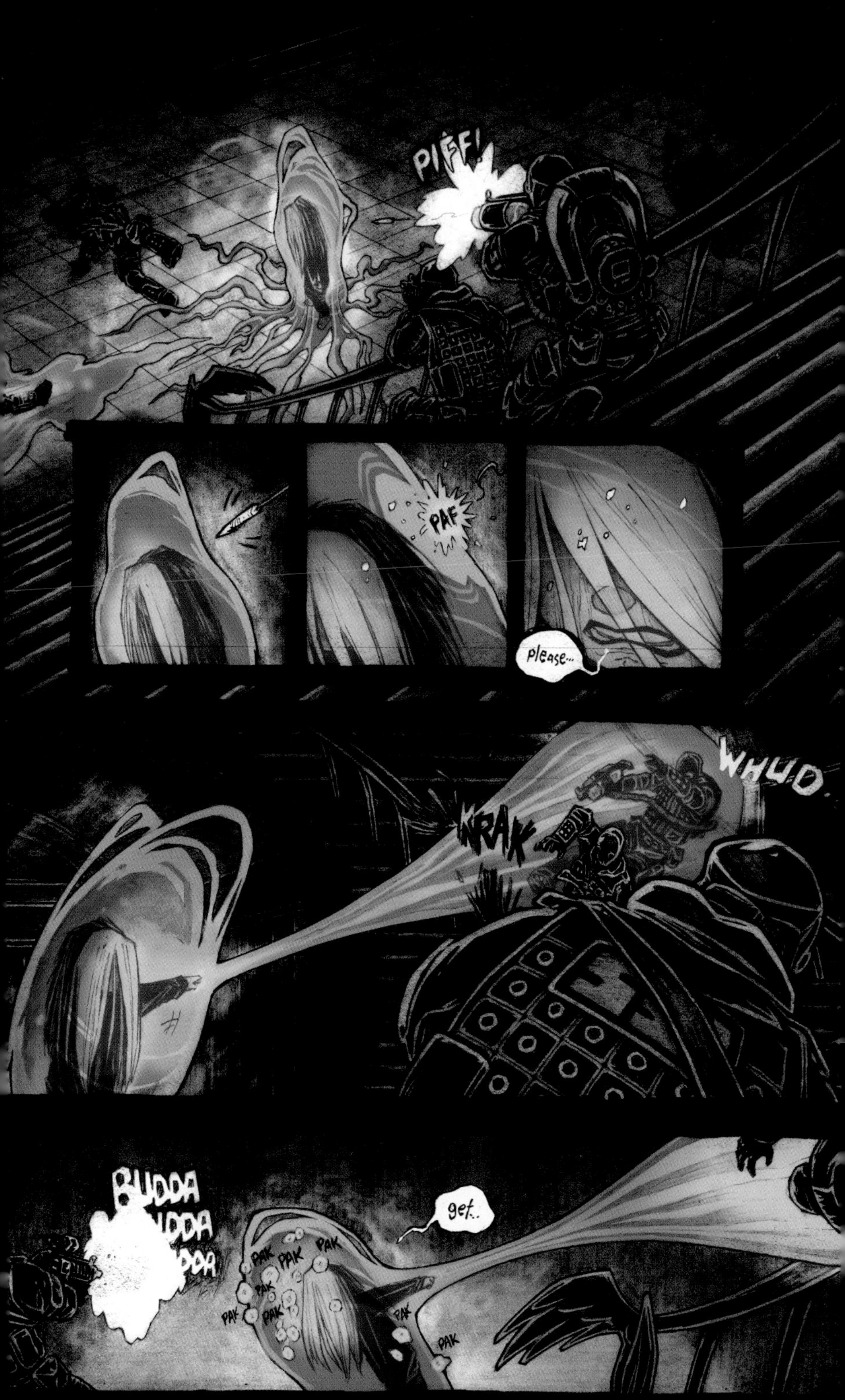
PIFF!
PAF
please...
KRAK
WHUD..
BUDDA
get..
PAK
PAK
PAK
PAK
PAK
PAK
PAK
PAK
PAK

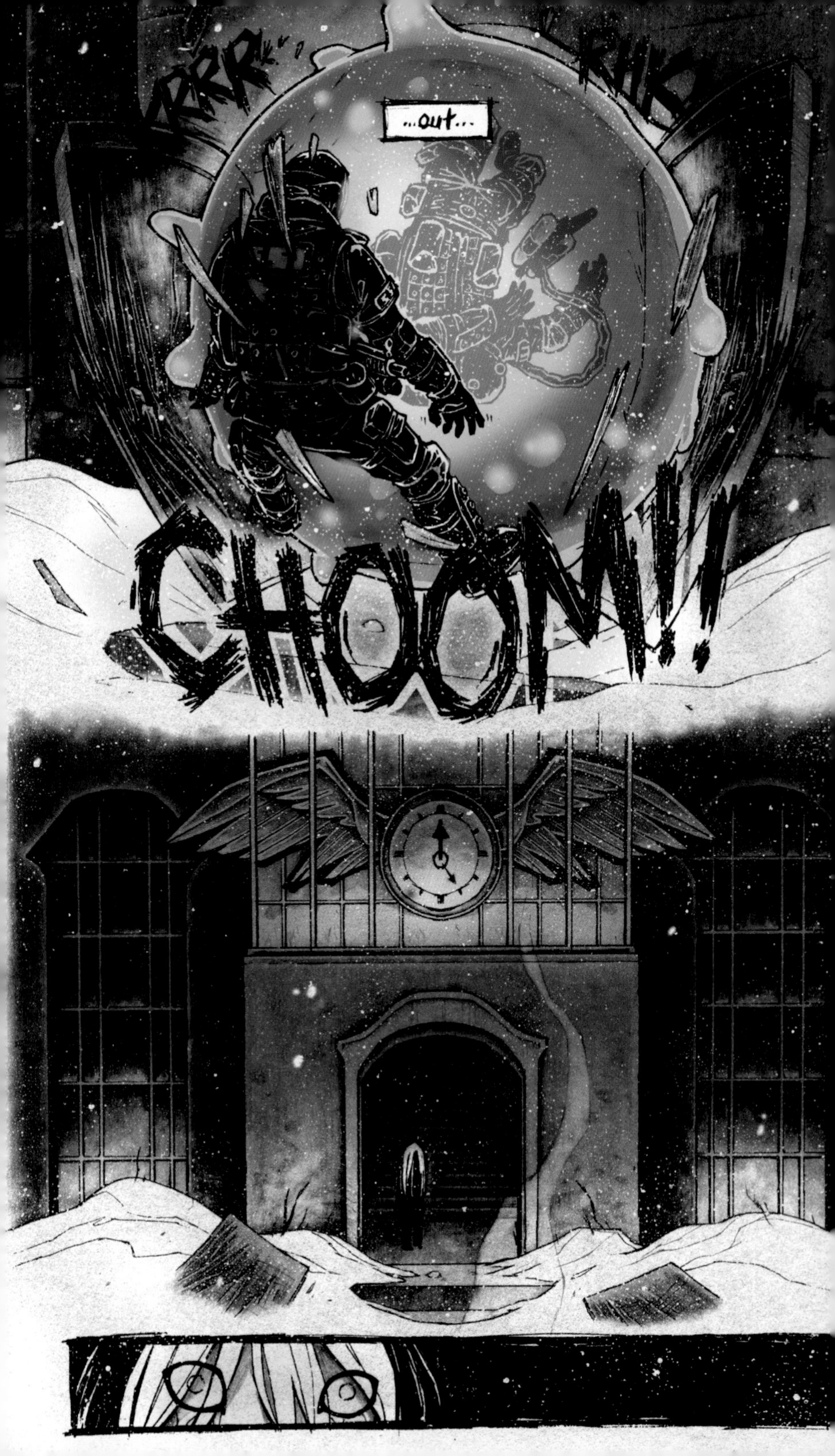

...out...
CHOOM!!

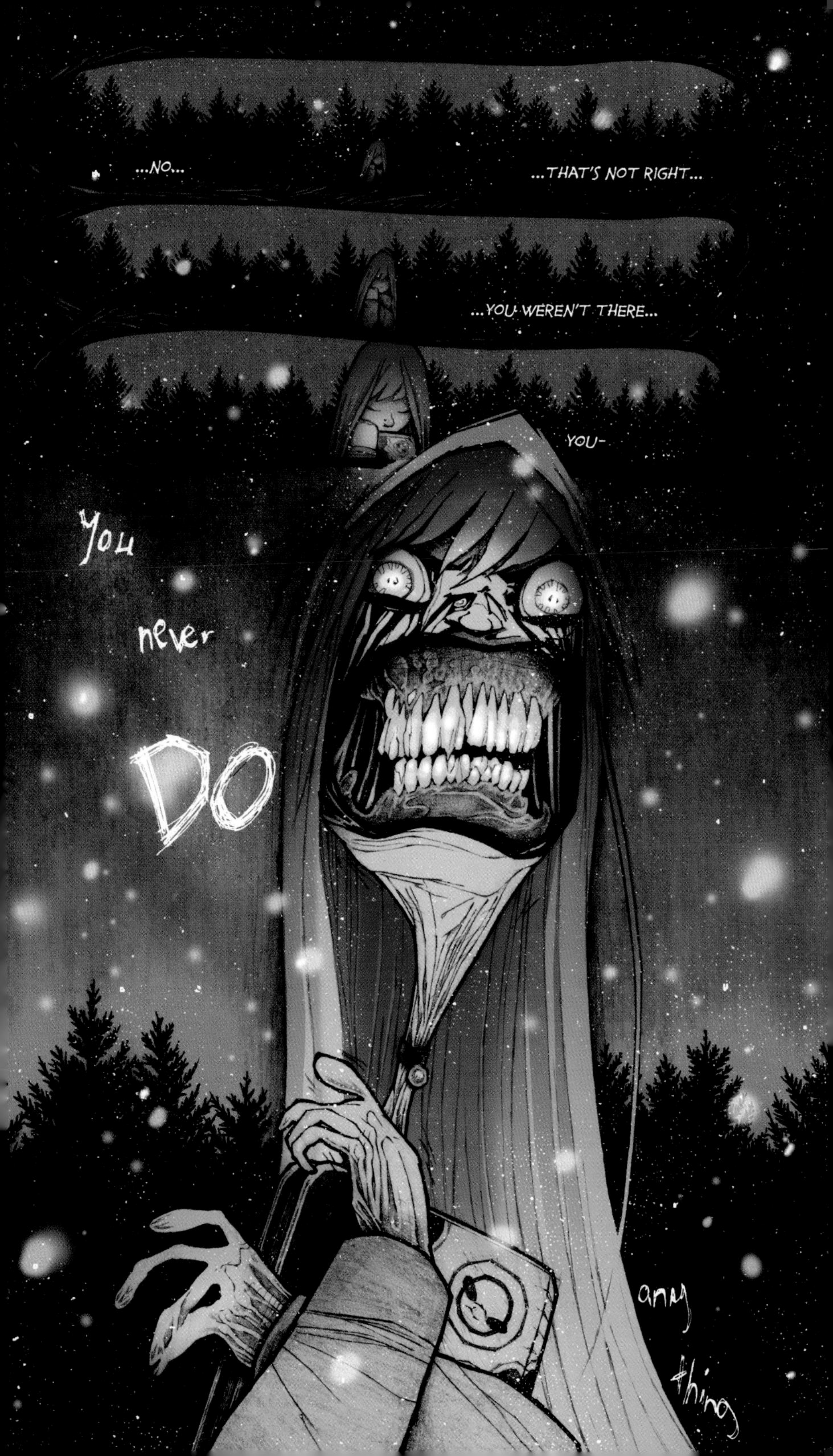
...NO...
...THAT'S NOT RIGHT...
...YOU WEREN'T THERE...
YOU-
You
never
DO
any
thing

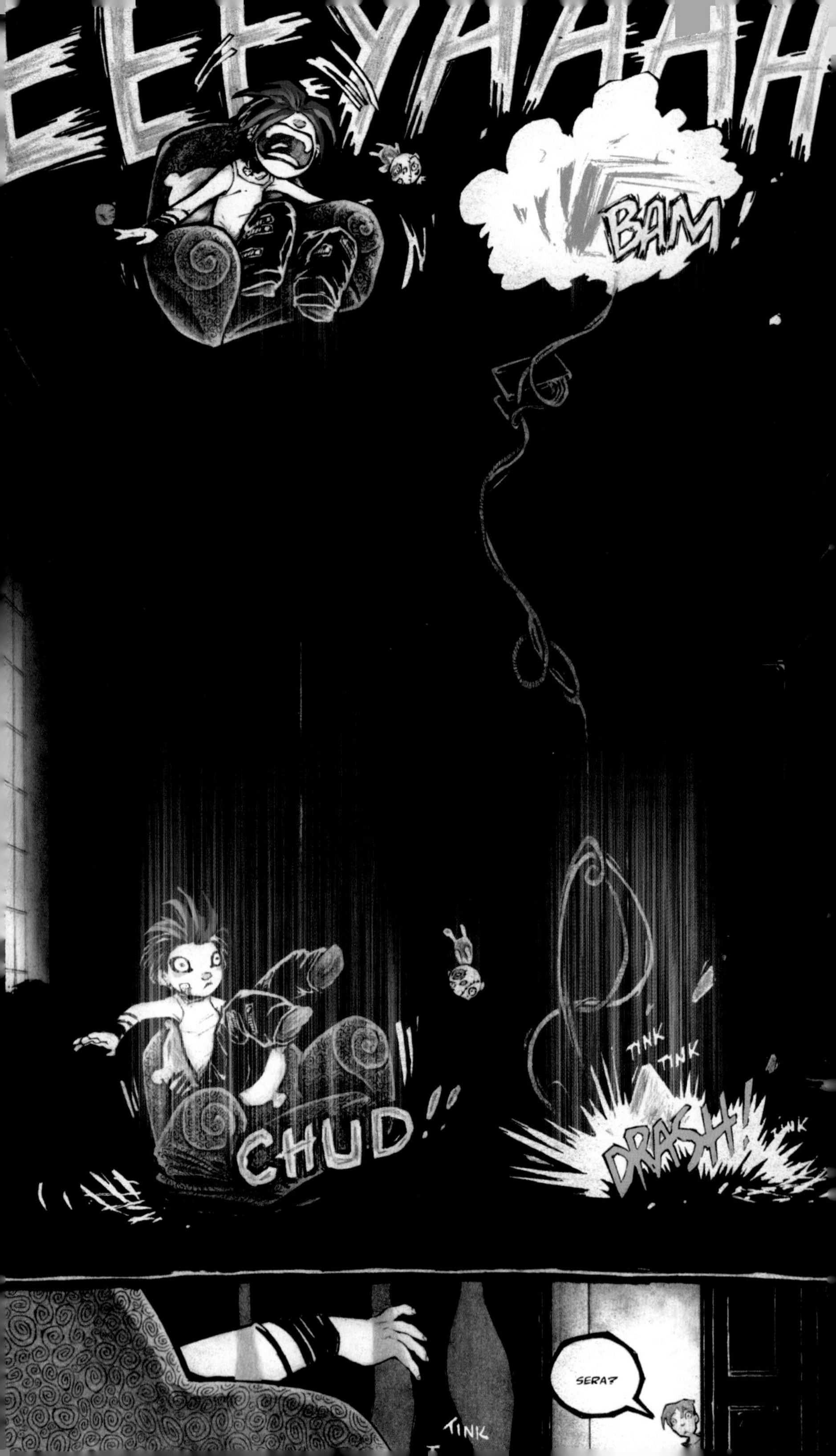
EEEYAAAH
BAM!
CHUD!!
TINK
TINK
DRASH!
TINK
SERA?
TINK

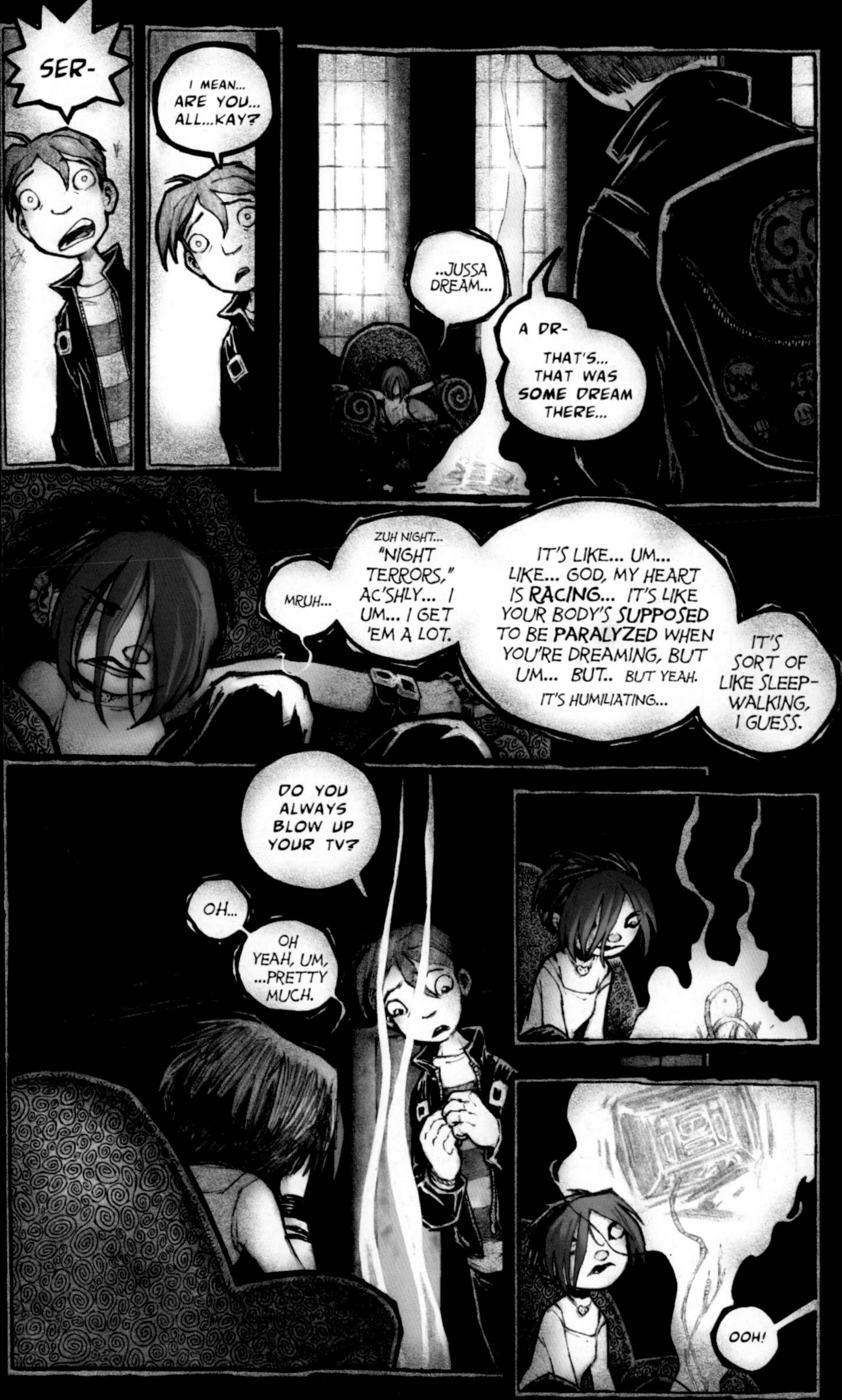
SER-
I MEAN... ARE YOU... ALL...KAY?
..JUSSA DREAM...
A DR-
THAT'S... THAT WAS SOME DREAM THERE...
MRUH...
ZUH NIGHT... "NIGHT TERRORS," AC'SHLY... I UM... I GET 'EM A LOT.
IT'S LIKE... UM... LIKE... GOD, MY HEART IS RACING... IT'S LIKE YOUR BODY'S SUPPOSED TO BE PARALYZED WHEN YOU'RE DREAMING, BUT UM... BUT.. BUT YEAH.
IT'S HUMILIATING...
IT'S SORT OF LIKE SLEEP-WALKING, I GUESS.
DO YOU ALWAYS BLOW UP YOUR TV?
OH...
OH YEAH, UM, ...PRETTY MUCH.
OOH!

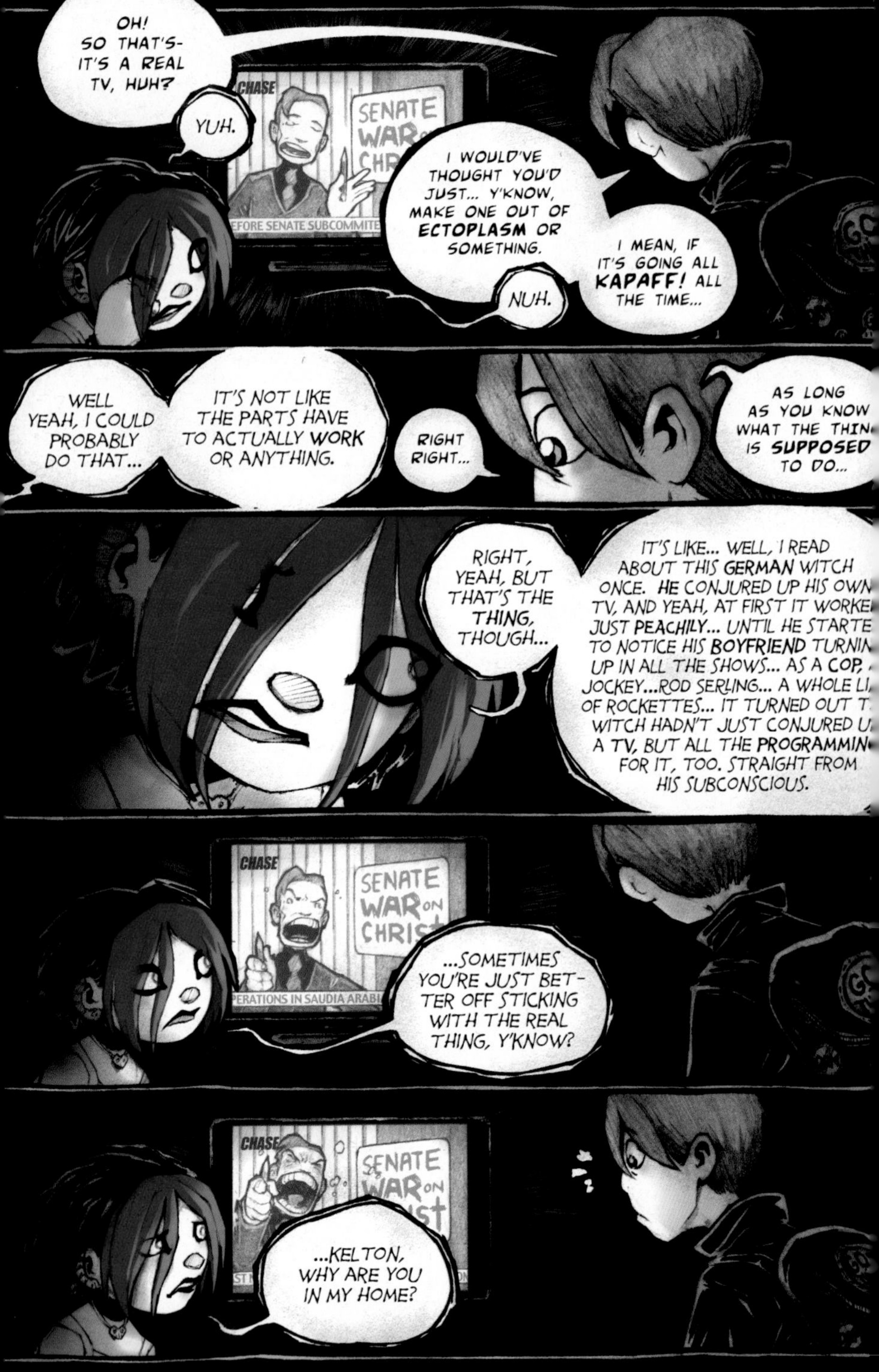
OH! SO THAT'S- IT'S A REAL TV, HUH?
YUH.
CHASE
SENATE WAR
I WOULD'VE THOUGHT YOU'D JUST... Y'KNOW, MAKE ONE OUT OF ECTOPLASM OR SOMETHING.
NUH.
I MEAN, IF IT'S GOING ALL KAPAFF! ALL THE TIME...
WELL YEAH, I COULD PROBABLY DO THAT...
IT'S NOT LIKE THE PARTS HAVE TO ACTUALLY WORK OR ANYTHING.
RIGHT RIGHT...
AS LONG AS YOU KNOW WHAT THE THIN IS SUPPOSED TO DO...
RIGHT, YEAH, BUT THAT'S THE THING, THOUGH...
IT'S LIKE... WELL, I READ ABOUT THIS GERMAN WITCH ONCE. HE CONJURED UP HIS OWN TV, AND YEAH, AT FIRST IT WORKE JUST PEACHILY... UNTIL HE STARTE TO NOTICE HIS BOYFRIEND TURNIN UP IN ALL THE SHOWS... AS A COP, JOCKEY...ROD SERLING... A WHOLE LI OF ROCKETTES... IT TURNED OUT T WITCH HADN'T JUST CONJURED U A TV, BUT ALL THE PROGRAMMIN FOR IT, TOO. STRAIGHT FROM HIS SUBCONSCIOUS.
CHASE
SENATE WAR ON CHRIS
PERATIONS IN SAUDIA ARABI
...SOMETIMES YOU'RE JUST BET-TER OFF STICKING WITH THE REAL THING, Y'KNOW?
CHASE
SENATE WAR ON
...KELTON, WHY ARE YOU IN MY HOME?

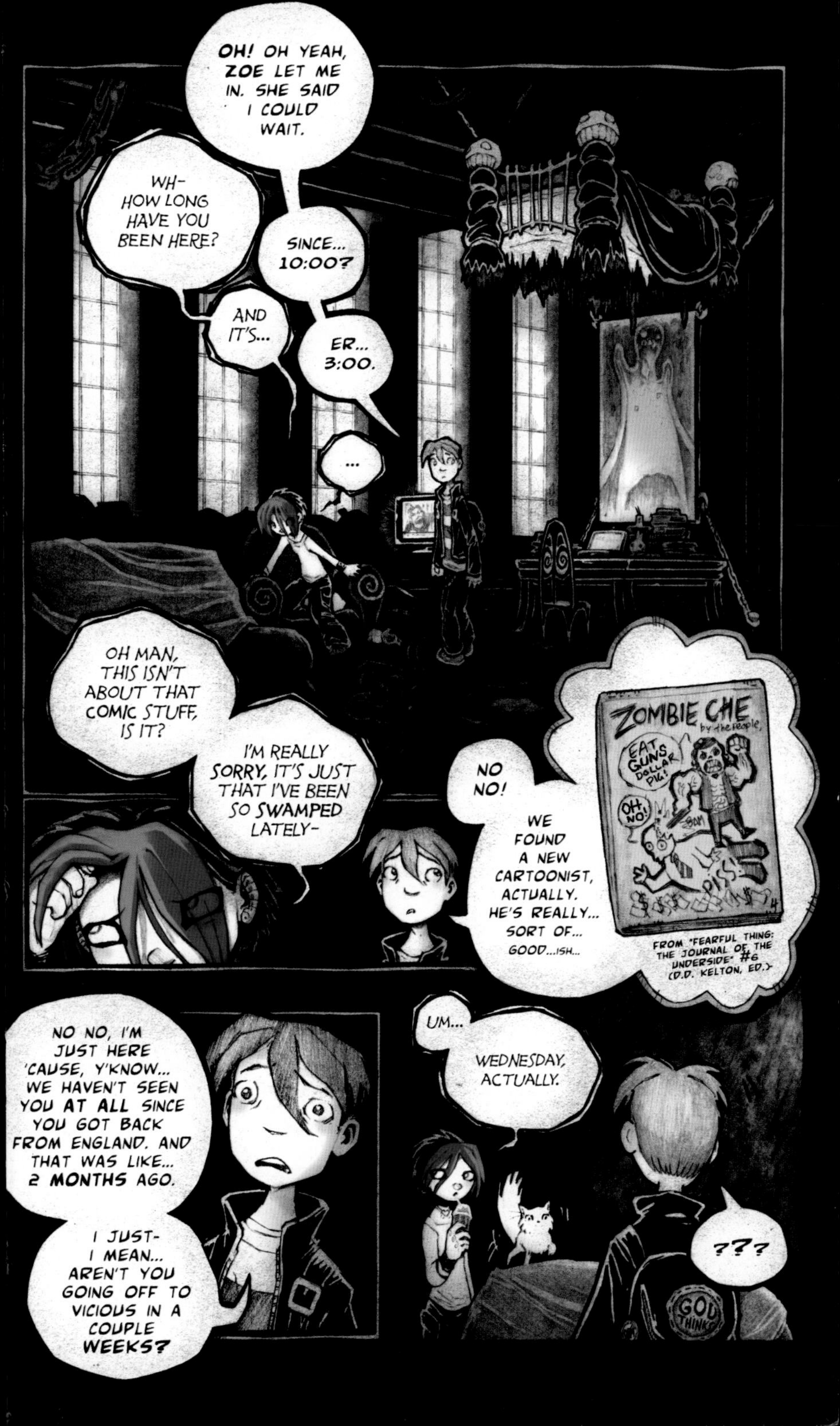
OH! OH YEAH, ZOE LET ME IN. SHE SAID I COULD WAIT.
WH- HOW LONG HAVE YOU BEEN HERE?
SINCE... 10:00?
AND IT'S...
ER... 3:00.
...
OH MAN, THIS ISN'T ABOUT THAT COMIC STUFF, IS IT?
I'M REALLY SORRY, IT'S JUST THAT I'VE BEEN SO SWAMPED LATELY-
NO NO!
WE FOUND A NEW CARTOONIST, ACTUALLY. HE'S REALLY... SORT OF... GOOD...ISH...
ZOMBIE CHE by the People
EAT GUNS DOLLAR PIG!
OH NO!
FROM "FEARFUL THING: THE JOURNAL OF THE UNDERSIDE" #6 (D.D. KELTON, ED.)
NO NO, I'M JUST HERE 'CAUSE, Y'KNOW... WE HAVEN'T SEEN YOU AT ALL SINCE YOU GOT BACK FROM ENGLAND. AND THAT WAS LIKE... 2 MONTHS AGO.
I JUST- I MEAN... AREN'T YOU GOING OFF TO VICIOUS IN A COUPLE WEEKS?
UM...
WEDNESDAY, ACTUALLY.
???
GOD THINKS

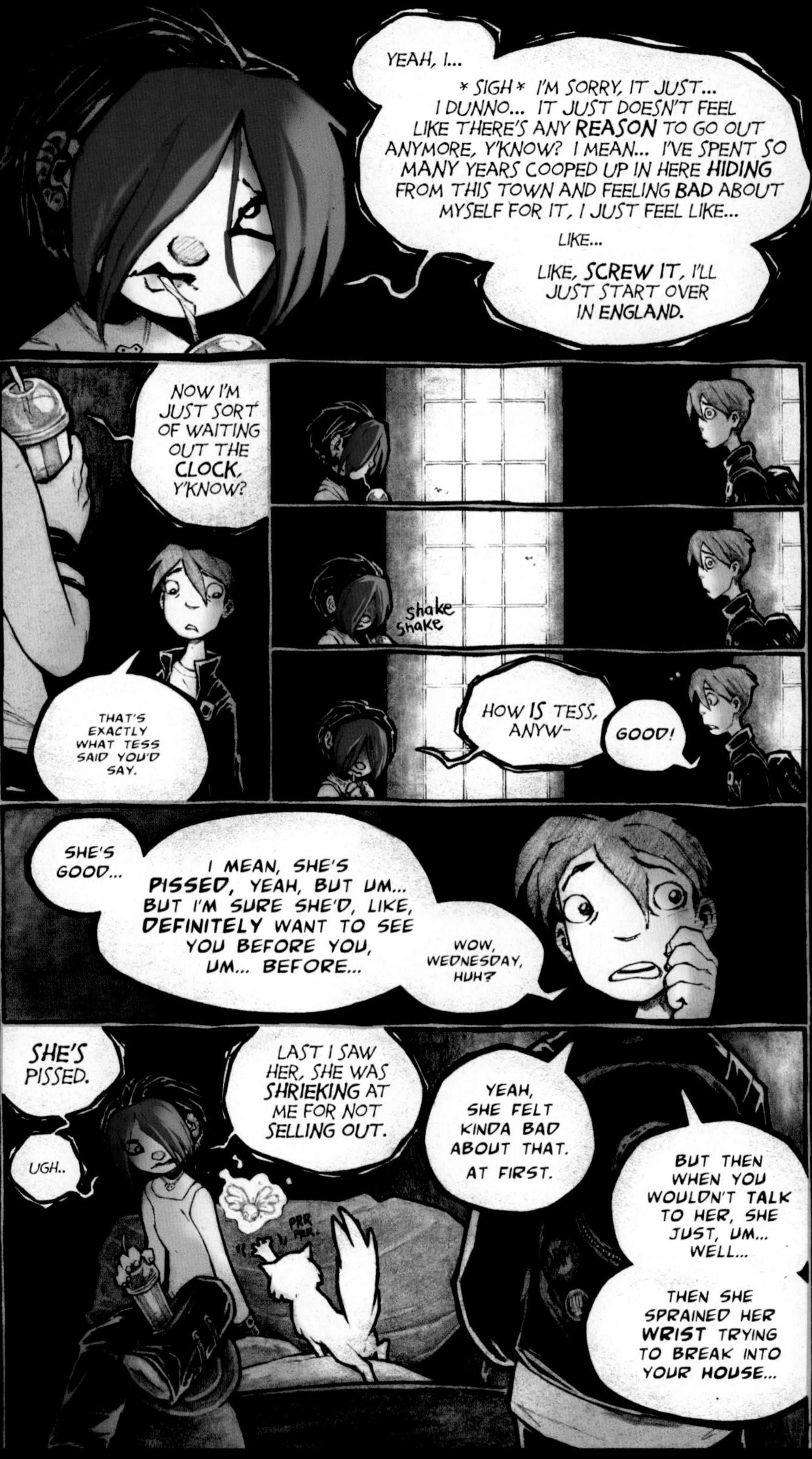
YEAH, I...
* SIGH * I'M SORRY, IT JUST... I DUNNO... IT JUST DOESN'T FEEL LIKE THERE'S ANY REASON TO GO OUT ANYMORE, Y'KNOW? I MEAN... I'VE SPENT SO MANY YEARS COOPED UP IN HERE HIDING FROM THIS TOWN AND FEELING BAD ABOUT MYSELF FOR IT, I JUST FEEL LIKE...
LIKE...
LIKE, SCREW IT, I'LL JUST START OVER IN ENGLAND.
NOW I'M JUST SORT OF WAITING OUT THE CLOCK, Y'KNOW?
THAT'S EXACTLY WHAT TESS SAID YOU'D SAY.
shake shake
HOW IS TESS, ANYW-
GOOD!
SHE'S GOOD...
I MEAN, SHE'S PISSED, YEAH, BUT UM... BUT I'M SURE SHE'D, LIKE, DEFINITELY WANT TO SEE YOU BEFORE YOU, UM... BEFORE...
WOW, WEDNESDAY, HUH?
SHE'S PISSED.
UGH..
LAST I SAW HER, SHE WAS SHRIEKING AT ME FOR NOT SELLING OUT.
YEAH, SHE FELT KINDA BAD ABOUT THAT. AT FIRST.
BUT THEN WHEN YOU WOULDN'T TALK TO HER, SHE JUST, UM... WELL...
THEN SHE SPRAINED HER WRIST TRYING TO BREAK INTO YOUR HOUSE...

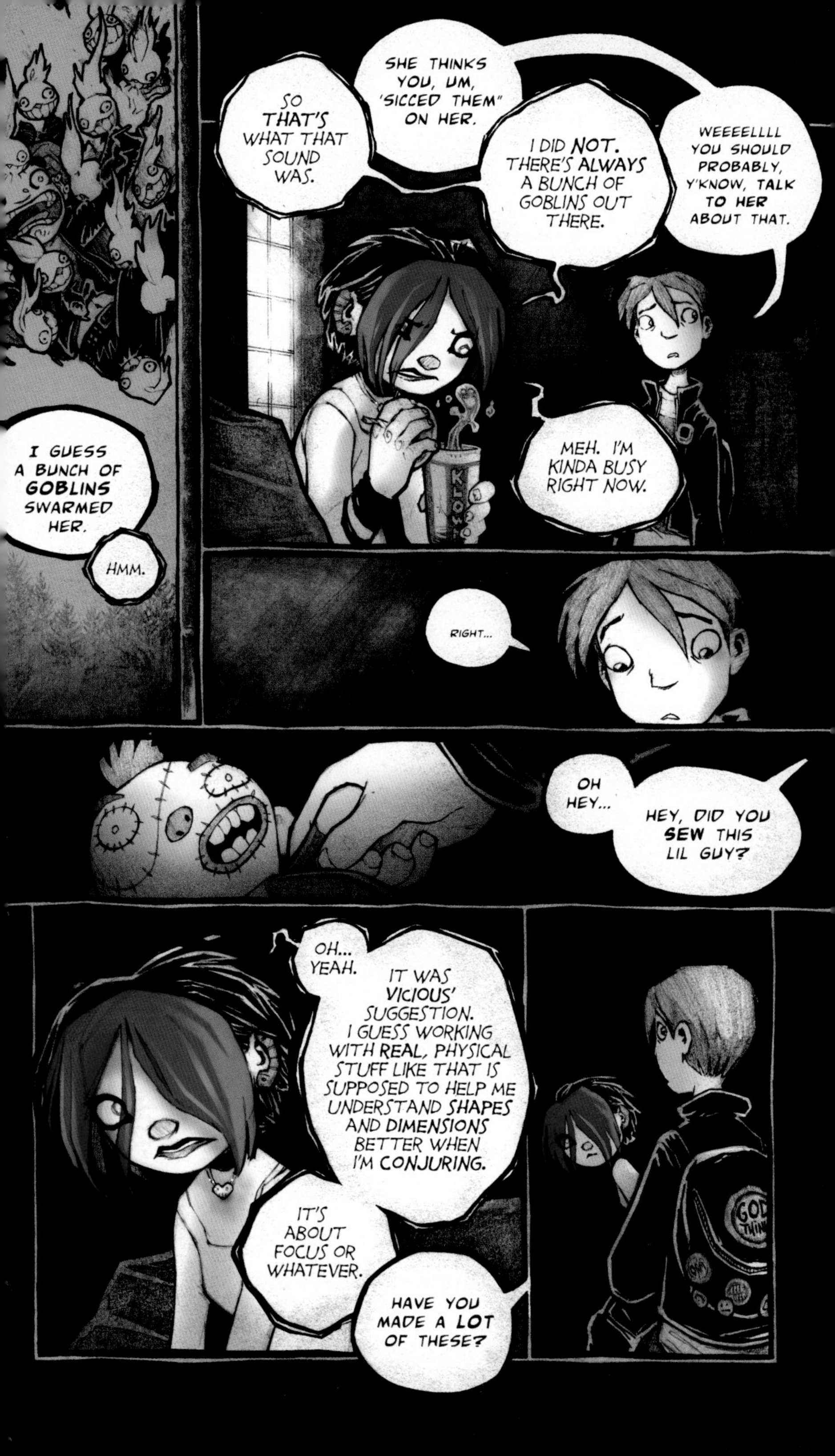
SO THAT'S WHAT THAT SOUND WAS.
SHE THINKS YOU, UM, 'SICCED THEM" ON HER.
I DID NOT. THERE'S ALWAYS A BUNCH OF GOBLINS OUT THERE.
WEEEELLLL YOU SHOULD PROBABLY, Y'KNOW, TALK TO HER ABOUT THAT.
I GUESS A BUNCH OF GOBLINS SWARMED HER.
HMM.
MEH. I'M KINDA BUSY RIGHT NOW.
RIGHT...
OH HEY...
HEY, DID YOU SEW THIS LIL GUY?
OH... YEAH.
IT WAS VICIOUS' SUGGESTION. I GUESS WORKING WITH REAL, PHYSICAL STUFF LIKE THAT IS SUPPOSED TO HELP ME UNDERSTAND SHAPES AND DIMENSIONS BETTER WHEN I'M CONJURING.
IT'S ABOUT FOCUS OR WHATEVER.
HAVE YOU MADE A LOT OF THESE?

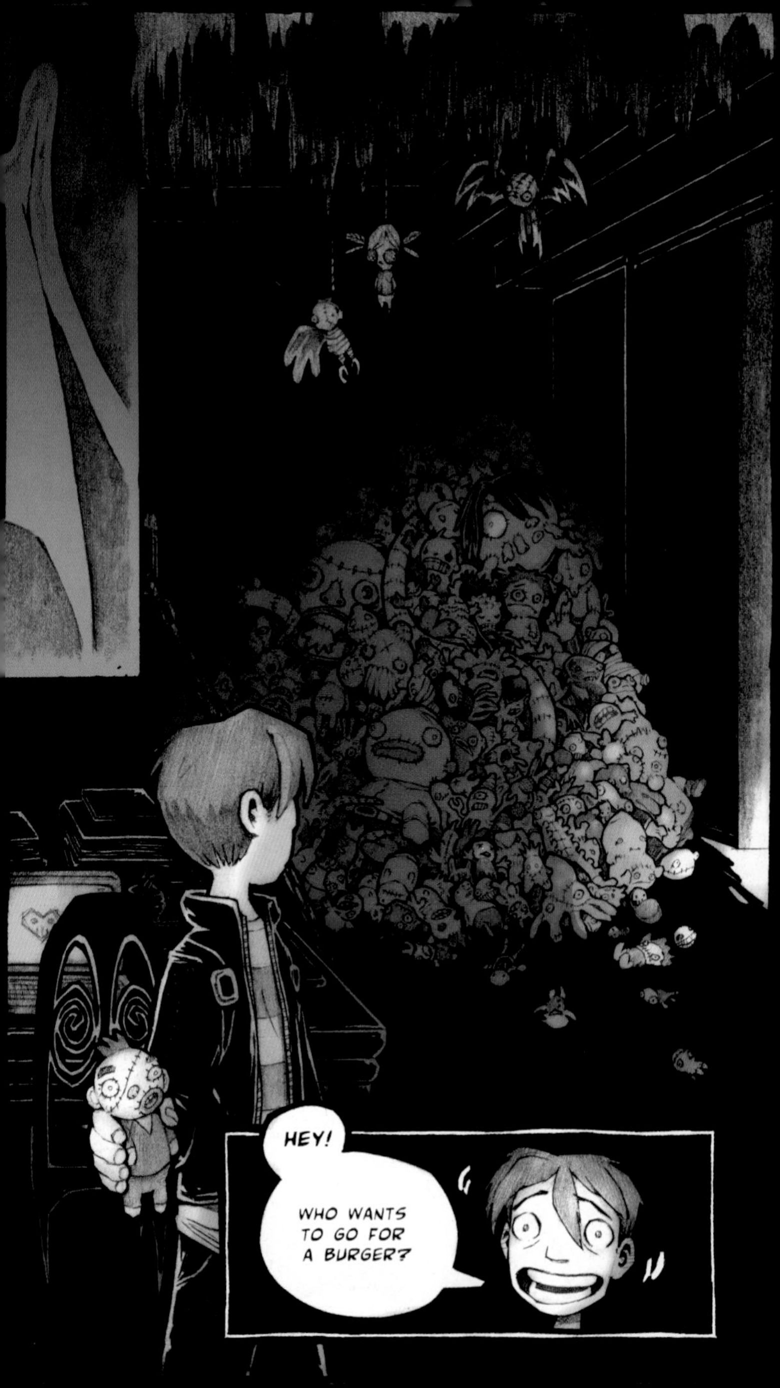
HEY!
WHO WANTS TO GO FOR A BURGER?

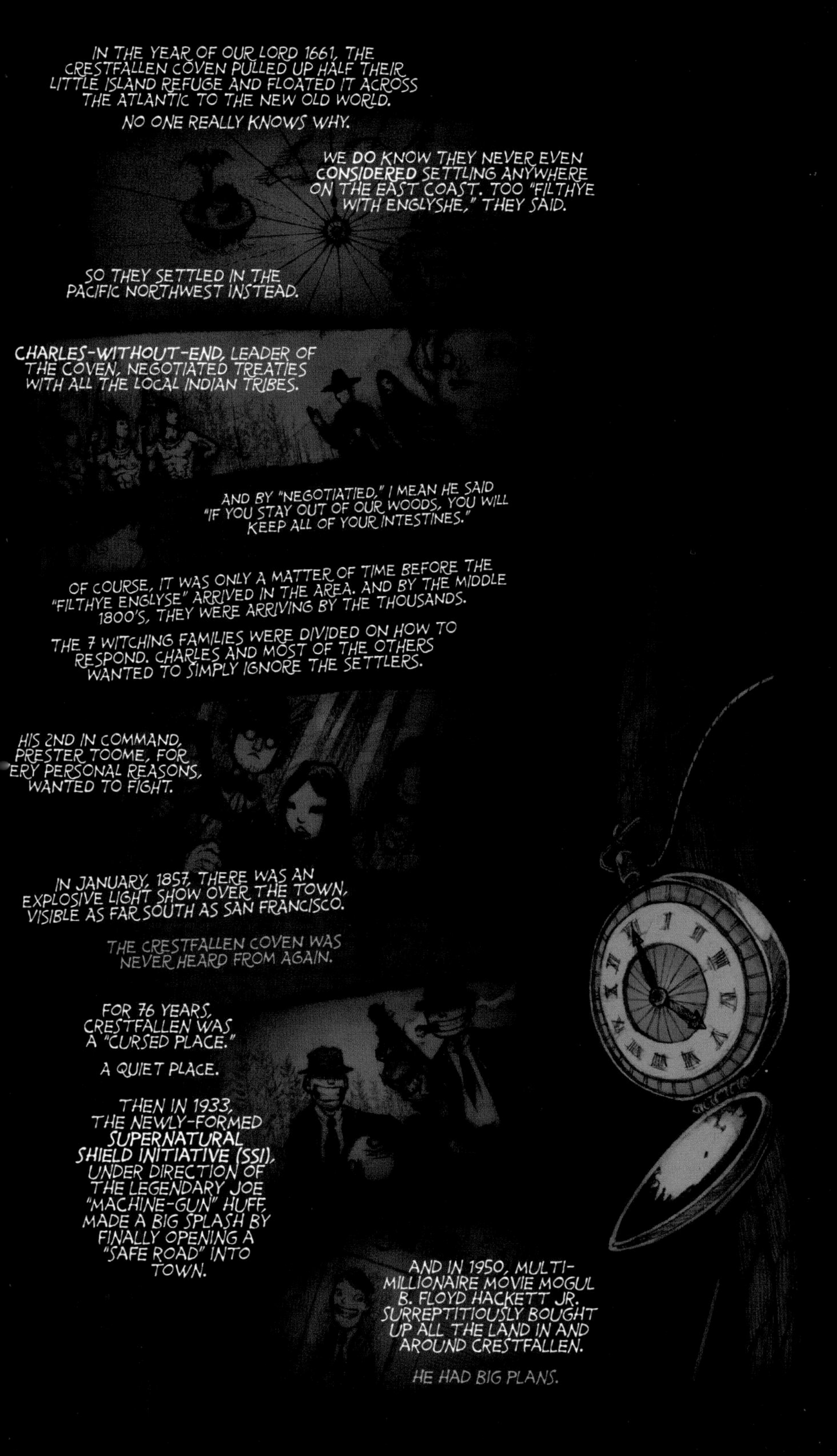
IN THE YEAR OF OUR LORD 1661, THE CRESTFALLEN COVEN PULLED UP HALF THEIR LITTLE ISLAND REFUGE AND FLOATED IT ACROSS THE ATLANTIC TO THE NEW OLD WORLD.
NO ONE REALLY KNOWS WHY.
WE **DO** KNOW THEY NEVER EVEN **CONSIDERED** SETTLING ANYWHERE ON THE EAST COAST. TOO "FILTHYE WITH ENGLYSHE," THEY SAID.
SO THEY SETTLED IN THE PACIFIC NORTHWEST INSTEAD.
CHARLES-WITHOUT-END, LEADER OF THE COVEN, NEGOTIATED TREATIES WITH ALL THE LOCAL INDIAN TRIBES.
AND BY "NEGOTIATIED," I MEAN HE SAID "IF YOU STAY OUT OF OUR WOODS, YOU WILL KEEP ALL OF YOUR INTESTINES."
OF COURSE, IT WAS ONLY A MATTER OF TIME BEFORE THE "FILTHYE ENGLYSE" ARRIVED IN THE AREA. AND BY THE MIDDLE 1800'S, THEY WERE ARRIVING BY THE THOUSANDS.
THE 7 WITCHING FAMILIES WERE DIVIDED ON HOW TO RESPOND. CHARLES AND MOST OF THE OTHERS WANTED TO SIMPLY IGNORE THE SETTLERS.
HIS 2ND IN COMMAND, PRESTER TOOME, FOR ERY PERSONAL REASONS, WANTED TO FIGHT.
IN JANUARY, 1857, THERE WAS AN EXPLOSIVE LIGHT SHOW OVER THE TOWN, VISIBLE AS FAR SOUTH AS SAN FRANCISCO.
THE CRESTFALLEN COVEN WAS NEVER HEARD FROM AGAIN.
FOR 76 YEARS, CRESTFALLEN WAS A "CURSED PLACE."
A QUIET PLACE.
THEN IN 1933, THE NEWLY-FORMED **SUPERNATURAL SHIELD INITIATIVE (SSI)**, UNDER DIRECTION OF THE LEGENDARY JOE "MACHINE-GUN" HUFF, MADE A BIG SPLASH BY FINALLY OPENING A "SAFE ROAD" INTO TOWN.
AND IN 1950, MULTI-MILLIONAIRE MOVIE MOGUL B. FLOYD HACKETT JR. SURREPTITIOUSLY BOUGHT UP ALL THE LAND IN AND AROUND CRESTFALLEN.
HE HAD BIG PLANS.

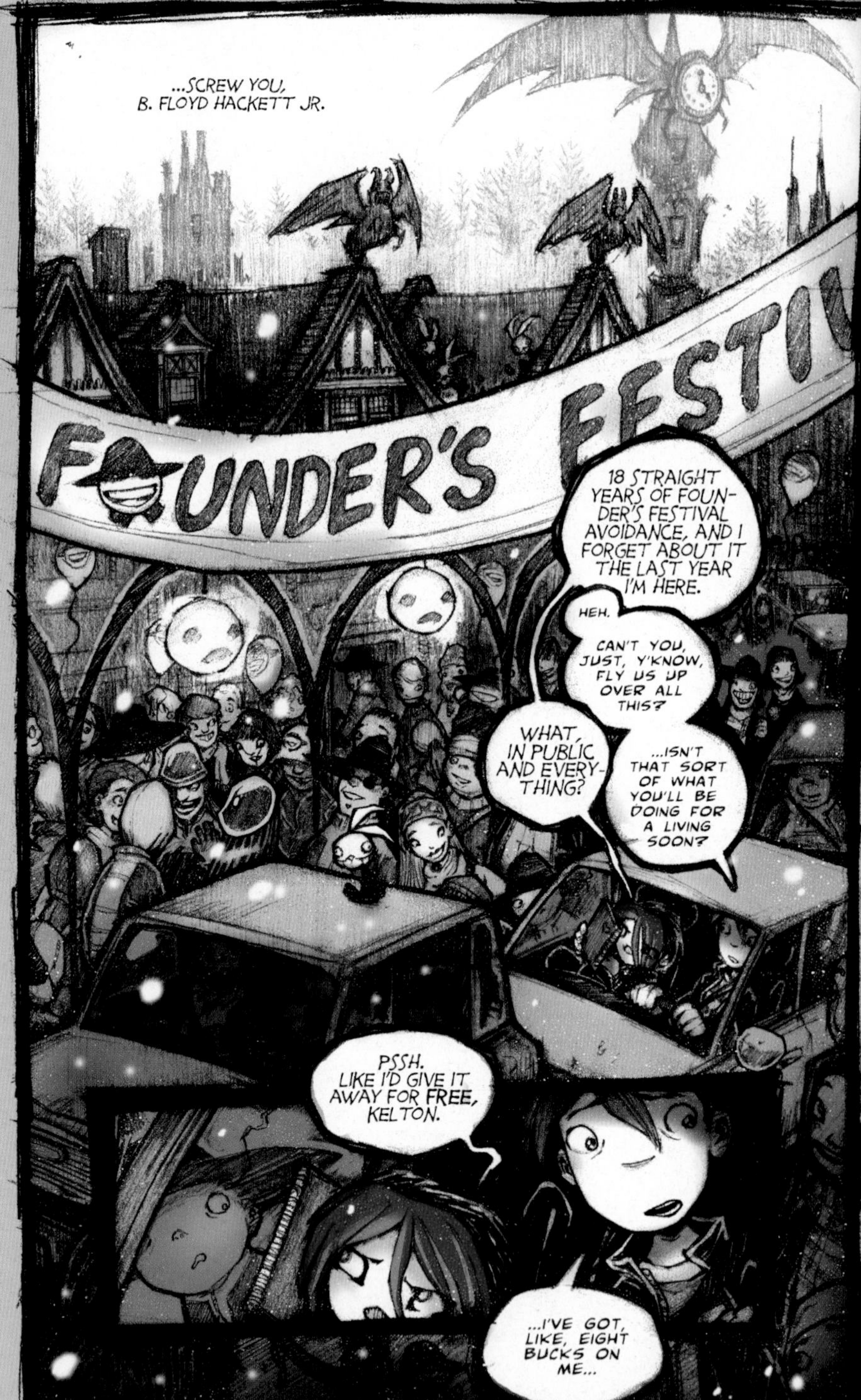
...SCREW YOU, B. FLOYD HACKETT JR.
FOUNDER'S FESTIV
18 STRAIGHT YEARS OF FOUN-DER'S FESTIVAL AVOIDANCE, AND I FORGET ABOUT IT THE LAST YEAR I'M HERE.
HEH.
CAN'T YOU, JUST, Y'KNOW, FLY US UP OVER ALL THIS?
WHAT, IN PUBLIC AND EVERY-THING?
...ISN'T THAT SORT OF WHAT YOU'LL BE DOING FOR A LIVING SOON?
PSSH. LIKE I'D GIVE IT AWAY FOR FREE, KELTON.
...I'VE GOT, LIKE, EIGHT BUCKS ON ME...

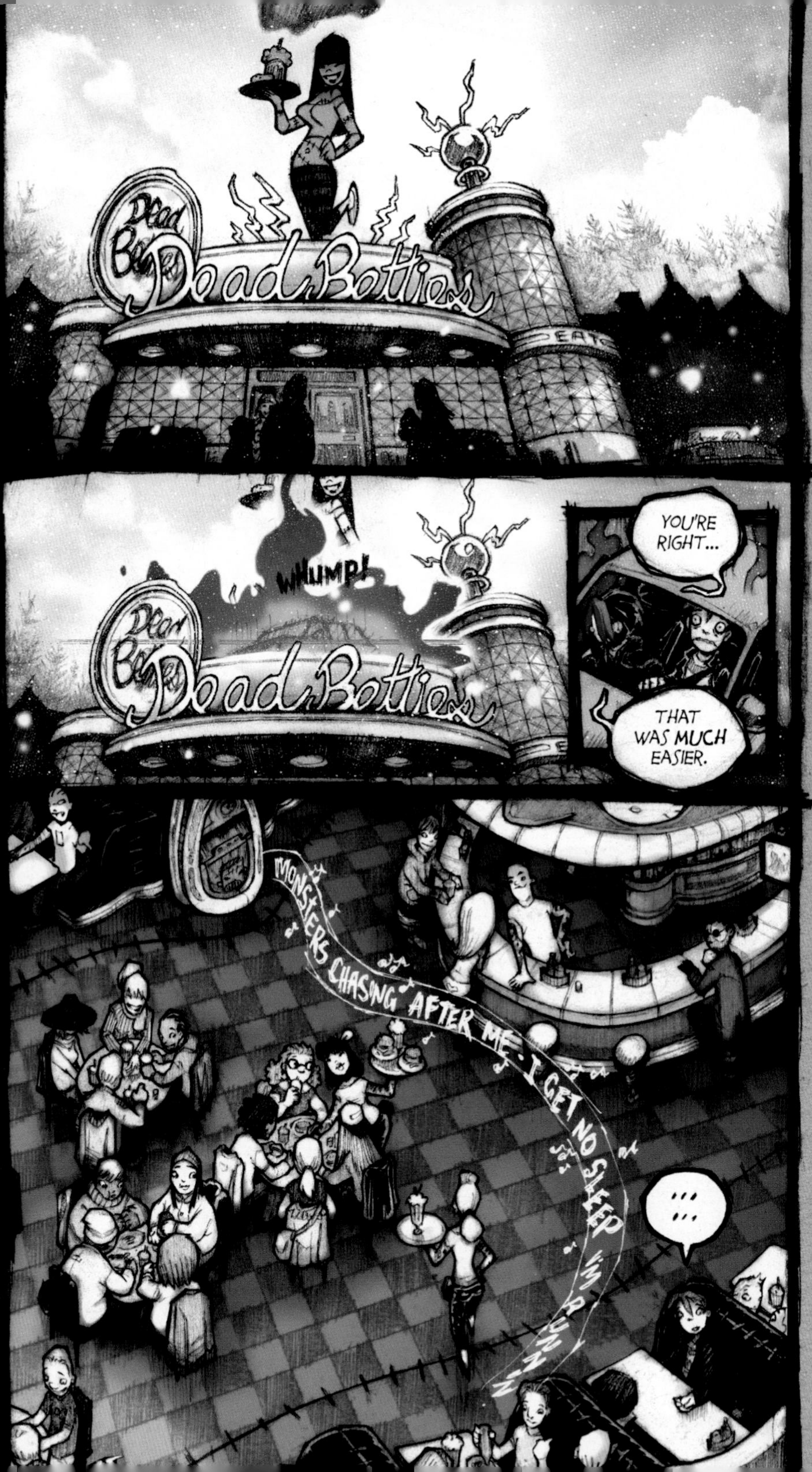
EAT
WHUMP!
YOU'RE RIGHT...
THAT WAS MUCH EASIER.
MONSTERS CHASING AFTER ME · I GET NO SLEEP I'M RUNNIN
...

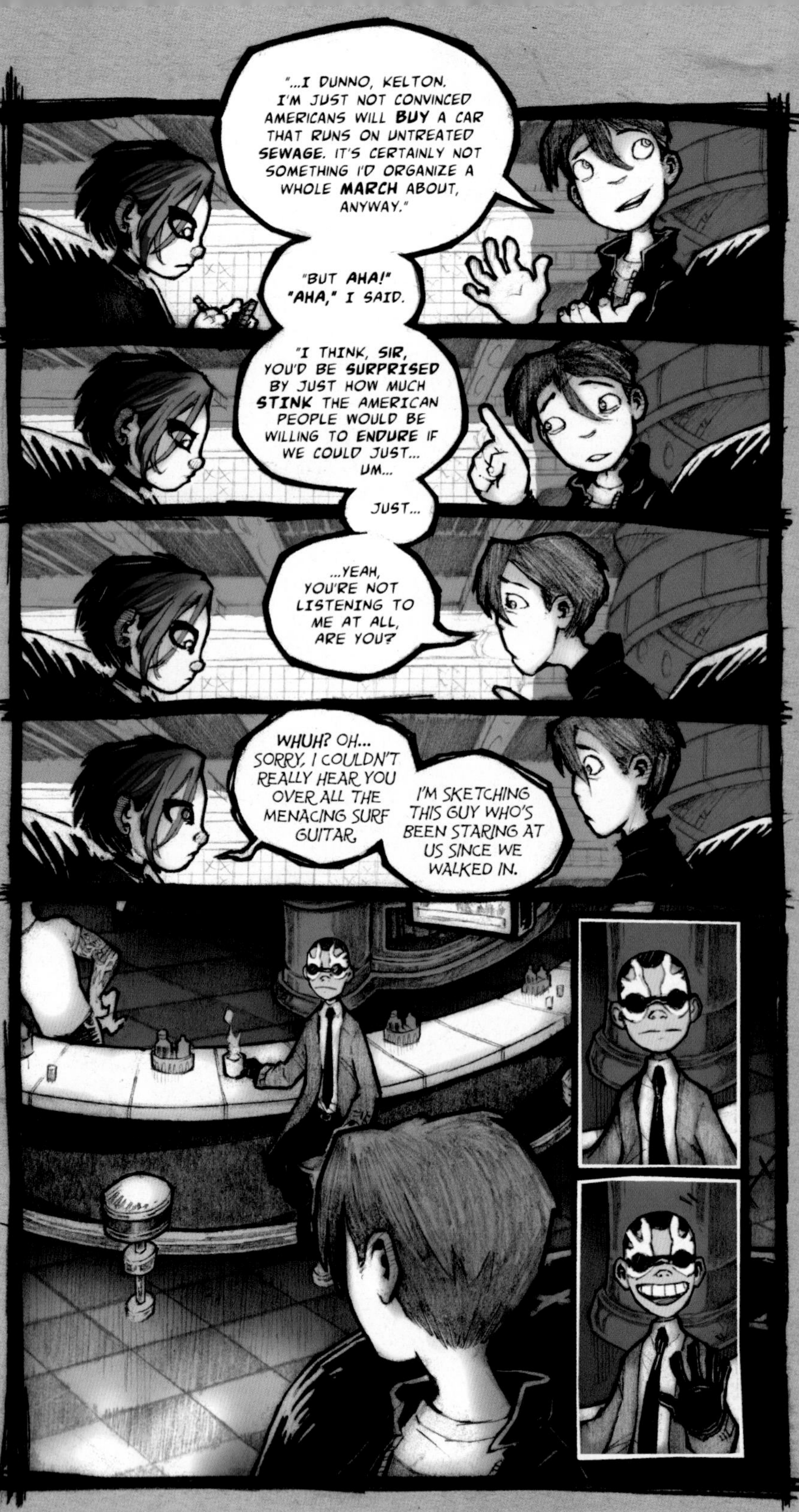
"...I DUNNO, KELTON. I'M JUST NOT CONVINCED AMERICANS WILL BUY A CAR THAT RUNS ON UNTREATED SEWAGE. IT'S CERTAINLY NOT SOMETHING I'D ORGANIZE A WHOLE MARCH ABOUT, ANYWAY."
"BUT AHA!" "AHA," I SAID.
"I THINK, SIR, YOU'D BE SURPRISED BY JUST HOW MUCH STINK THE AMERICAN PEOPLE WOULD BE WILLING TO ENDURE IF WE COULD JUST... UM...
JUST...
...YEAH, YOU'RE NOT LISTENING TO ME AT ALL, ARE YOU?
WHUH? OH... SORRY, I COULDN'T REALLY HEAR YOU OVER ALL THE MENACING SURF GUITAR.
I'M SKETCHING THIS GUY WHO'S BEEN STARING AT US SINCE WE WALKED IN.

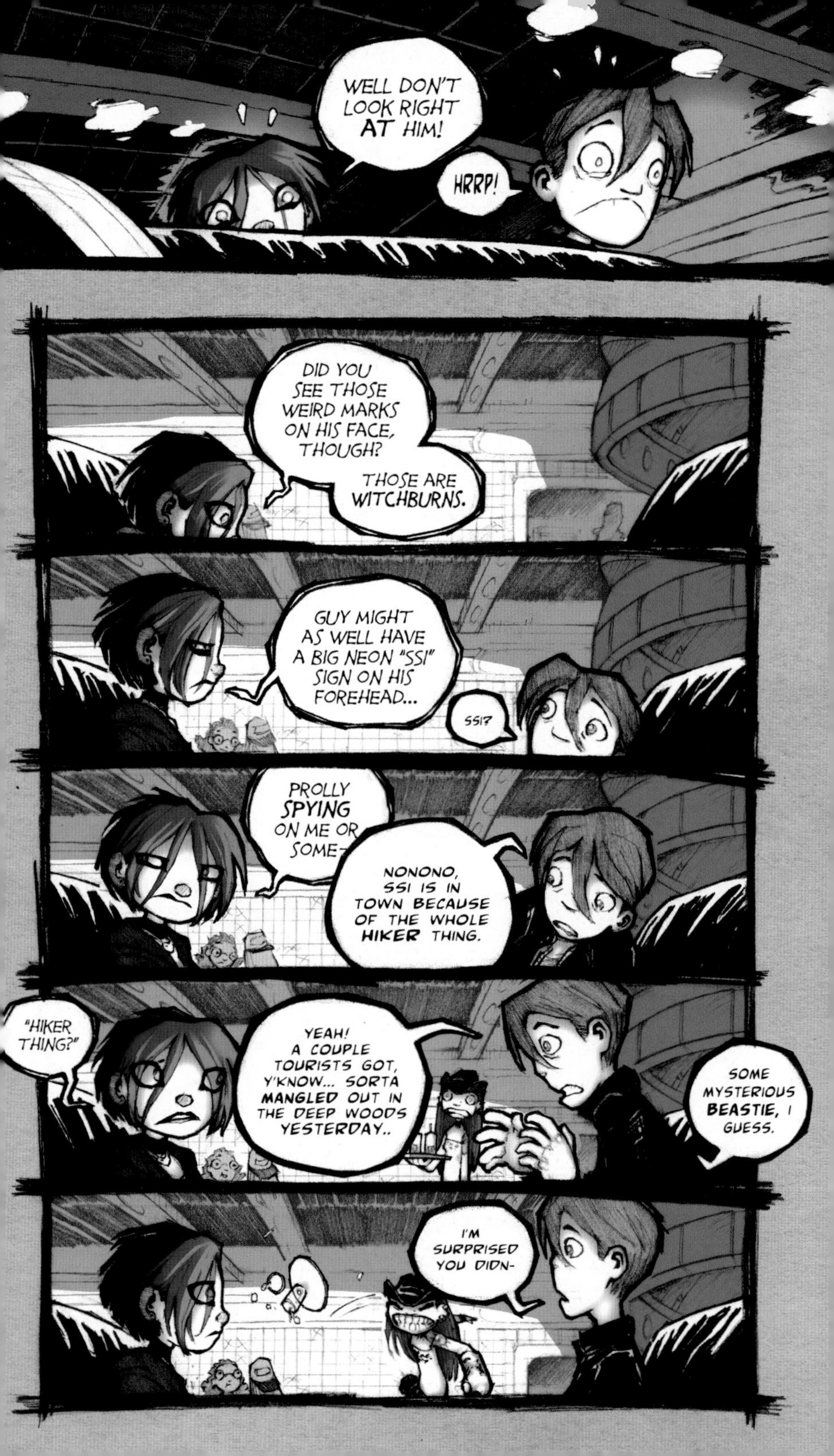
WELL DON'T LOOK RIGHT AT HIM!
HRRP!
DID YOU SEE THOSE WEIRD MARKS ON HIS FACE, THOUGH?
THOSE ARE WITCHBURNS.
GUY MIGHT AS WELL HAVE A BIG NEON "SSI" SIGN ON HIS FOREHEAD...
SSI?
PROLLY SPYING ON ME OR SOME-
NONONO, SSI IS IN TOWN BECAUSE OF THE WHOLE HIKER THING.
"HIKER THING?"
YEAH! A COUPLE TOURISTS GOT, Y'KNOW... SORTA MANGLED OUT IN THE DEEP WOODS YESTERDAY..
SOME MYSTERIOUS BEASTIE, I GUESS.
I'M SURPRISED YOU DIDN-

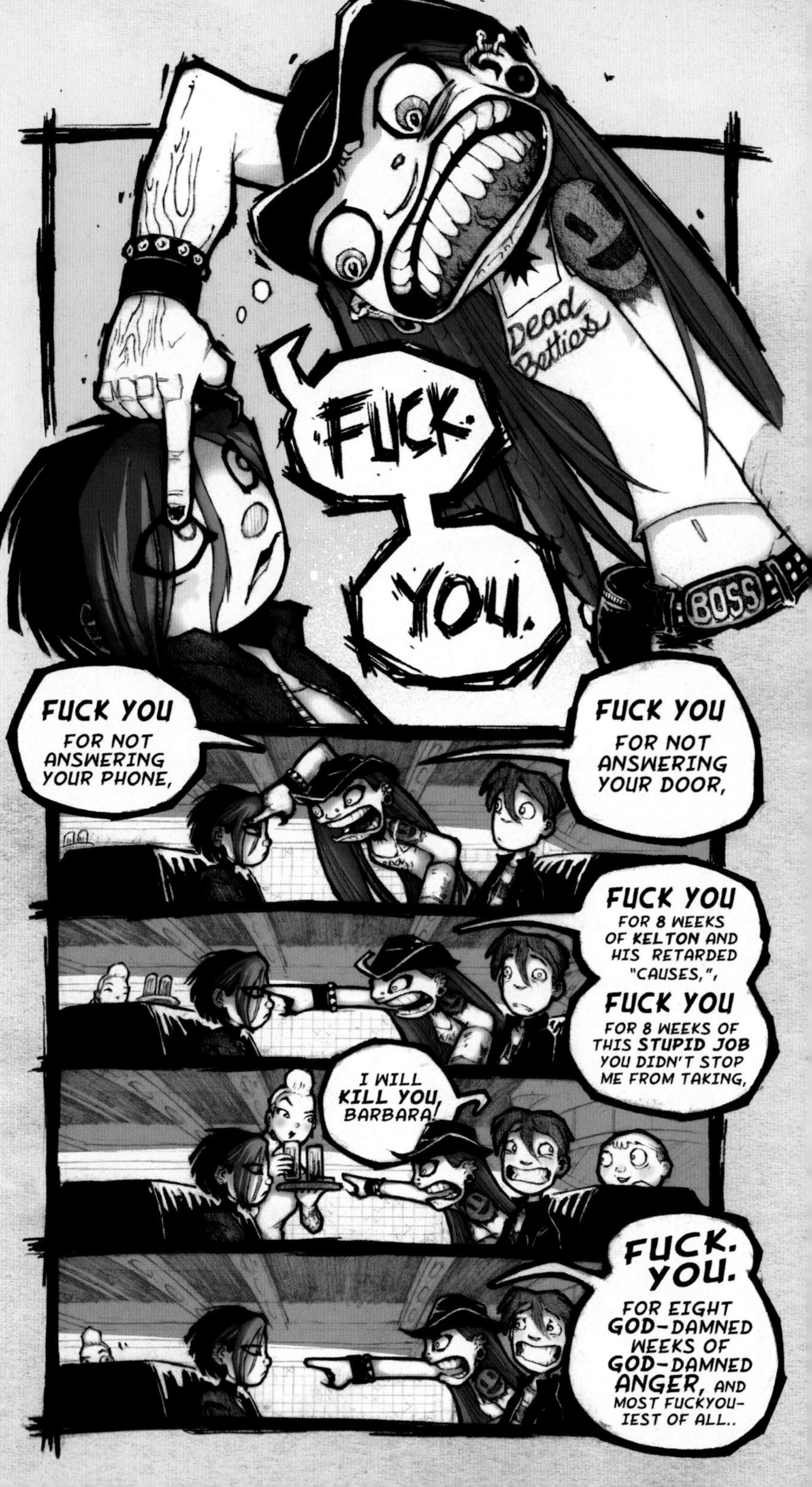

FUCK. YOU.
Dead Betties
BOSS
FUCK YOU FOR NOT ANSWERING YOUR PHONE,
FUCK YOU FOR NOT ANSWERING YOUR DOOR,
FUCK YOU FOR 8 WEEKS OF KELTON AND HIS RETARDED "CAUSES,",
FUCK YOU FOR 8 WEEKS OF THIS STUPID JOB YOU DIDN'T STOP ME FROM TAKING,
I WILL KILL YOU, BARBARA!
FUCK. YOU.
FOR EIGHT GOD-DAMNED WEEKS OF GOD-DAMNED ANGER, AND MOST FUCKYOU-IEST OF ALL..

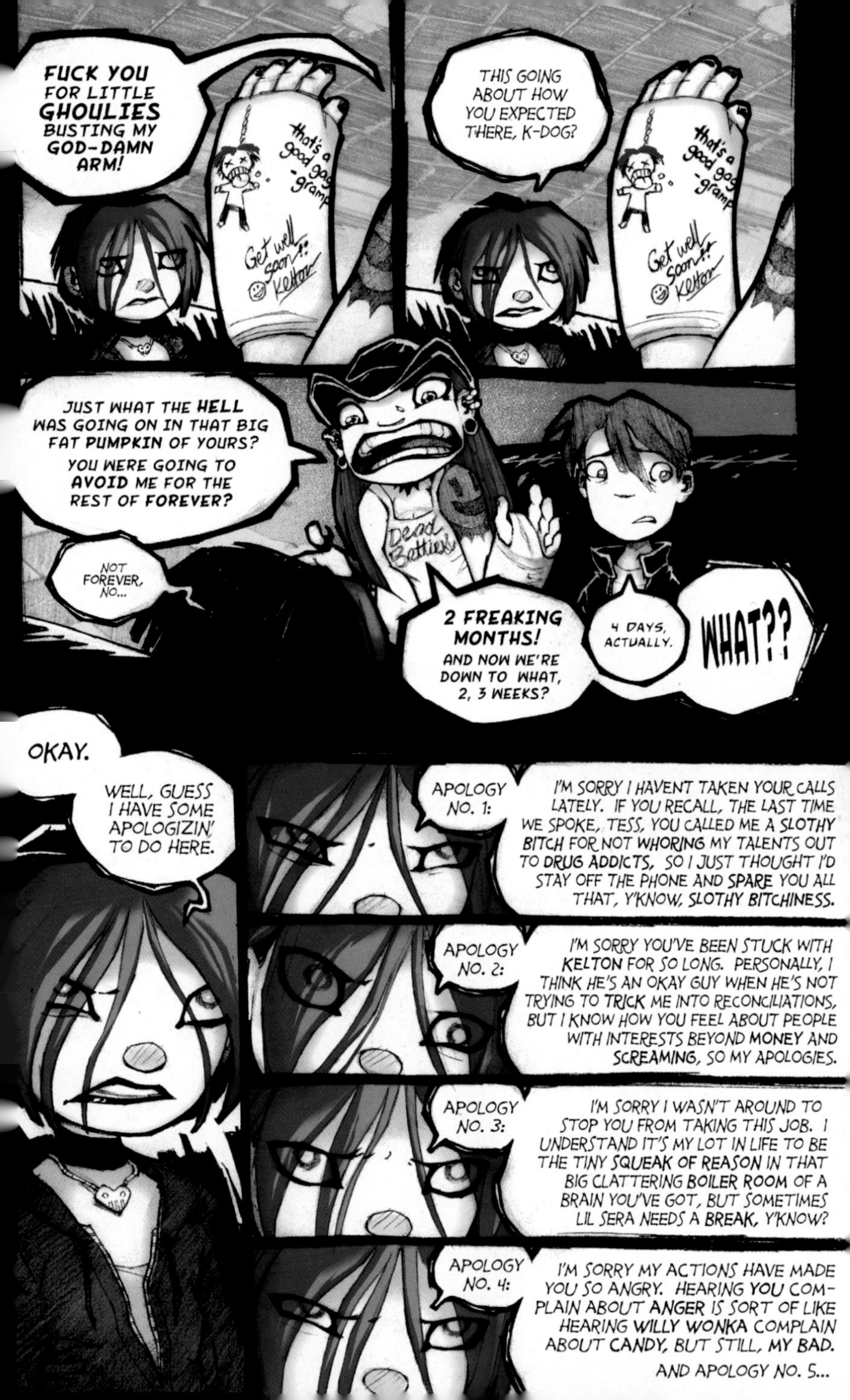

FUCK YOU FOR LITTLE GHOULIES BUSTING MY GOD-DAMN ARM!
that's a good gag -gramp
Get well soon!! Kelton
THIS GOING ABOUT HOW YOU EXPECTED THERE, K-DOG?
JUST WHAT THE HELL WAS GOING ON IN THAT BIG FAT PUMPKIN OF YOURS?
YOU WERE GOING TO AVOID ME FOR THE REST OF FOREVER?
NOT FOREVER, NO...
Dead Batties
2 FREAKING MONTHS!
AND NOW WE'RE DOWN TO WHAT, 2, 3 WEEKS?
4 DAYS, ACTUALLY.
WHAT??
OKAY.
WELL, GUESS I HAVE SOME APOLOGIZIN' TO DO HERE.
APOLOGY NO. 1:
I'M SORRY I HAVENT TAKEN YOUR CALLS LATELY. IF YOU RECALL, THE LAST TIME WE SPOKE, TESS, YOU CALLED ME A SLOTHY BITCH FOR NOT WHORING MY TALENTS OUT TO DRUG ADDICTS, SO I JUST THOUGHT I'D STAY OFF THE PHONE AND SPARE YOU ALL THAT, Y'KNOW, SLOTHY BITCHINESS.
APOLOGY NO. 2:
I'M SORRY YOU'VE BEEN STUCK WITH KELTON FOR SO LONG. PERSONALLY, I THINK HE'S AN OKAY GUY WHEN HE'S NOT TRYING TO TRICK ME INTO RECONCILIATIONS, BUT I KNOW HOW YOU FEEL ABOUT PEOPLE WITH INTERESTS BEYOND MONEY AND SCREAMING, SO MY APOLOGIES.
APOLOGY NO. 3:
I'M SORRY I WASN'T AROUND TO STOP YOU FROM TAKING THIS JOB. I UNDERSTAND IT'S MY LOT IN LIFE TO BE THE TINY SQUEAK OF REASON IN THAT BIG CLATTERING BOILER ROOM OF A BRAIN YOU'VE GOT, BUT SOMETIMES LIL SERA NEEDS A BREAK, Y'KNOW?
APOLOGY NO. 4:
I'M SORRY MY ACTIONS HAVE MADE YOU SO ANGRY. HEARING YOU COMPLAIN ABOUT ANGER IS SORT OF LIKE HEARING WILLY WONKA COMPLAIN ABOUT CANDY, BUT STILL, MY BAD.
AND APOLOGY NO. 5...

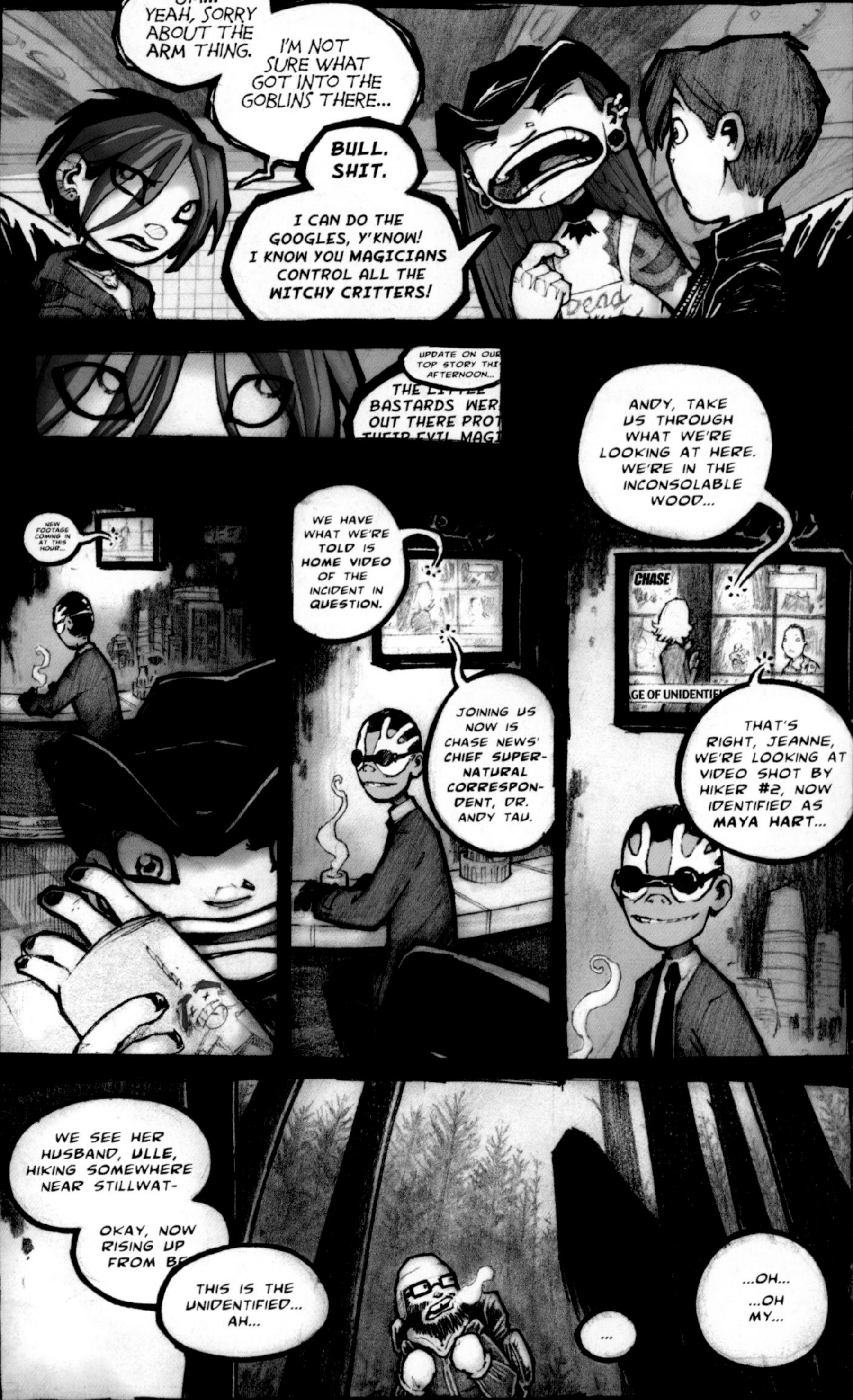
UM... YEAH, SORRY ABOUT THE ARM THING.
I'M NOT SURE WHAT GOT INTO THE GOBLINS THERE...
BULL. SHIT.
I CAN DO THE GOOGLES, Y'KNOW! I KNOW YOU MAGICIANS CONTROL ALL THE WITCHY CRITTERS!
UPDATE ON OUR TOP STORY THI AFTERNOON...
BASTARDS WER OUT THERE PROT
ANDY, TAKE US THROUGH WHAT WE'RE LOOKING AT HERE. WE'RE IN THE INCONSOLABLE WOOD...
NEW FOOTAGE COMING IN AT THIS HOUR...
WE HAVE WHAT WE'RE TOLD IS HOME VIDEO OF THE INCIDENT IN QUESTION.
CHASE
GE OF UNIDENTI
JOINING US NOW IS CHASE NEWS' CHIEF SUPER-NATURAL CORRESPON-DENT, DR. ANDY TAU.
THAT'S RIGHT, JEANNE, WE'RE LOOKING AT VIDEO SHOT BY HIKER #2, NOW IDENTIFIED AS MAYA HART...
WE SEE HER HUSBAND, ULLE, HIKING SOMEWHERE NEAR STILLWAT-
OKAY, NOW RISING UP FROM B
THIS IS THE UNIDENTIFIED... AH...
...
...OH... ...OH MY...

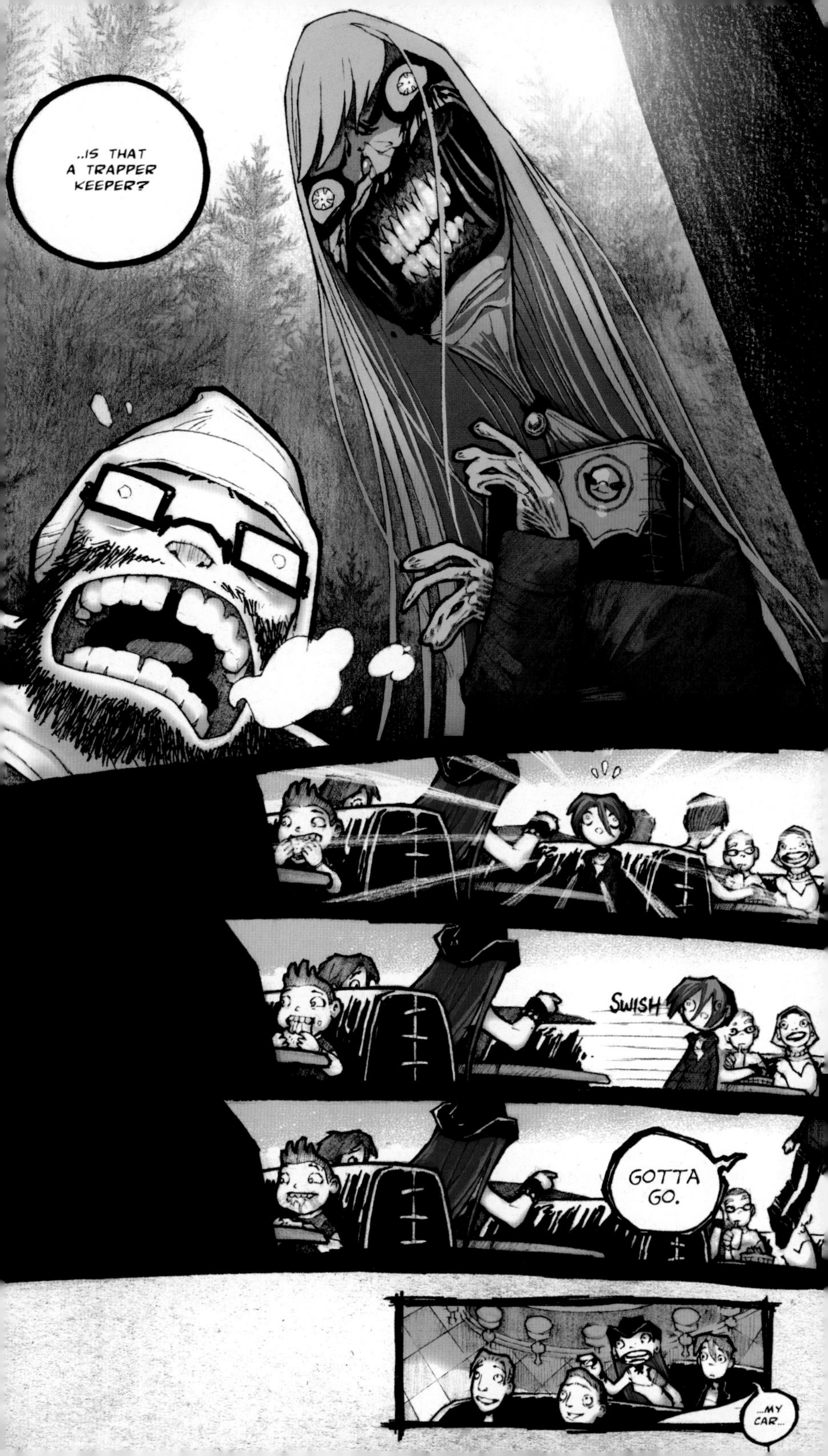
..IS THAT A TRAPPER KEEPER?
SWISH
GOTTA GO.
...MY CAR...

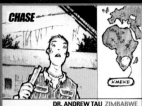

SIX WEEKS AGO...

CHASE
KMEKE
DR. ANDREW TAU ZIMBABWE
ATURAL CREATURES DISCOVERED IN ABANDONED DIAMOND MIN
CHASE
DIAMOND MINE MYSTERY
ESTERN ZIMBABWE... VAN VEDEKER COMPANY HAS "NO COMME
CHASE
DIAMOND MINE MYSTERY
SSIBLE CONNECTIONS TO THE UNEXPLAINED DEATHS OF THEO AN
CHASE
DR. ANDREW TAU ZIMBABWE
CHRISTIANNE VON VEDEKER TWO YEARS AGO IN THE SAME REGIO
CHASE
SSI
LOWIE OOSTERHAGEN SSI
SI INTERNATIONAL HAS CALLED IN EXPERTS TO STUDY "HEIROGL
CHASE
SSI
LOWIE OOSTERHAGEN SSI
ON THE TUNNEL WALLS... POP DIVA BRITNEY SPEARS HAS BEEN

MONSTERS IN MATOBO!

INSPECTORS WERE **SHOCKED** BY WHAT THEY DISCOVERED IN **THIS** ABANDONED DIAMOND MINE IN SOUTHWESTERN ZIMBABWE

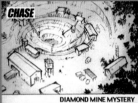

THE MATOBO MINE WAS SHUT DOWN BY THE TROUBLED **VAN VEDEKER** COMPANY NEARLY 20 YEARS AGO. BUT LAST WEEK THE COMPANY'S NEW OWNERS **RE-OPENED** THE SUBTERRANEAN SECTIONS OF THE SITE... AND GOT A **DISTURBING** SURPRISE.

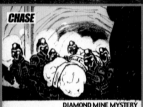

SSI INTERNATIONAL HAS PULLED NEARLY **300** APPARENTLY **SPELLCAST** CREATURES OUT OF THE TUNNELS SINCE SUNDAY, WITH NO TELLING **HOW** MANY ARE LEFT TO FIND.

SO FAR WE HAVE FEW DETAILS ON THE NATURE OF THESE CREATURES, THOUGH ONE OFFICIAL **DID** DESCRIBE THEM AS "HIGHLY DISTURBING."

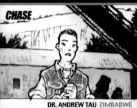

AND IT SEEMS SUPERNATURAL **BEASTIES** ARE NOT THE ONLY THING THE AUTHORITIES HAVE FOUND IN THE TUNNELS.

EXPERTS HAVE BEEN FLOWN IN TO EXAMINE WHAT SSI IS CALLING **"HEIROGLYPHICS"** SPREAD THROUGHOUT THE SYSTEM, ...AND TO CATALOG SEVERAL **HUNDRED** SCATTERED PERSONAL ITEMS, AS WELL.

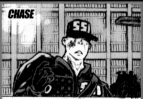

"COATS, BLANKETS... SOME **BUCKETS**, CUTLERY, KNIVES...

BOOKS. SOME BOOKS...

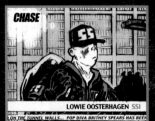

...CHILDREN'S BOOKS..."

Part Two

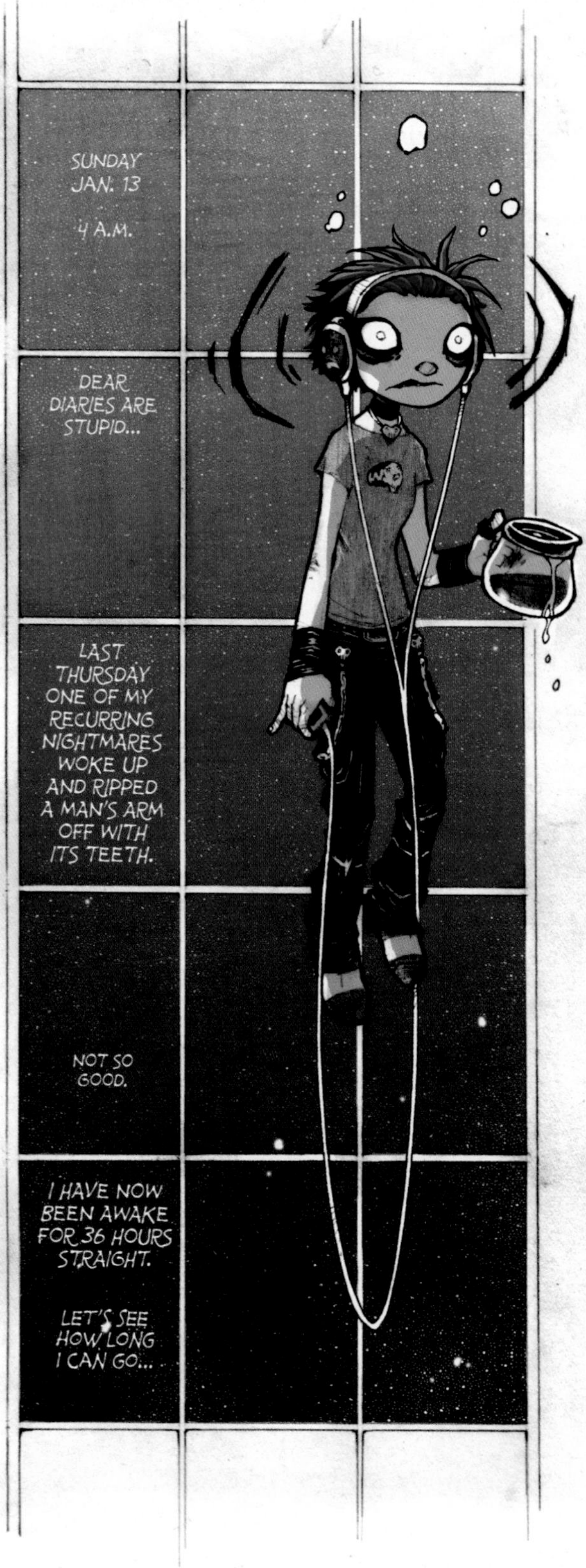
SUNDAY JAN. 13
4 A.M.
DEAR DIARIES ARE STUPID...
LAST THURSDAY ONE OF MY RECURRING NIGHTMARES WOKE UP AND RIPPED A MAN'S ARM OFF WITH ITS TEETH.
NOT SO GOOD.
I HAVE NOW BEEN AWAKE FOR 36 HOURS STRAIGHT.
LET'S SEE HOW LONG I CAN GO...

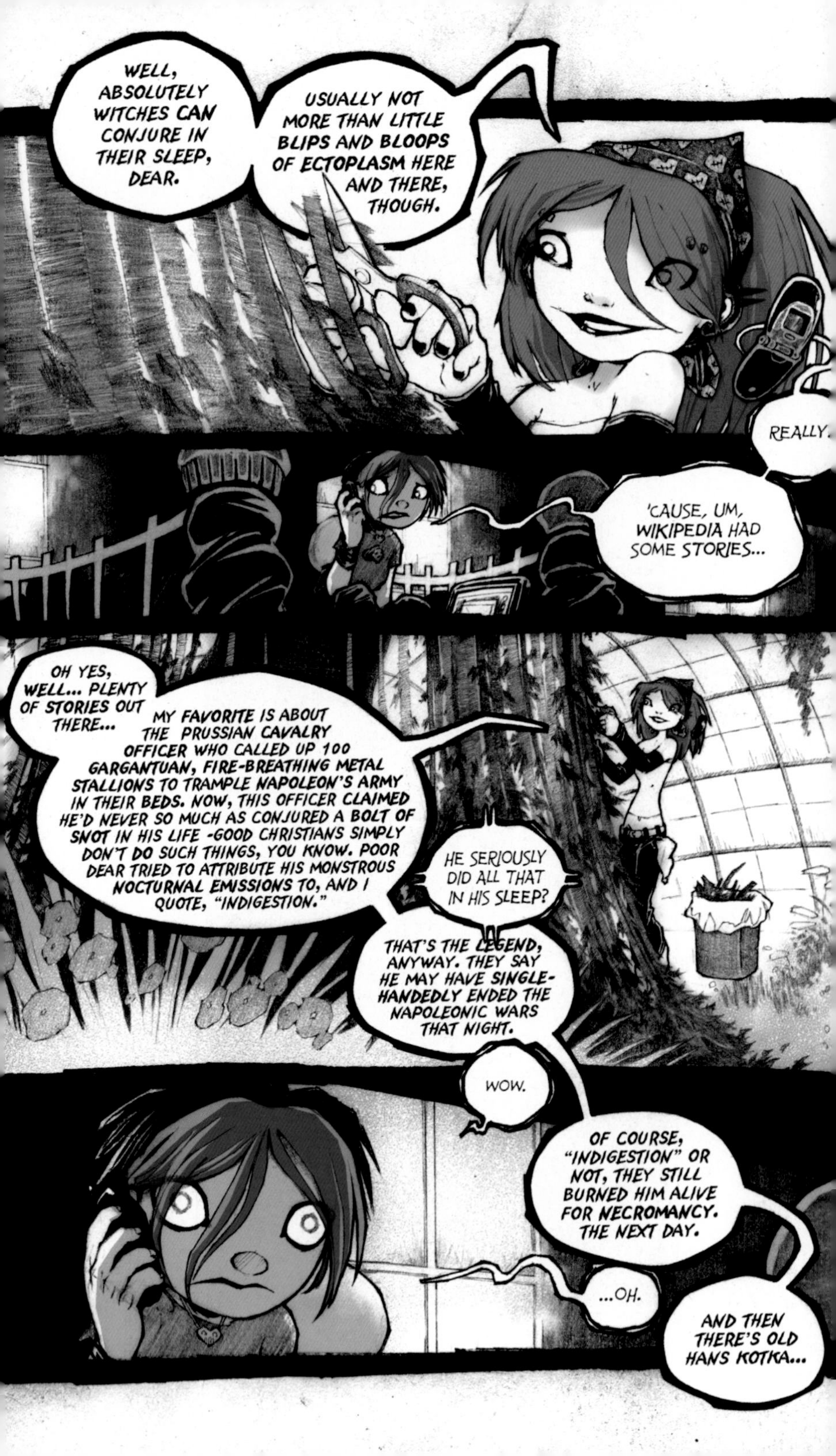
WELL, ABSOLUTELY WITCHES CAN CONJURE IN THEIR SLEEP, DEAR.
USUALLY NOT MORE THAN LITTLE BLIPS AND BLOOPS OF ECTOPLASM HERE AND THERE, THOUGH.
REALLY.
'CAUSE, UM, WIKIPEDIA HAD SOME STORIES...
OH YES, WELL... PLENTY OF STORIES OUT THERE...
MY FAVORITE IS ABOUT THE PRUSSIAN CAVALRY OFFICER WHO CALLED UP 100 GARGANTUAN, FIRE-BREATHING METAL STALLIONS TO TRAMPLE NAPOLEON'S ARMY IN THEIR BEDS. NOW, THIS OFFICER CLAIMED HE'D NEVER SO MUCH AS CONJURED A BOLT OF SNOT IN HIS LIFE -GOOD CHRISTIANS SIMPLY DON'T DO SUCH THINGS, YOU KNOW. POOR DEAR TRIED TO ATTRIBUTE HIS MONSTROUS NOCTURNAL EMISSIONS TO, AND I QUOTE, "INDIGESTION."
HE SERIOUSLY DID ALL THAT IN HIS SLEEP?
THAT'S THE LEGEND, ANYWAY. THEY SAY HE MAY HAVE SINGLE-HANDEDLY ENDED THE NAPOLEONIC WARS THAT NIGHT.
WOW.
OF COURSE, "INDIGESTION" OR NOT, THEY STILL BURNED HIM ALIVE FOR NECROMANCY. THE NEXT DAY.
...OH.
AND THEN THERE'S OLD HANS KOTKA...

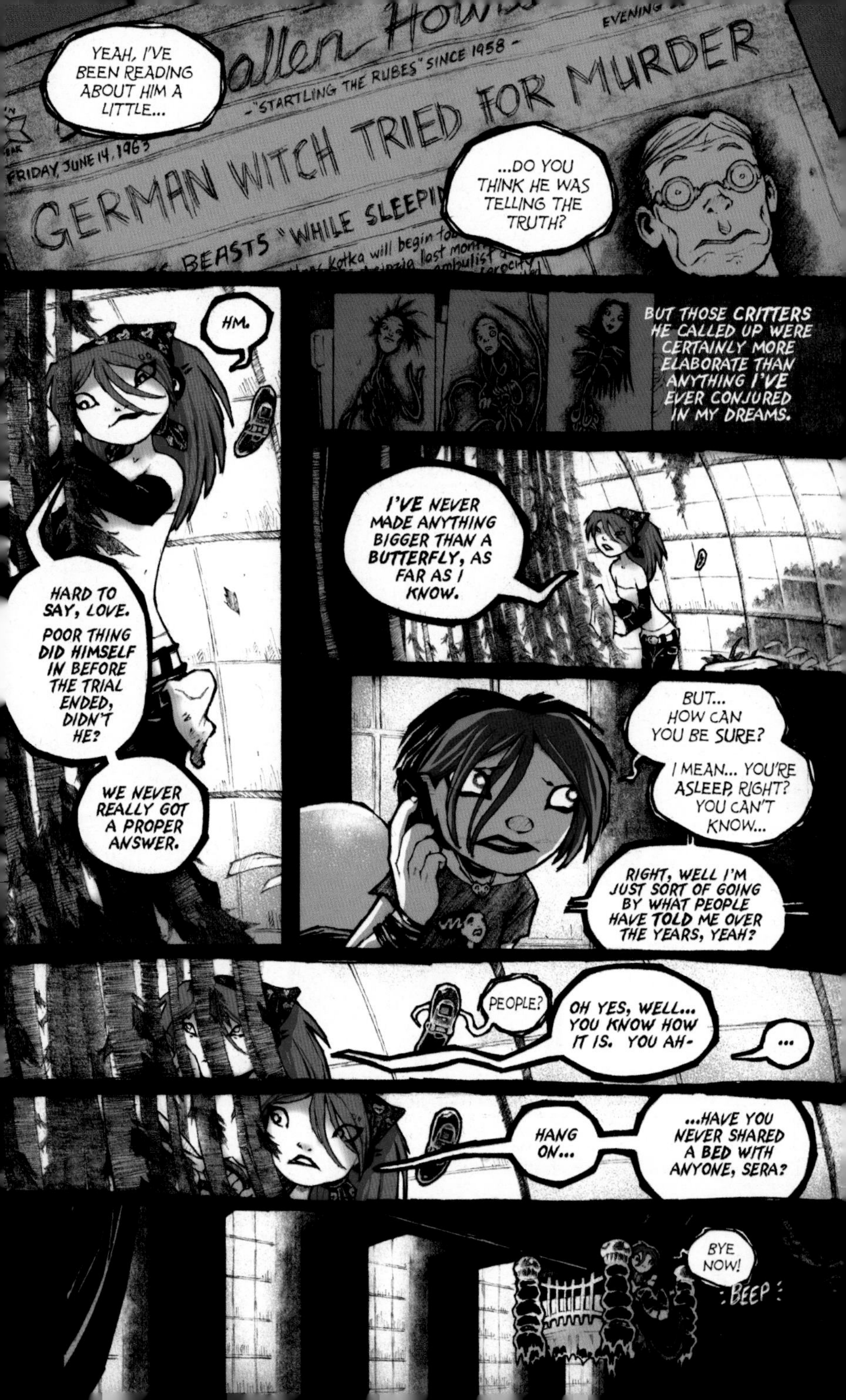
Fallen Hows
EVENING
- "STARTLING THE RUBES" SINCE 1958 -
FRIDAY, JUNE 14, 1963
GERMAN WITCH TRIED FOR MURDER
YEAH, I'VE BEEN READING ABOUT HIM A LITTLE...
...DO YOU THINK HE WAS TELLING THE TRUTH?
HM.
BUT THOSE CRITTERS HE CALLED UP WERE CERTAINLY MORE ELABORATE THAN ANYTHING I'VE EVER CONJURED IN MY DREAMS.
I'VE NEVER MADE ANYTHING BIGGER THAN A BUTTERFLY, AS FAR AS I KNOW.
HARD TO SAY, LOVE.
POOR THING DID HIMSELF IN BEFORE THE TRIAL ENDED, DIDN'T HE?
WE NEVER REALLY GOT A PROPER ANSWER.
BUT... HOW CAN YOU BE SURE?
I MEAN... YOU'RE ASLEEP, RIGHT? YOU CAN'T KNOW...
RIGHT, WELL I'M JUST SORT OF GOING BY WHAT PEOPLE HAVE TOLD ME OVER THE YEARS, YEAH?
PEOPLE?
OH YES, WELL... YOU KNOW HOW IT IS. YOU AH-
...
HANG ON...
...HAVE YOU NEVER SHARED A BED WITH ANYONE, SERA?
BYE NOW!
BEEP

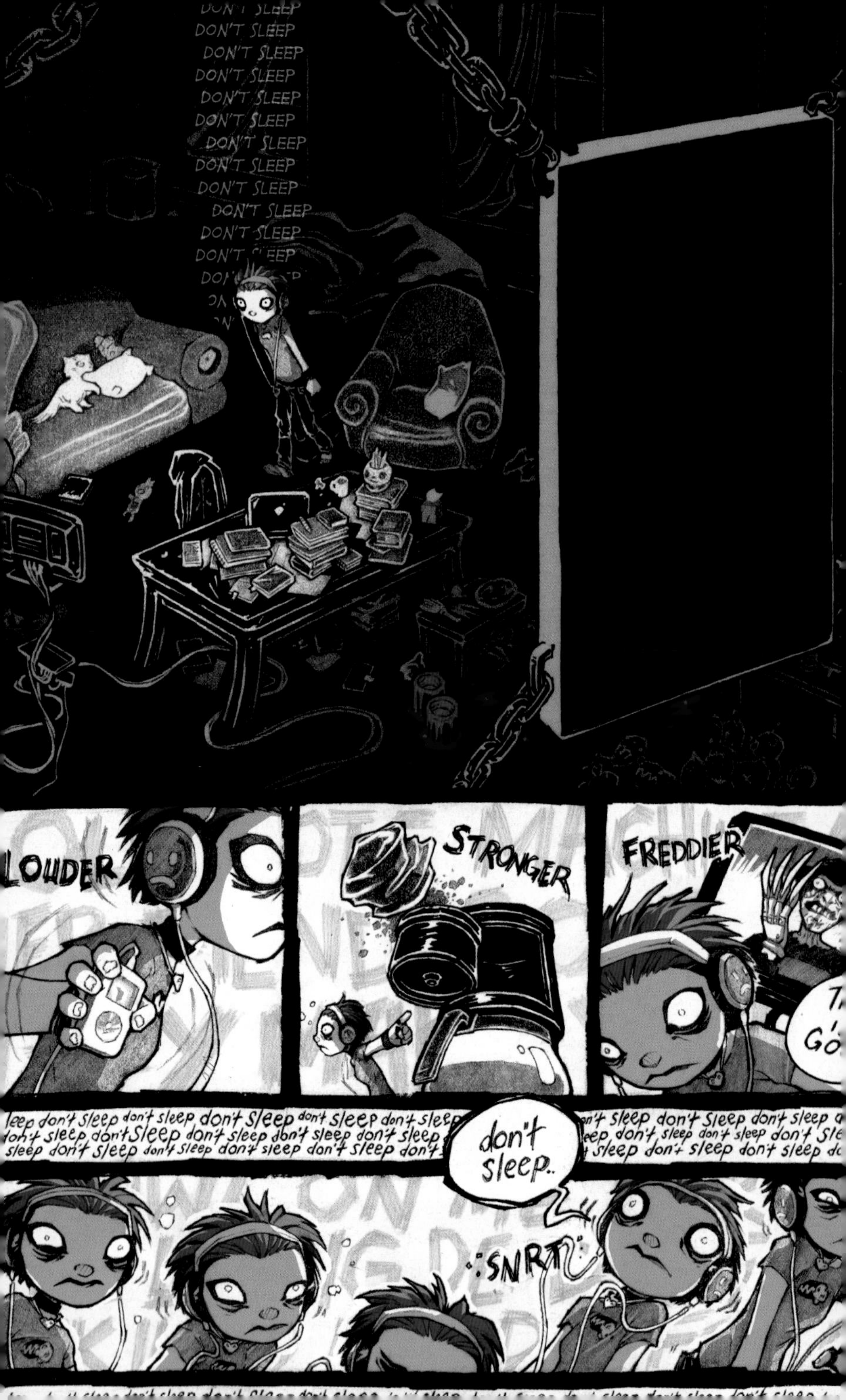
DON'T SLEEP
DON'T SLEEP
DON'T SLEEP
DON'T SLEEP
DON'T SLEEP
DON'T SLEEP
DON'T SLEEP
DON'T SLEEP
DON'T SLEEP
DON'T SLEEP
DON'T SLEEP
LOUDER
STRONGER
FREDDIER
leep don't sleep don't sleep don't sleep don't sleep don't sleep
don't sleep don't sleep don't sleep don't sleep don't sleep don't sleep
sleep don't sleep don't sleep don't sleep don't sleep don't
don't sleep..
n't sleep don't sleep don't sleep
eep don't sleep don't sleep don't sleep don't sle
t sleep don't sleep don't sleep don't sleep do
:SNRT:

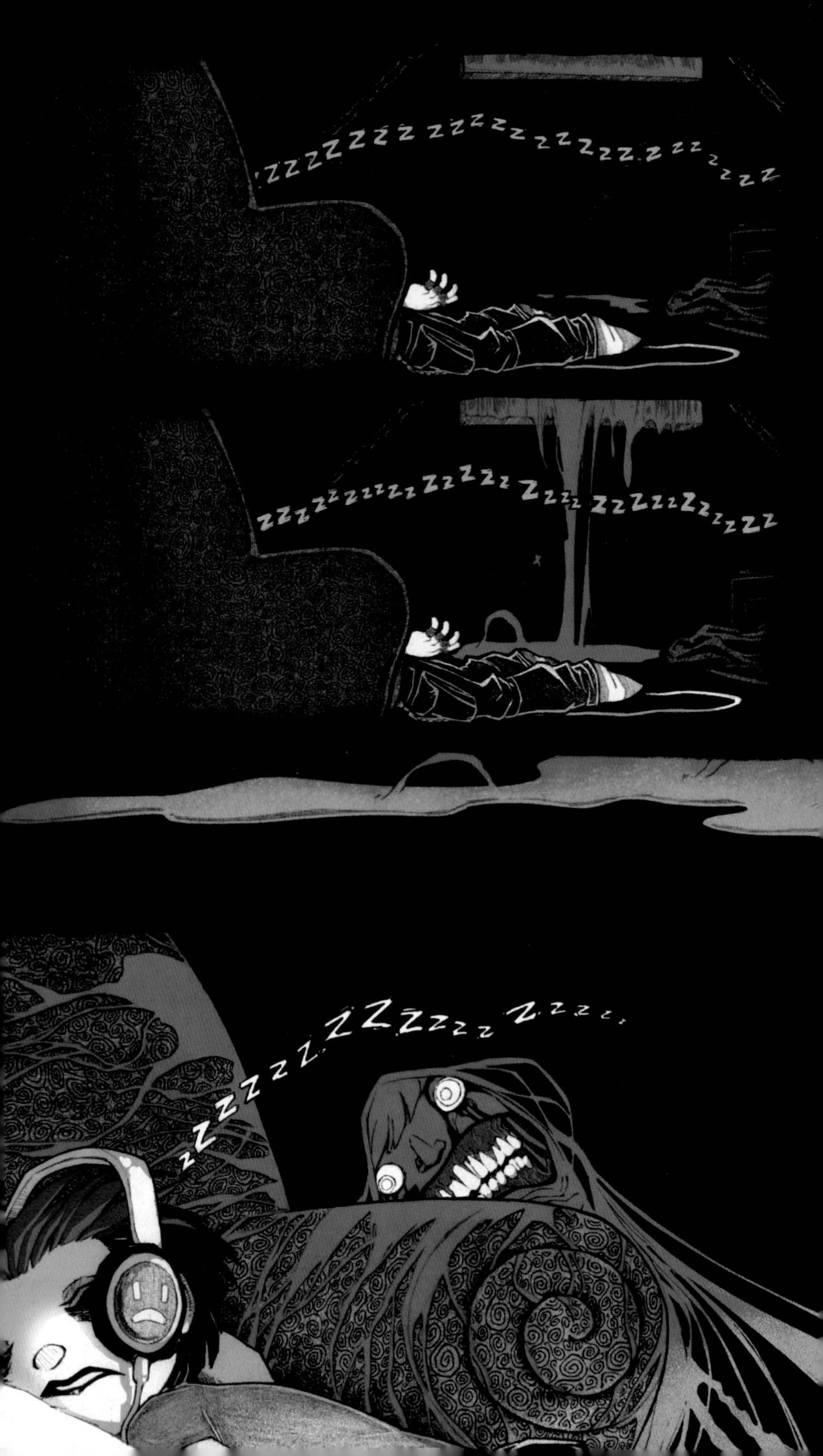

SER-

SERA!

SERA, MY GOD! ARE YOU ALL RIGHT?

THISH... ...HASH OTTA STOB...

MY GOD, SERA!

THE NIGHT TERRORS AGAIN?

MMM...

MM I THOUD... UM... IF I STAYED UP LONG ENOUGH I'D BE TOO EXHAUSTED FOR DREAMING, BUT UM...

BUT YEAH, DIDN'T WORK.

ONLY YOU WOULD USE INDUSTRIAL ROCK AND HORROR MOVIES AS A CURE FOR NIGHT TERRORS.

HORROR STUFF DOESN'T GIVE ME BAD DREAMS, ZOE.

OH, I KNOW THAT.

BUT PERHA WE OUGHT HAVE A LITTLE, "SLEEP STRAT SESSION AT S POINT, YEA

ANYWAY, THE SHERIFF IS HERE TO SEE YOU.

YUP.

OH, AND HERE SHE IS NOW, BARGING INTO PEOPLE'S ROOMS WITHOU PERMISSION. HOW NICE FOR EVERYONE!

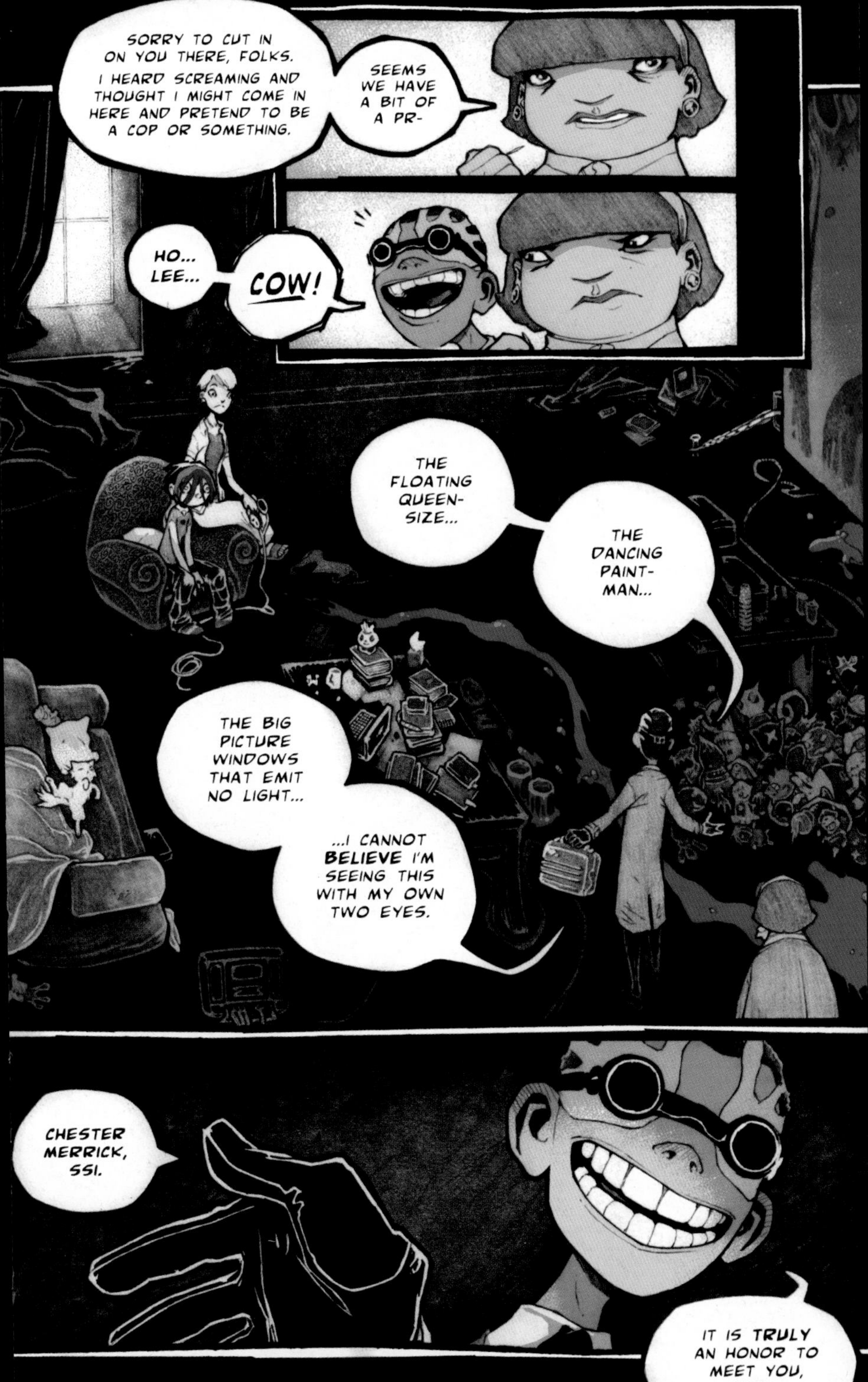

SORRY TO CUT IN ON YOU THERE, FOLKS.
I HEARD SCREAMING AND THOUGHT I MIGHT COME IN HERE AND PRETEND TO BE A COP OR SOMETHING.
SEEMS WE HAVE A BIT OF A PR-
HO... LEE...
COW!
THE FLOATING QUEEN-SIZE...
THE DANCING PAINT-MAN...
THE BIG PICTURE WINDOWS THAT EMIT NO LIGHT...
...I CANNOT BELIEVE I'M SEEING THIS WITH MY OWN TWO EYES.
CHESTER MERRICK, SSI.
IT IS TRULY AN HONOR TO MEET YOU, SERA.

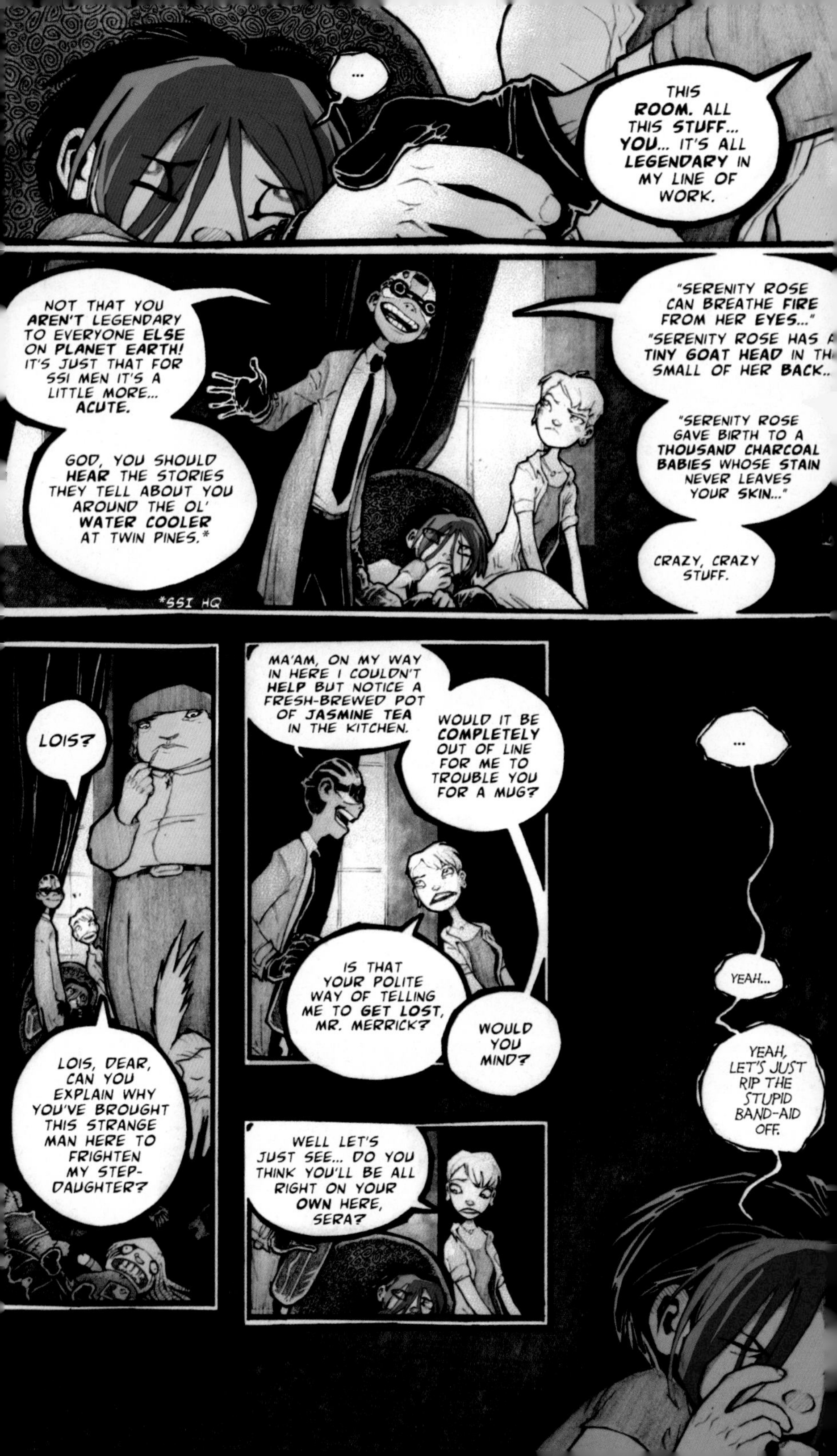
...
THIS ROOM. ALL THIS STUFF... YOU... IT'S ALL LEGENDARY IN MY LINE OF WORK.
NOT THAT YOU AREN'T LEGENDARY TO EVERYONE ELSE ON PLANET EARTH! IT'S JUST THAT FOR SSI MEN IT'S A LITTLE MORE... ACUTE.
GOD, YOU SHOULD HEAR THE STORIES THEY TELL ABOUT YOU AROUND THE OL' WATER COOLER AT TWIN PINES.*
"SERENITY ROSE CAN BREATHE FIRE FROM HER EYES..." "SERENITY ROSE HAS A TINY GOAT HEAD IN THE SMALL OF HER BACK..
"SERENITY ROSE GAVE BIRTH TO A THOUSAND CHARCOAL BABIES WHOSE STAIN NEVER LEAVES YOUR SKIN..."
CRAZY, CRAZY STUFF.
*SSI HQ
LOIS?
LOIS, DEAR, CAN YOU EXPLAIN WHY YOU'VE BROUGHT THIS STRANGE MAN HERE TO FRIGHTEN MY STEP-DAUGHTER?
MA'AM, ON MY WAY IN HERE I COULDN'T HELP BUT NOTICE A FRESH-BREWED POT OF JASMINE TEA IN THE KITCHEN.
WOULD IT BE COMPLETELY OUT OF LINE FOR ME TO TROUBLE YOU FOR A MUG?
IS THAT YOUR POLITE WAY OF TELLING ME TO GET LOST, MR. MERRICK?
WOULD YOU MIND?
WELL LET'S JUST SEE... DO YOU THINK YOU'LL BE ALL RIGHT ON YOUR OWN HERE, SERA?
...
YEAH...
YEAH, LET'S JUST RIP THE STUPID BAND-AID OFF.

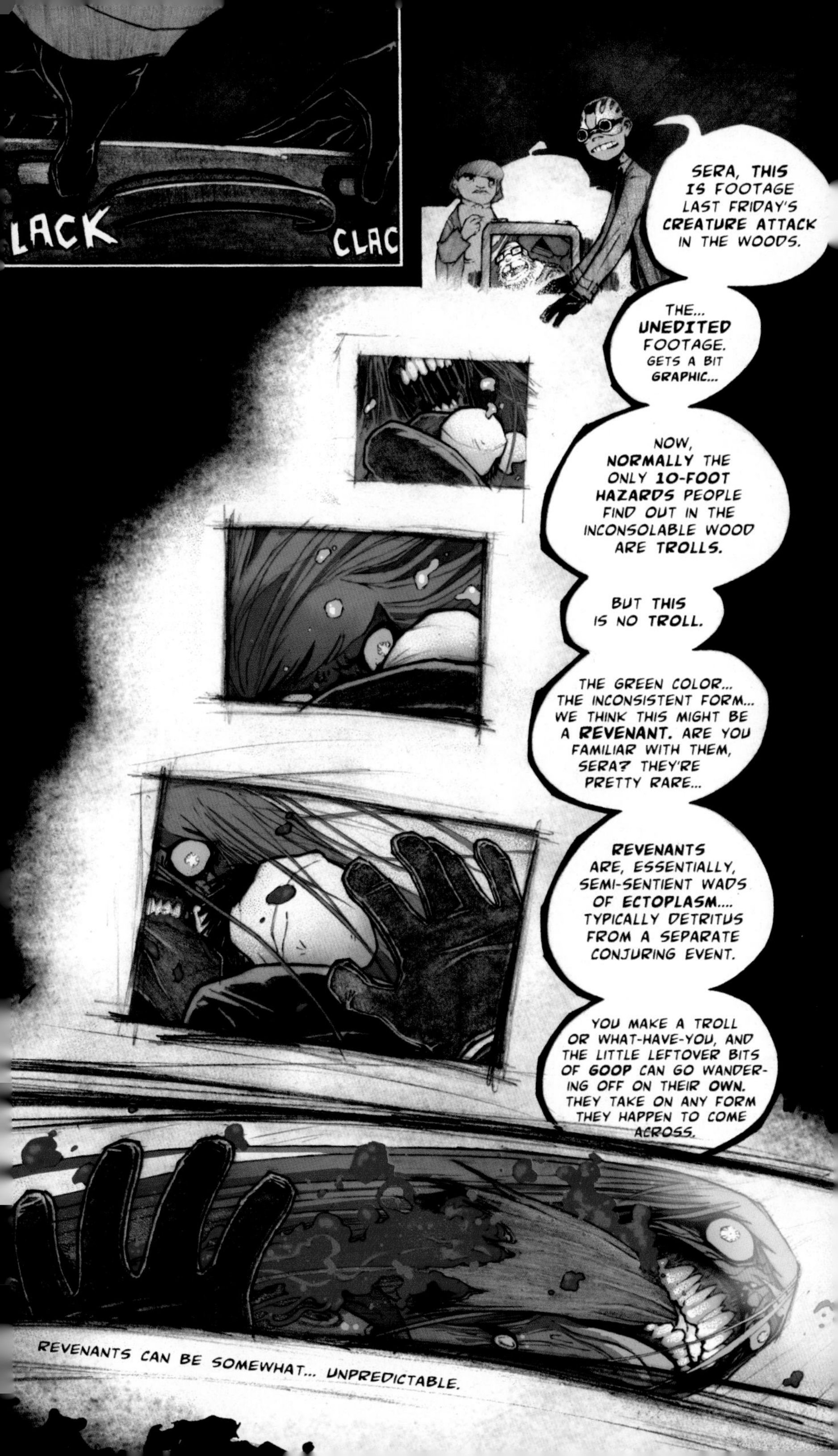

LACK
CLAC
SERA, THIS IS FOOTAGE LAST FRIDAY'S CREATURE ATTACK IN THE WOODS.
THE... UNEDITED FOOTAGE. GETS A BIT GRAPHIC...
NOW, NORMALLY THE ONLY 10-FOOT HAZARDS PEOPLE FIND OUT IN THE INCONSOLABLE WOOD ARE TROLLS.
BUT THIS IS NO TROLL.
THE GREEN COLOR... THE INCONSISTENT FORM... WE THINK THIS MIGHT BE A REVENANT. ARE YOU FAMILIAR WITH THEM, SERA? THEY'RE PRETTY RARE...
REVENANTS ARE, ESSENTIALLY, SEMI-SENTIENT WADS OF ECTOPLASM.... TYPICALLY DETRITUS FROM A SEPARATE CONJURING EVENT.
YOU MAKE A TROLL OR WHAT-HAVE-YOU, AND THE LITTLE LEFTOVER BITS OF GOOP CAN GO WANDER-ING OFF ON THEIR OWN. THEY TAKE ON ANY FORM THEY HAPPEN TO COME ACROSS.
REVENANTS CAN BE SOMEWHAT... UNPREDICTABLE.

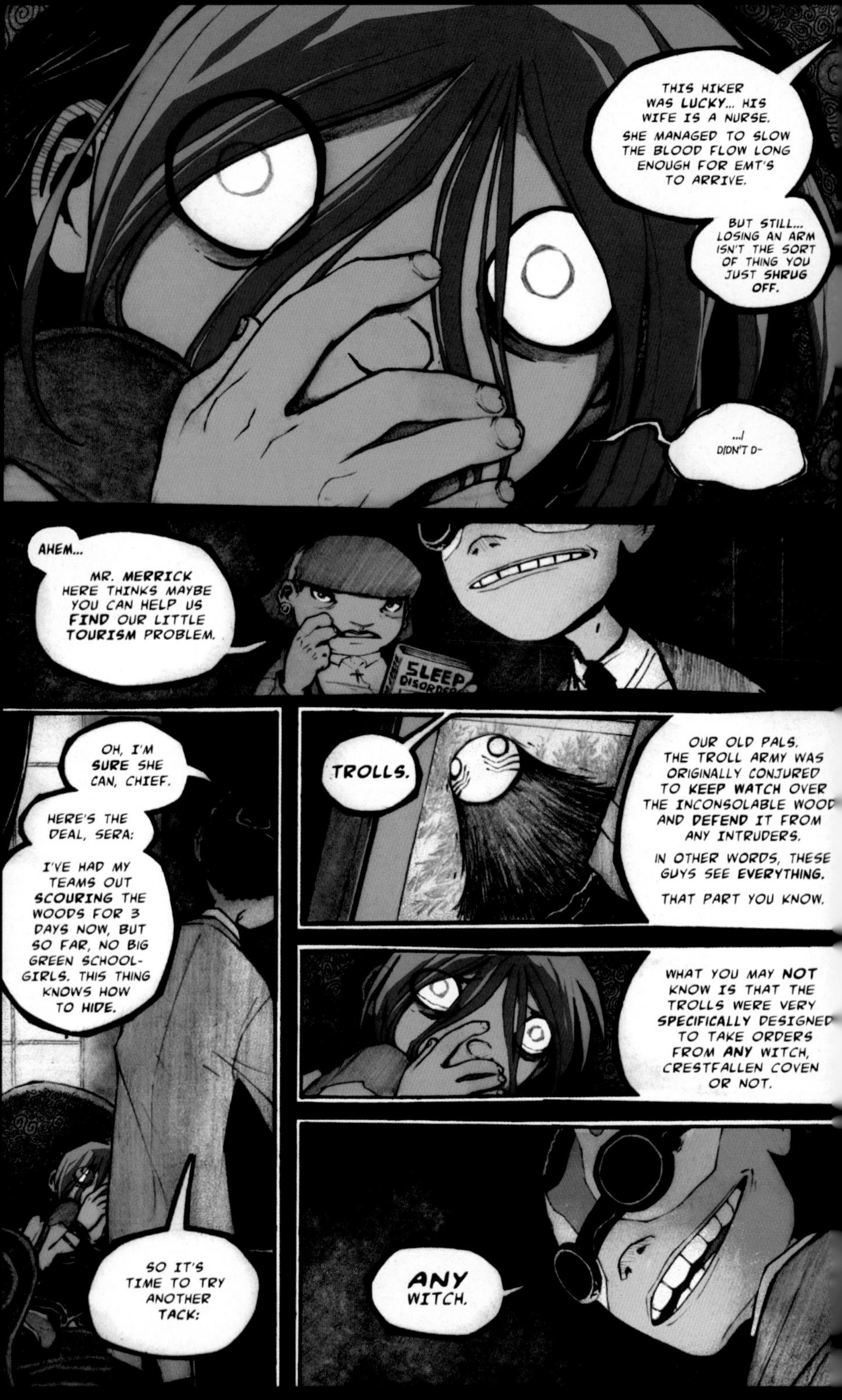
THIS HIKER WAS LUCKY... HIS WIFE IS A NURSE.
SHE MANAGED TO SLOW THE BLOOD FLOW LONG ENOUGH FOR EMT'S TO ARRIVE.
BUT STILL... LOSING AN ARM ISN'T THE SORT OF THING YOU JUST SHRUG OFF.
...I DIDN'T D-
AHEM...
MR. MERRICK HERE THINKS MAYBE YOU CAN HELP US FIND OUR LITTLE TOURISM PROBLEM.
SLEEP DISORDE
OH, I'M SURE SHE CAN, CHIEF.
HERE'S THE DEAL, SERA:
I'VE HAD MY TEAMS OUT SCOURING THE WOODS FOR 3 DAYS NOW, BUT SO FAR, NO BIG GREEN SCHOOL-GIRLS. THIS THING KNOWS HOW TO HIDE.
SO IT'S TIME TO TRY ANOTHER TACK:
TROLLS.
OUR OLD PALS. THE TROLL ARMY WAS ORIGINALLY CONJURED TO KEEP WATCH OVER THE INCONSOLABLE WOOD AND DEFEND IT FROM ANY INTRUDERS.
IN OTHER WORDS, THESE GUYS SEE EVERYTHING.
THAT PART YOU KNOW.
WHAT YOU MAY NOT KNOW IS THAT THE TROLLS WERE VERY SPECIFICALLY DESIGNED TO TAKE ORDERS FROM ANY WITCH, CRESTFALLEN COVEN OR NOT.
ANY WITCH.

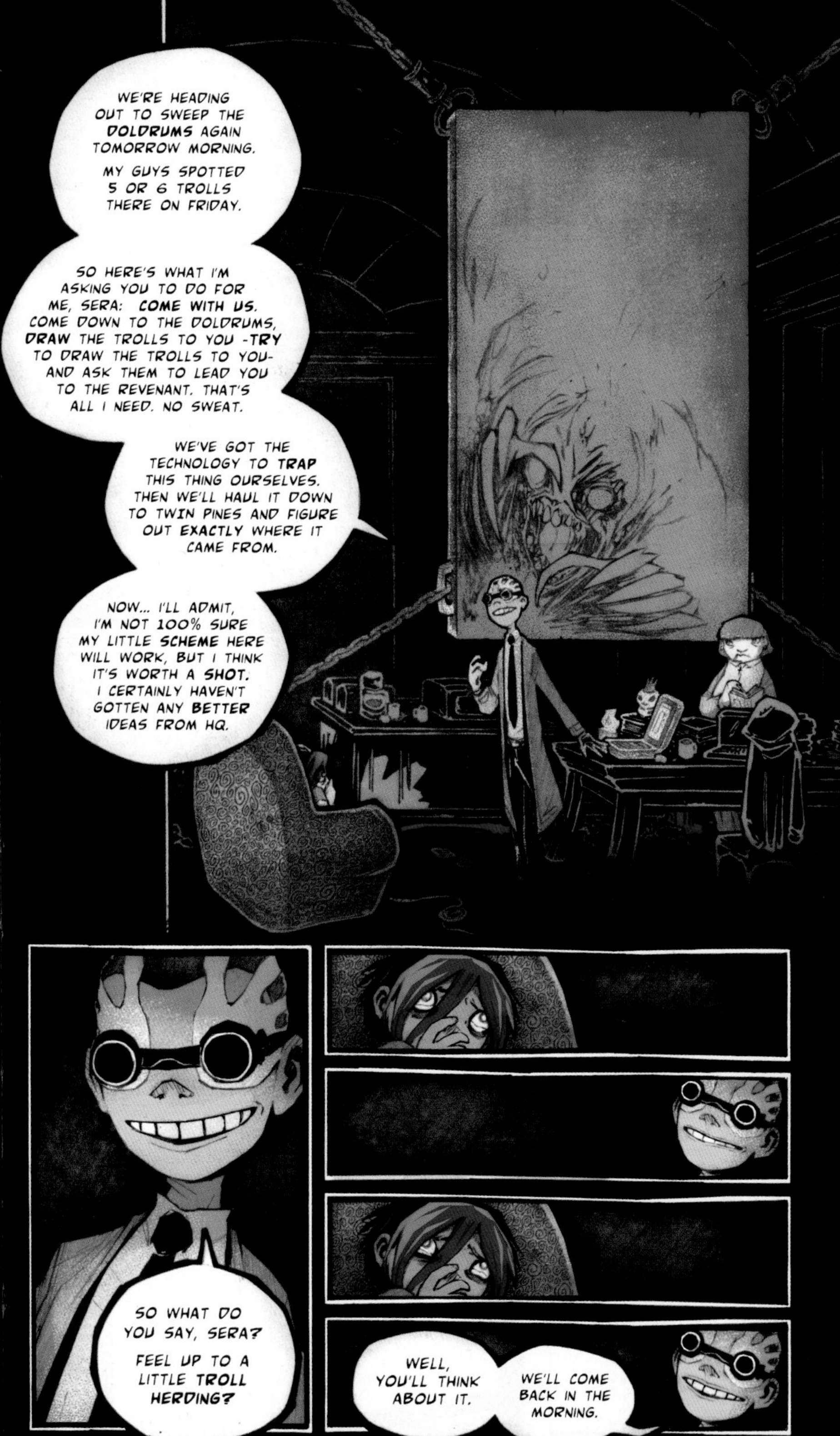
WE'RE HEADING OUT TO SWEEP THE **DOLDRUMS** AGAIN TOMORROW MORNING.
MY GUYS SPOTTED 5 OR 6 TROLLS THERE ON FRIDAY.
SO HERE'S WHAT I'M ASKING YOU TO DO FOR ME, SERA: **COME WITH US.** COME DOWN TO THE DOLDRUMS, **DRAW** THE TROLLS TO YOU -**TRY** TO DRAW THE TROLLS TO YOU- AND ASK THEM TO LEAD YOU TO THE REVENANT. THAT'S ALL I NEED. NO SWEAT.
WE'VE GOT THE TECHNOLOGY TO **TRAP** THIS THING OURSELVES. THEN WE'LL HAUL IT DOWN TO TWIN PINES AND FIGURE OUT **EXACTLY** WHERE IT CAME FROM.
NOW... I'LL ADMIT, I'M NOT 100% SURE MY LITTLE **SCHEME** HERE WILL WORK, BUT I THINK IT'S WORTH A **SHOT.** I CERTAINLY HAVEN'T GOTTEN ANY **BETTER** IDEAS FROM HQ.
SO WHAT DO YOU SAY, SERA?
FEEL UP TO A LITTLE **TROLL HERDING?**
WELL, YOU'LL THINK ABOUT IT.
WE'LL COME BACK IN THE MORNING.

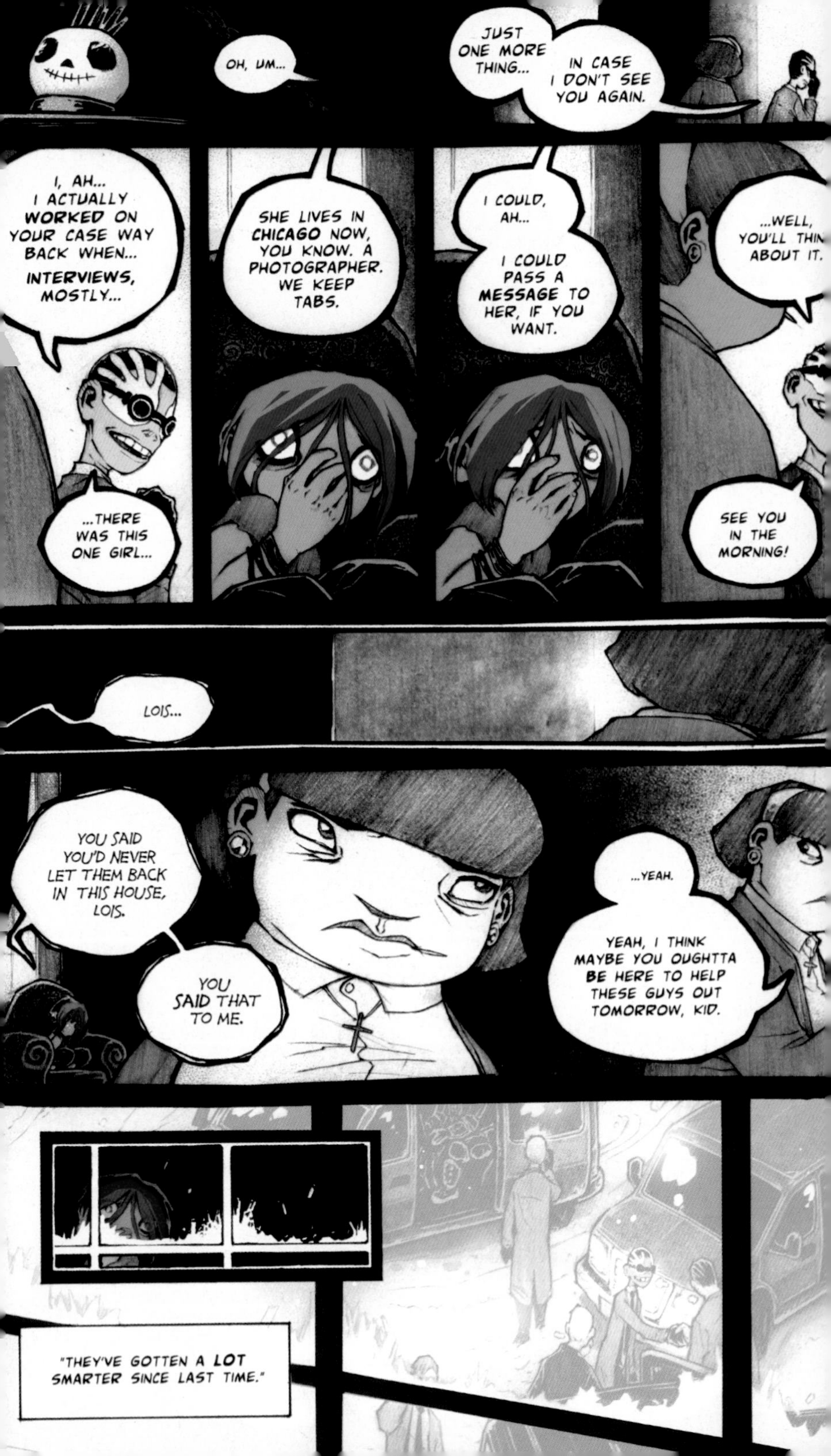
OH, UM...
JUST ONE MORE THING...
IN CASE I DON'T SEE YOU AGAIN.
I, AH... I ACTUALLY WORKED ON YOUR CASE WAY BACK WHEN... INTERVIEWS, MOSTLY...
...THERE WAS THIS ONE GIRL...
SHE LIVES IN CHICAGO NOW, YOU KNOW. A PHOTOGRAPHER. WE KEEP TABS.
I COULD, AH...
I COULD PASS A MESSAGE TO HER, IF YOU WANT.
...WELL, YOU'LL THIN ABOUT IT.
SEE YOU IN THE MORNING!
LOIS...
YOU SAID YOU'D NEVER LET THEM BACK IN THIS HOUSE, LOIS.
YOU SAID THAT TO ME.
...YEAH.
YEAH, I THINK MAYBE YOU OUGHTTA BE HERE TO HELP THESE GUYS OUT TOMORROW, KID.
"THEY'VE GOTTEN A LOT SMARTER SINCE LAST TIME."

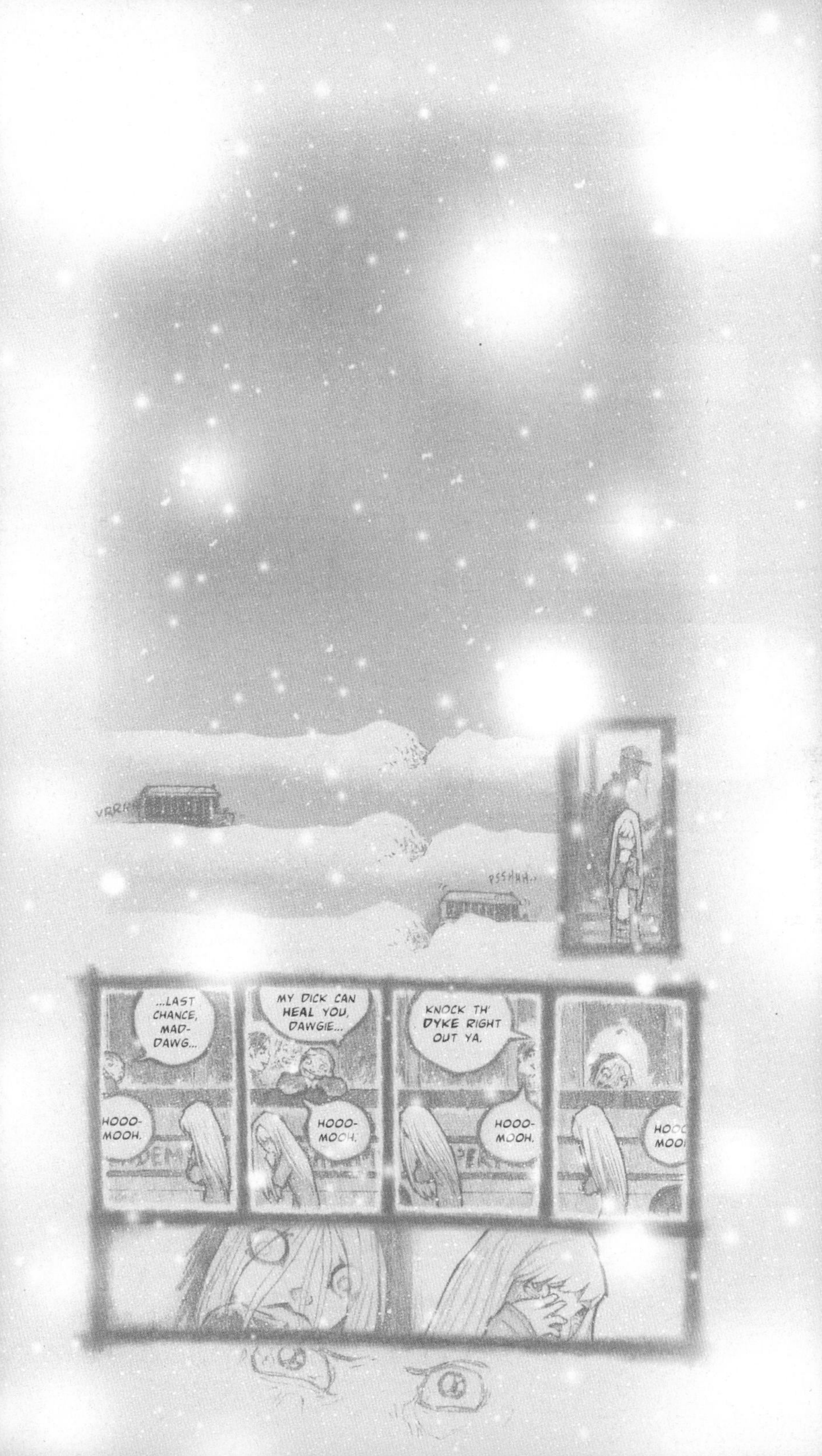
...LAST CHANCE, MAD-DAWG...
HOOO-MOOH.
MY DICK CAN HEAL YOU, DAWGIE...
HOOO-MOOH.
KNOCK TH' DYKE RIGHT OUT YA.
HOOO-MOOH.

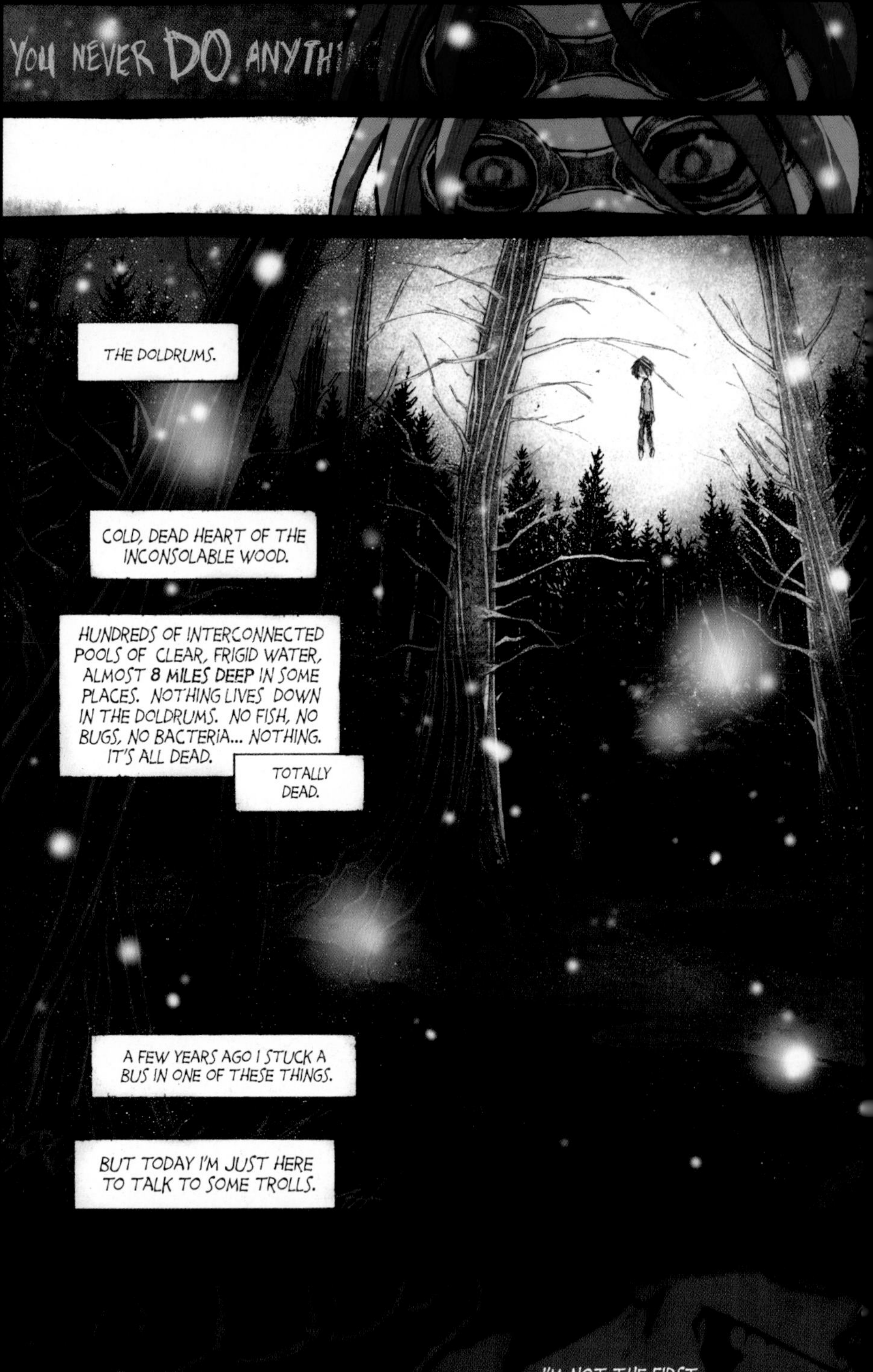
YOU NEVER DO ANYTHI
THE DOLDRUMS.
COLD, DEAD HEART OF THE INCONSOLABLE WOOD.
HUNDREDS OF INTERCONNECTED POOLS OF CLEAR, FRIGID WATER, ALMOST 8 MILES DEEP IN SOME PLACES. NOTHING LIVES DOWN IN THE DOLDRUMS. NO FISH, NO BUGS, NO BACTERIA... NOTHING. IT'S ALL DEAD.
TOTALLY DEAD.
A FEW YEARS AGO I STUCK A BUS IN ONE OF THESE THINGS.
BUT TODAY I'M JUST HERE TO TALK TO SOME TROLLS.
I'M NOT THE FIRST WITCH TO DO THIS...

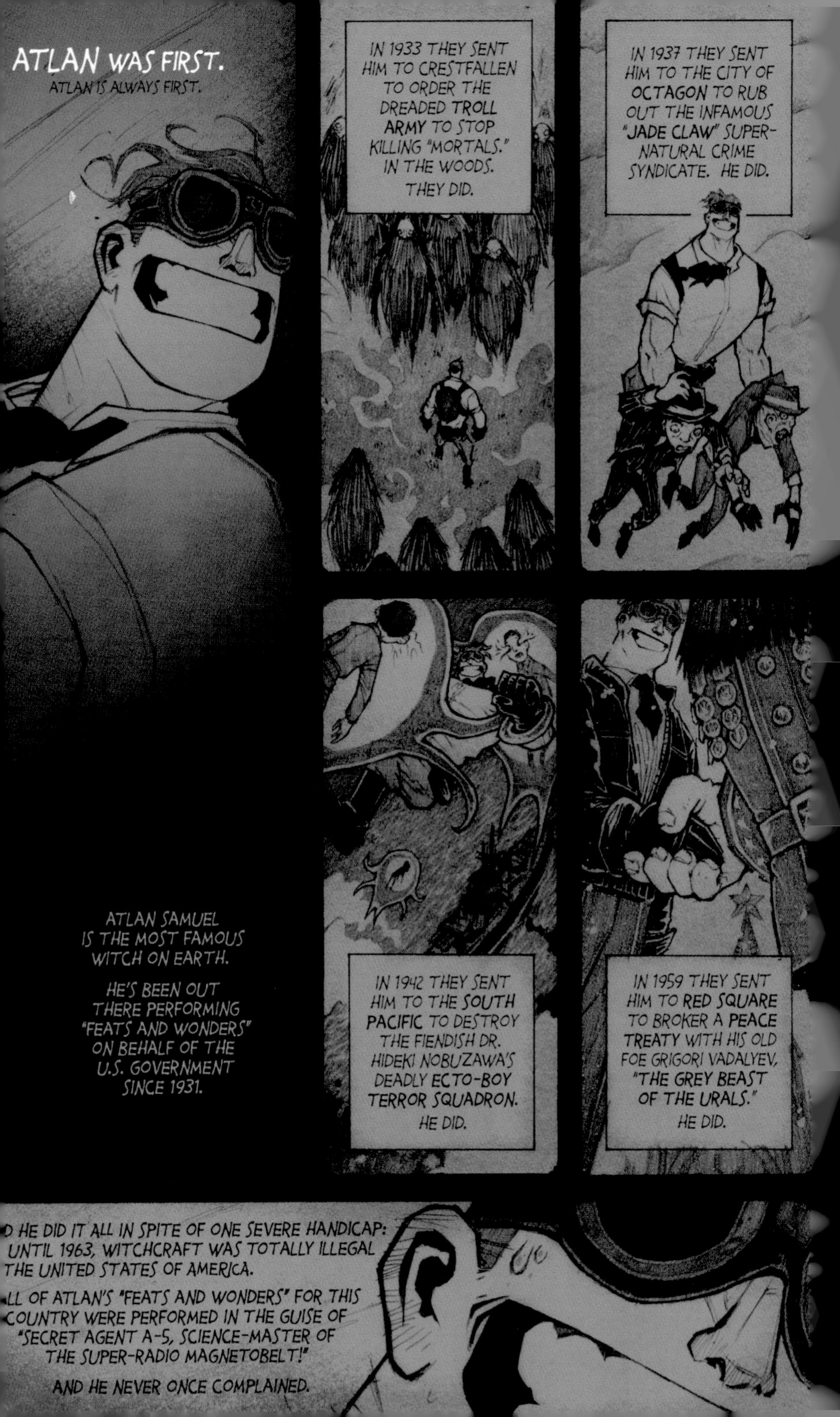
ATLAN WAS FIRST.
ATLAN IS ALWAYS FIRST.
ATLAN SAMUEL IS THE MOST FAMOUS WITCH ON EARTH.
HE'S BEEN OUT THERE PERFORMING "FEATS AND WONDERS" ON BEHALF OF THE U.S. GOVERNMENT SINCE 1931.
IN 1933 THEY SENT HIM TO CRESTFALLEN TO ORDER THE DREADED TROLL ARMY TO STOP KILLING "MORTALS." IN THE WOODS.
THEY DID.
IN 1937 THEY SENT HIM TO THE CITY OF OCTAGON TO RUB OUT THE INFAMOUS "JADE CLAW" SUPER-NATURAL CRIME SYNDICATE. HE DID.
IN 1942 THEY SENT HIM TO THE SOUTH PACIFIC TO DESTROY THE FIENDISH DR. HIDEKI NOBUZAWA'S DEADLY ECTO-BOY TERROR SQUADRON.
HE DID.
IN 1959 THEY SENT HIM TO RED SQUARE TO BROKER A PEACE TREATY WITH HIS OLD FOE GRIGORI VADALYEV, "THE GREY BEAST OF THE URALS."
HE DID.
D HE DID IT ALL IN SPITE OF ONE SEVERE HANDICAP: UNTIL 1963, WITCHCRAFT WAS TOTALLY ILLEGAL THE UNITED STATES OF AMERICA.
LL OF ATLAN'S "FEATS AND WONDERS" FOR THIS COUNTRY WERE PERFORMED IN THE GUISE OF "SECRET AGENT A-5, SCIENCE-MASTER OF THE SUPER-RADIO MAGNETOBELT!"
AND HE NEVER ONCE COMPLAINED.

I'M NOT ONE TENTH THE WITCH ATLAN IS.

I NEVER WILL BE.

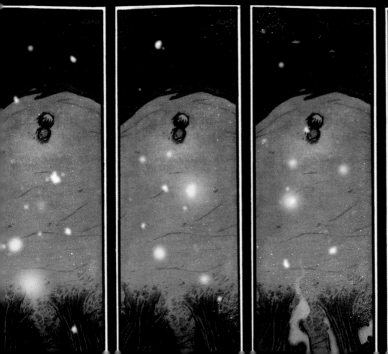
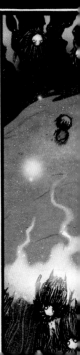

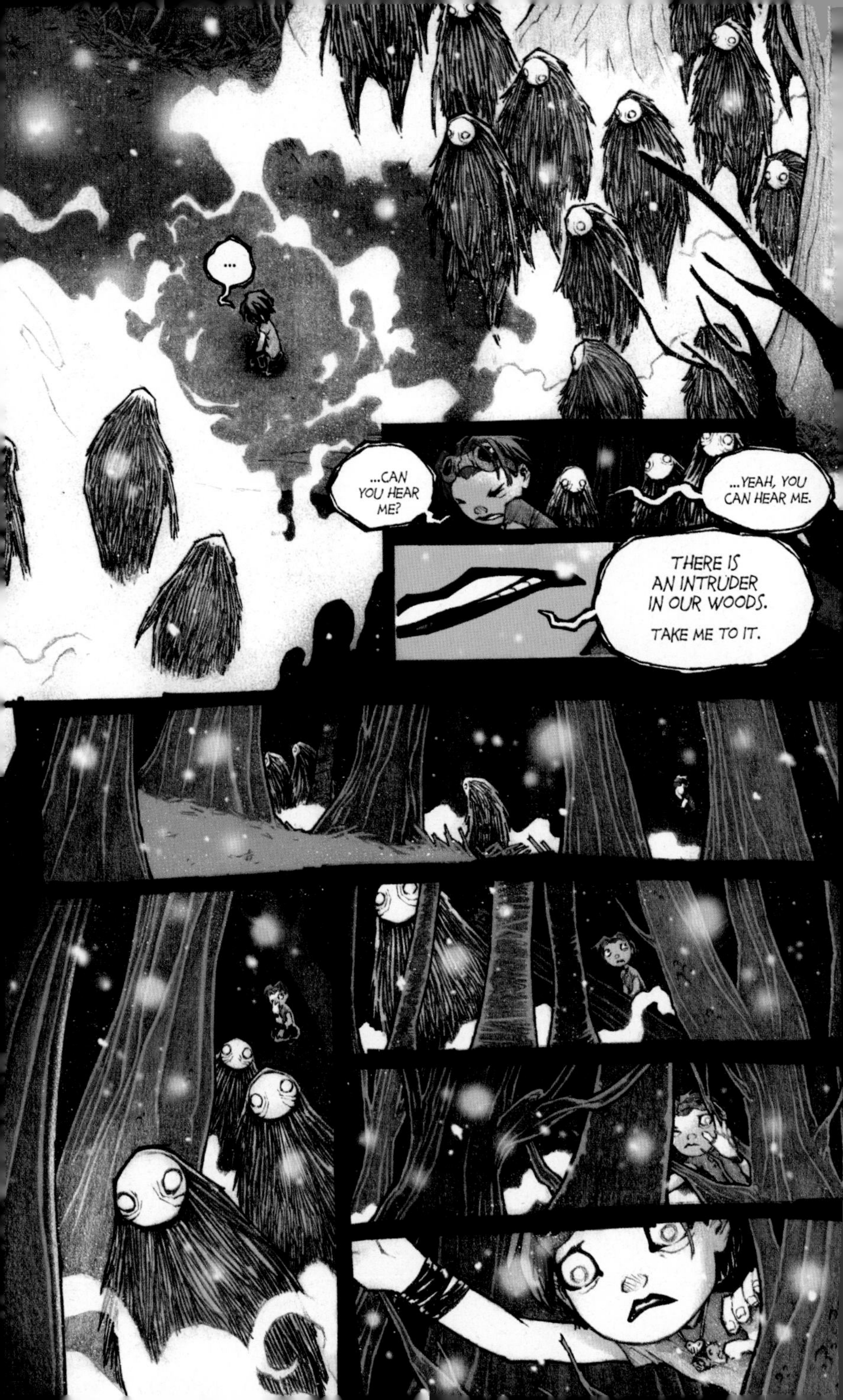
...
...CAN YOU HEAR ME?
...YEAH, YOU CAN HEAR ME.
THERE IS AN INTRUDER IN OUR WOODS.
TAKE ME TO IT.

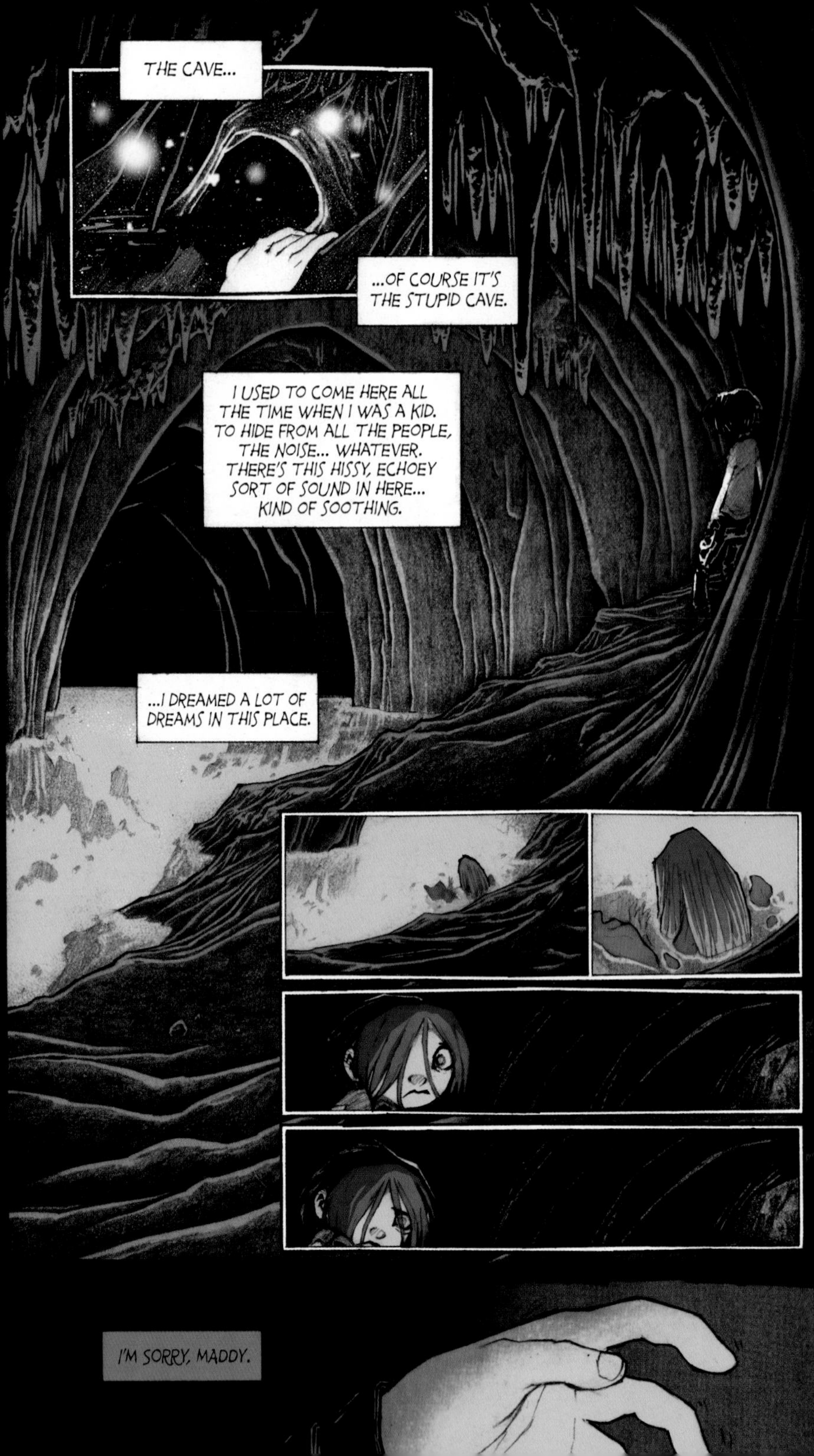
THE CAVE...
...OF COURSE IT'S THE STUPID CAVE.
I USED TO COME HERE ALL THE TIME WHEN I WAS A KID. TO HIDE FROM ALL THE PEOPLE, THE NOISE... WHATEVER. THERE'S THIS HISSY, ECHOEY SORT OF SOUND IN HERE... KIND OF SOOTHING.
...I DREAMED A LOT OF DREAMS IN THIS PLACE.
I'M SORRY, MADDY.

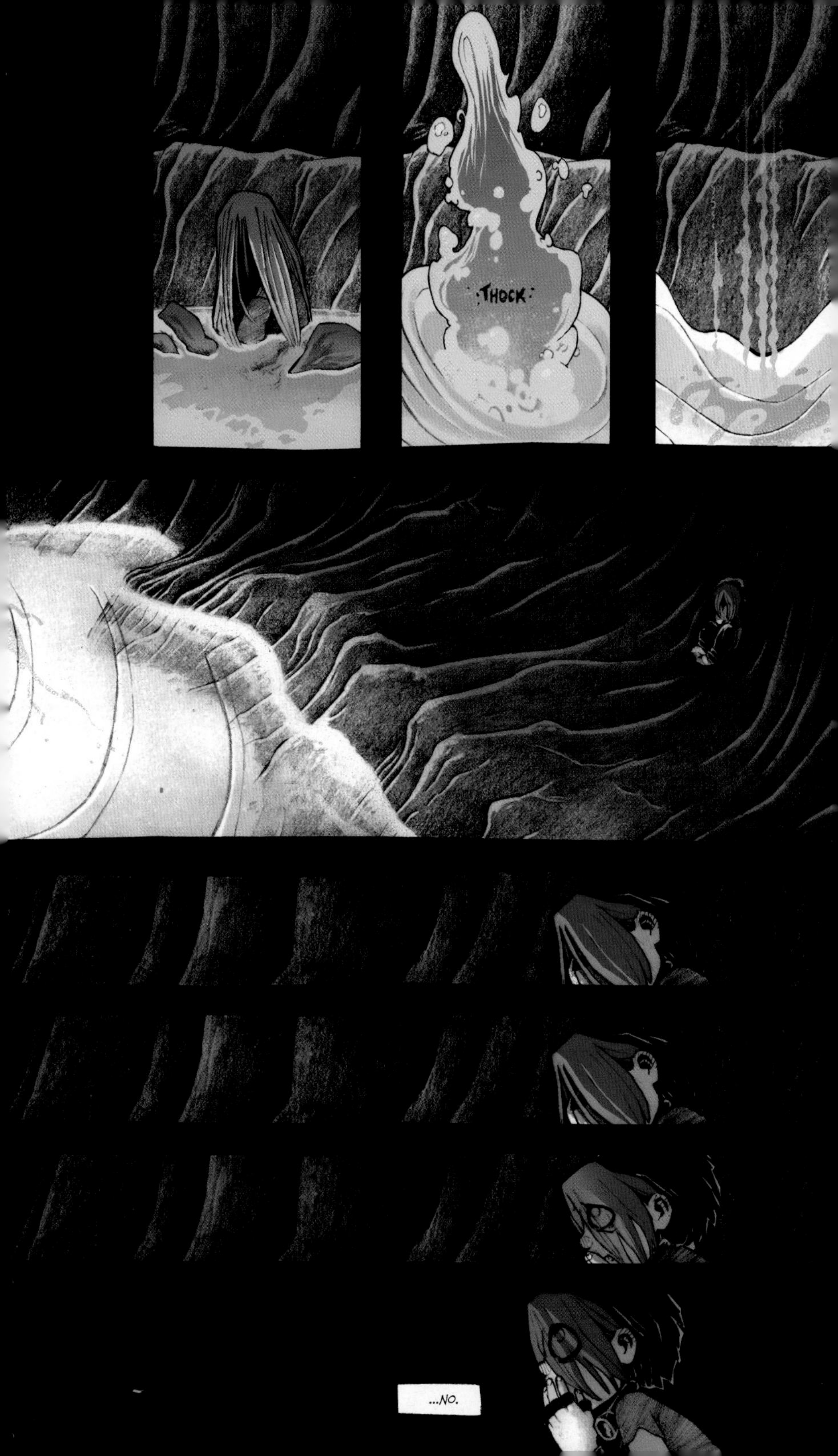
THOCK
...NO.

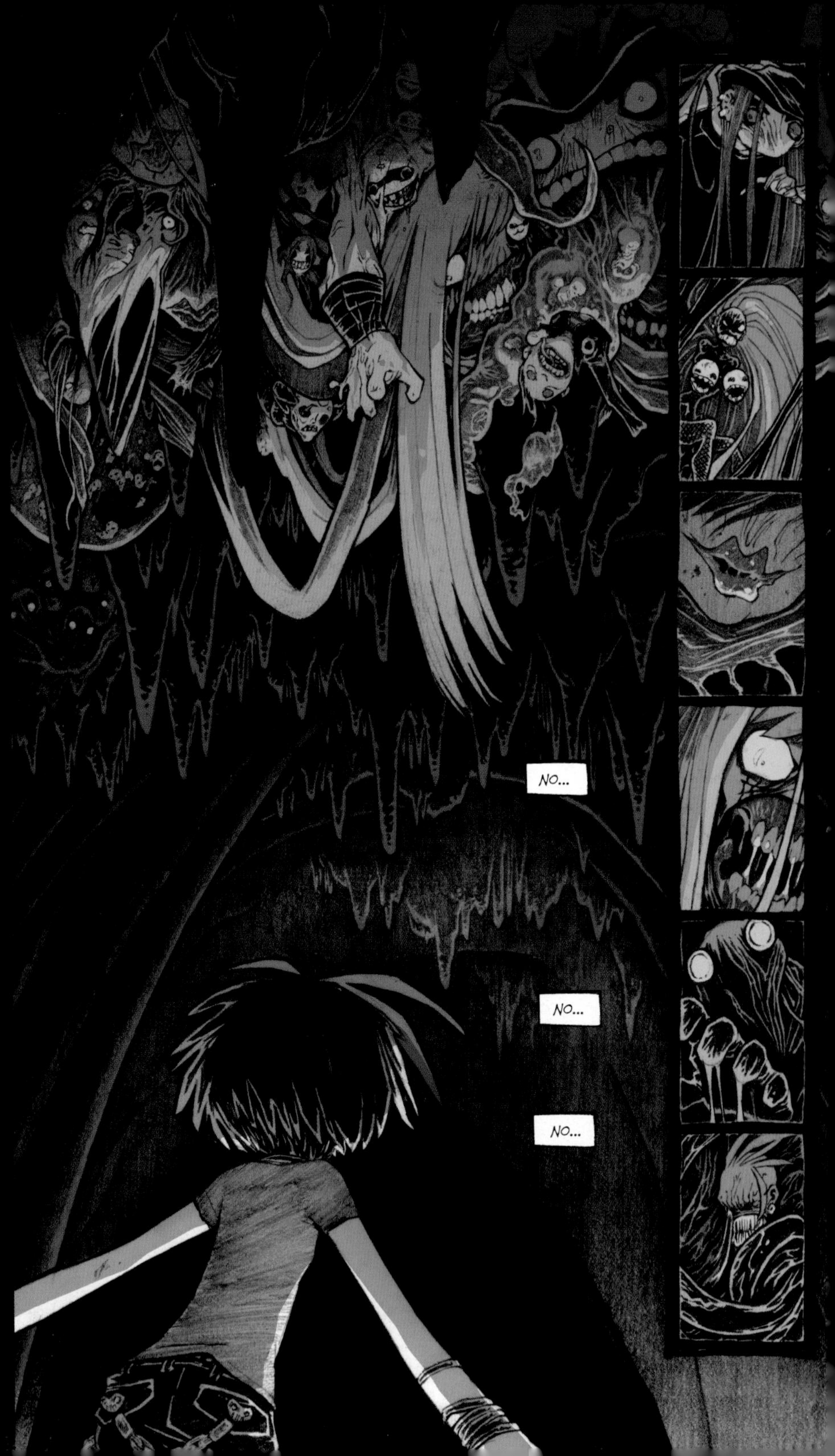
NO...
NO...
NO...

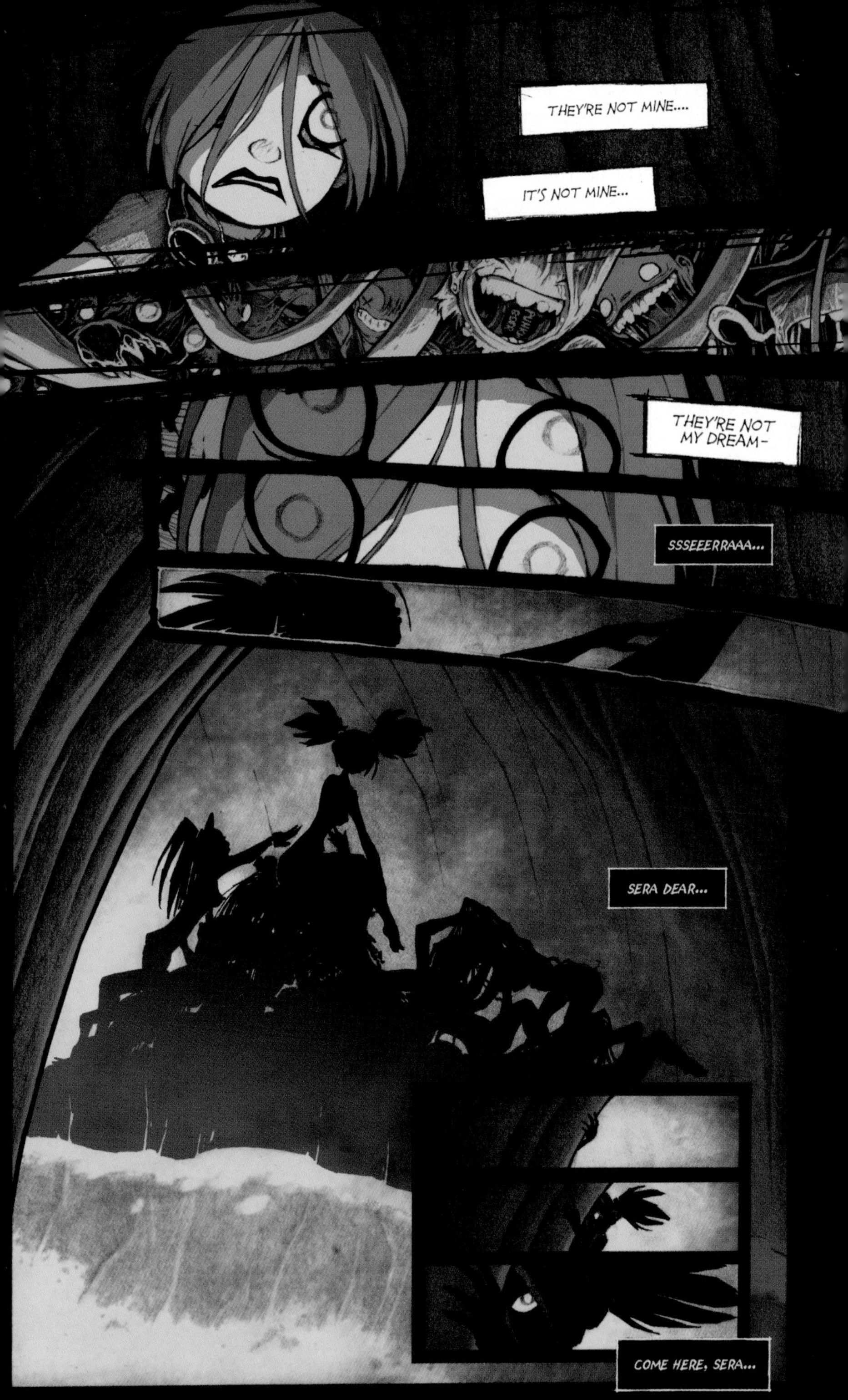
THEY'RE NOT MINE....
IT'S NOT MINE...
THEY'RE NOT MY DREAM-
SSSEEERRAAA...
SERA DEAR...
COME HERE, SERA...

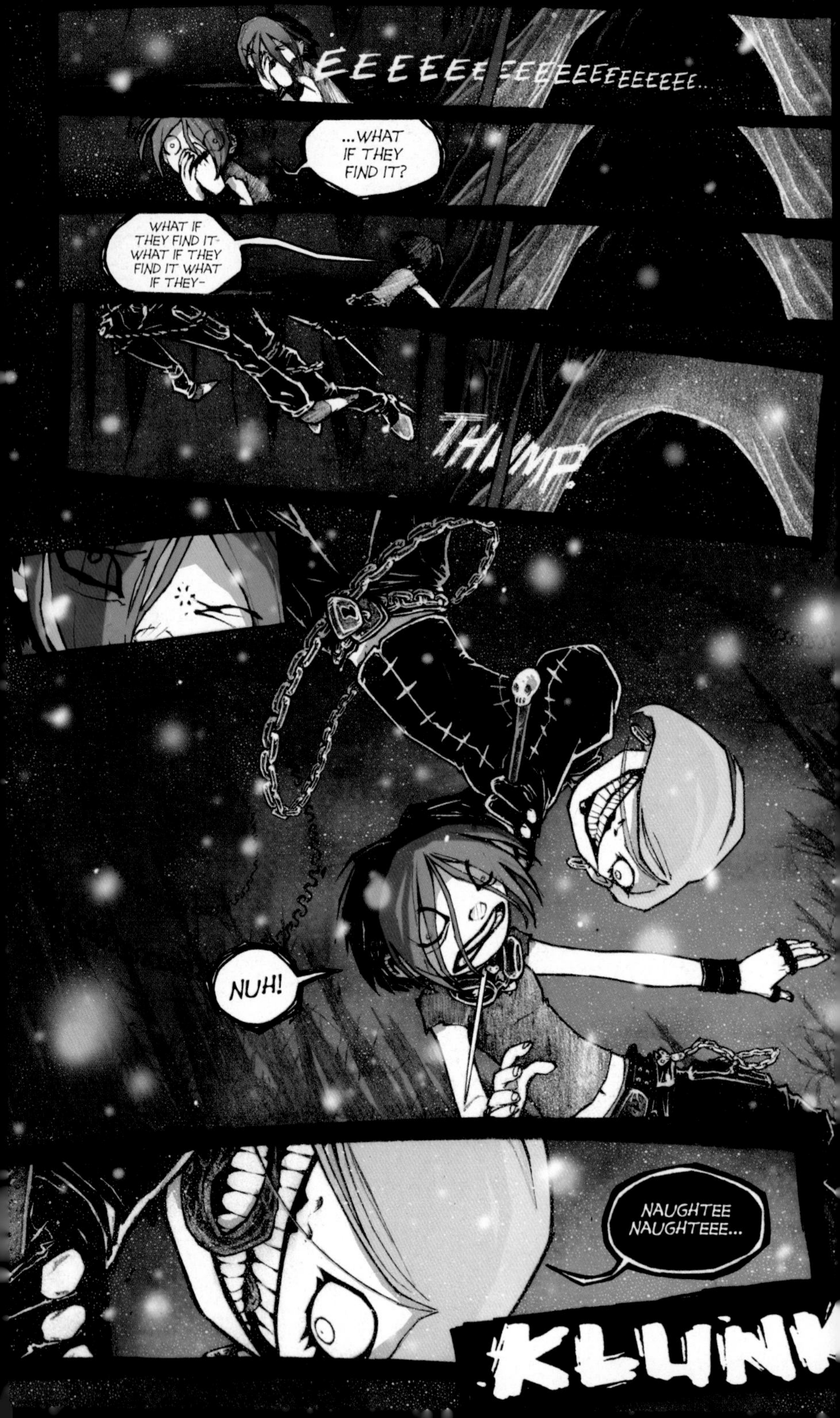
EEEEEEEEEEEEEEEEEEE...
...WHAT IF THEY FIND IT?
WHAT IF THEY FIND IT- WHAT IF THEY FIND IT WHAT IF THEY-
THUMP
NUH!
NAUGHTEE NAUGHTEEE...
KLUNK

FOUR WEEKS AGO...

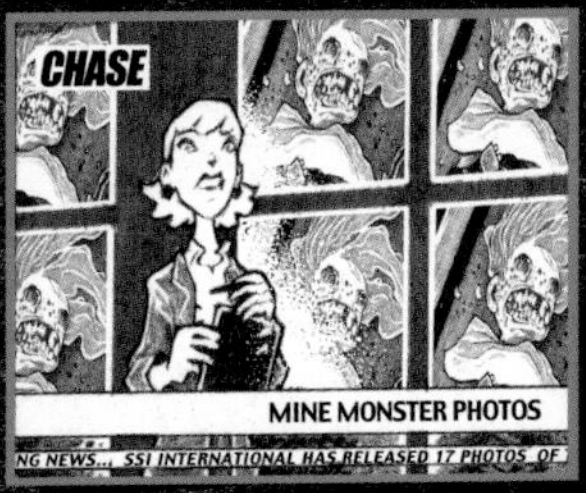

CHASE
MINE MONSTER PHOTOS
NG NEWS... SSI INTERNATIONAL HAS RELEASED 17 PHOTOS OF

"BREAKING NEWS AT THIS HOUR!

CHASE NEWS HAS RECEIVED **PHOTOS** OF THE MYSTERIOUS **"MATOBO MONSTERS"** DISCOVERED IN AN ABANDONED ZIMBABWEAN **DIAMOND MINE** TWO WEEKS AGO...

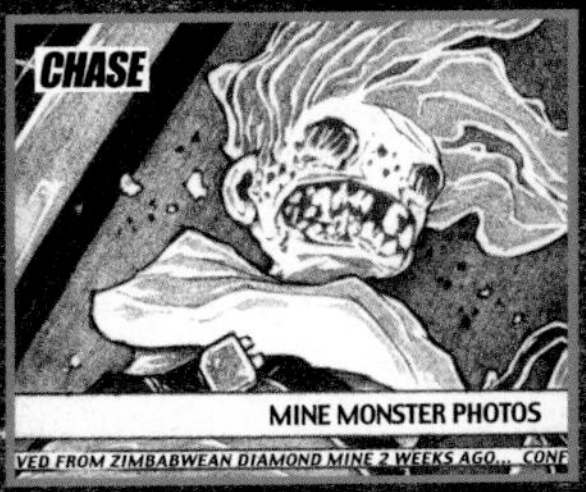

CHASE
MINE MONSTER PHOTOS
VED FROM ZIMBABWEAN DIAMOND MINE 2 WEEKS AGO... CONF

SSI INTERNATIONAL RELEASED THESE IMAGES JUST **MOMENTS AGO...**

OFFICIALS ARE NOW **CONFIRMING** THE CREATURES ARE INDEED **SPELLCAST**, BUT THEIR **ORIGIN** REMAINS UNKNOWN....

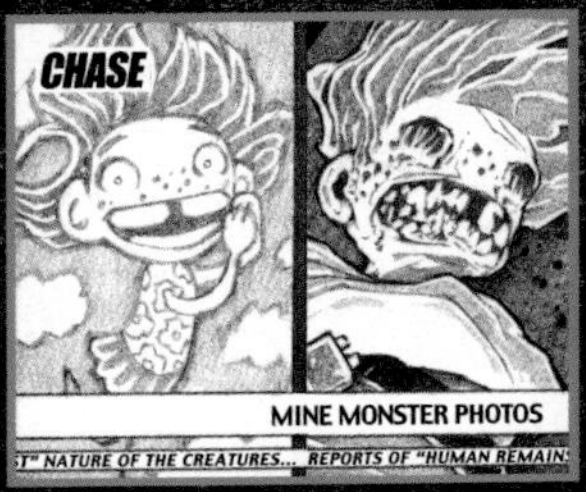

CHASE
MINE MONSTER PHOTOS
T" NATURE OF THE CREATURES... REPORTS OF "HUMAN REMAINS

EARLIER RUMORS POINTED TO **SIMILARITIES** BETWEEN THE CREATURES AND CHARACTERS IN **CHILDREN'S BOOKS** RECOVERED FROM THE SITE...

THESE PHOTOS CERTAINLY ADD **CREDENCE** TO THOSE REPORTS.

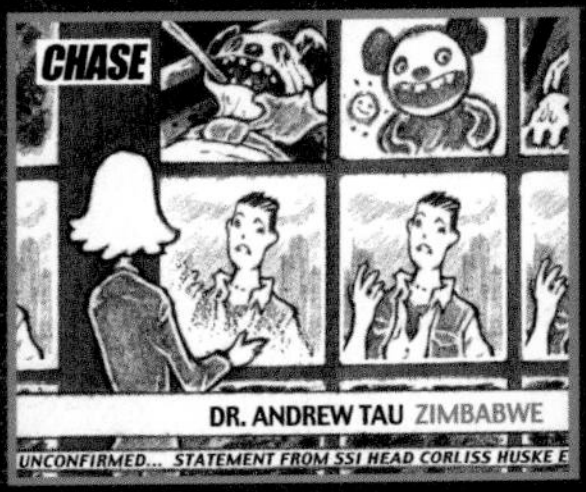

CHASE
DR. ANDREW TAU ZIMBABWE
UNCONFIRMED... STATEMENT FROM SSI HEAD CORLISS HUSKE E

JOINING US AGAIN FROM ZIMBABWE IS CHASE **SUPERNATURAL CORRESPONDENT** DR. ANDREW TAU... ANDY... JUST WHAT ARE WE TO MAKE OF THESE NEW IMAGES?"

"THAT'S AN EXCELLENT QUESTION, JEANNE.

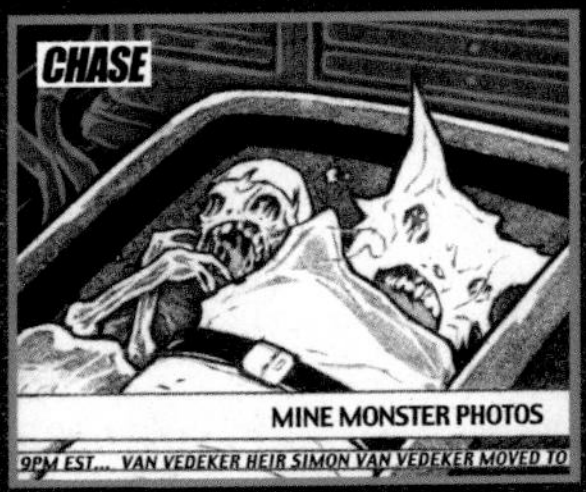

CHASE
MINE MONSTER PHOTOS
9PM EST... VAN VEDEKER HEIR SIMON VAN VEDEKER MOVED TO

WHAT **ARE** THESE THINGS?

WHY DO THEY LOOK LIKE DISTORTED **CHILDREN'S** CHARACTERS?

HOW ARE THEY CONNECTED TO LAST WEEK'S **RUMORS** OF **HUMAN REMAINS** FOUND IN THE TUNNELS?

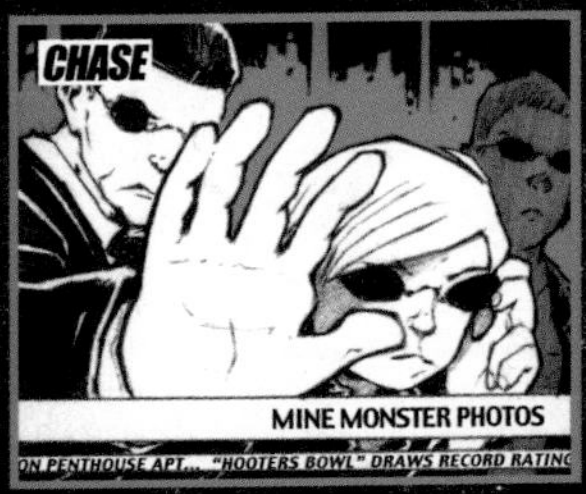

CHASE
MINE MONSTER PHOTOS
ON PENTHOUSE APT... "HOOTERS BOWL" DRAWS RECORD RATING

THE **ONLY** PEOPLE WHO CAN ANSWER THESE QUESTIONS?

THE VAN VEDEKER COMPANY.

AND TO THIS DAY THEY'VE RELEASED **NO STATEMENT** ABOUT THIS **HIDDEN ARMY OF MONSTERS** IN THEIR FORMER DIAMOND MINE..."

part three..

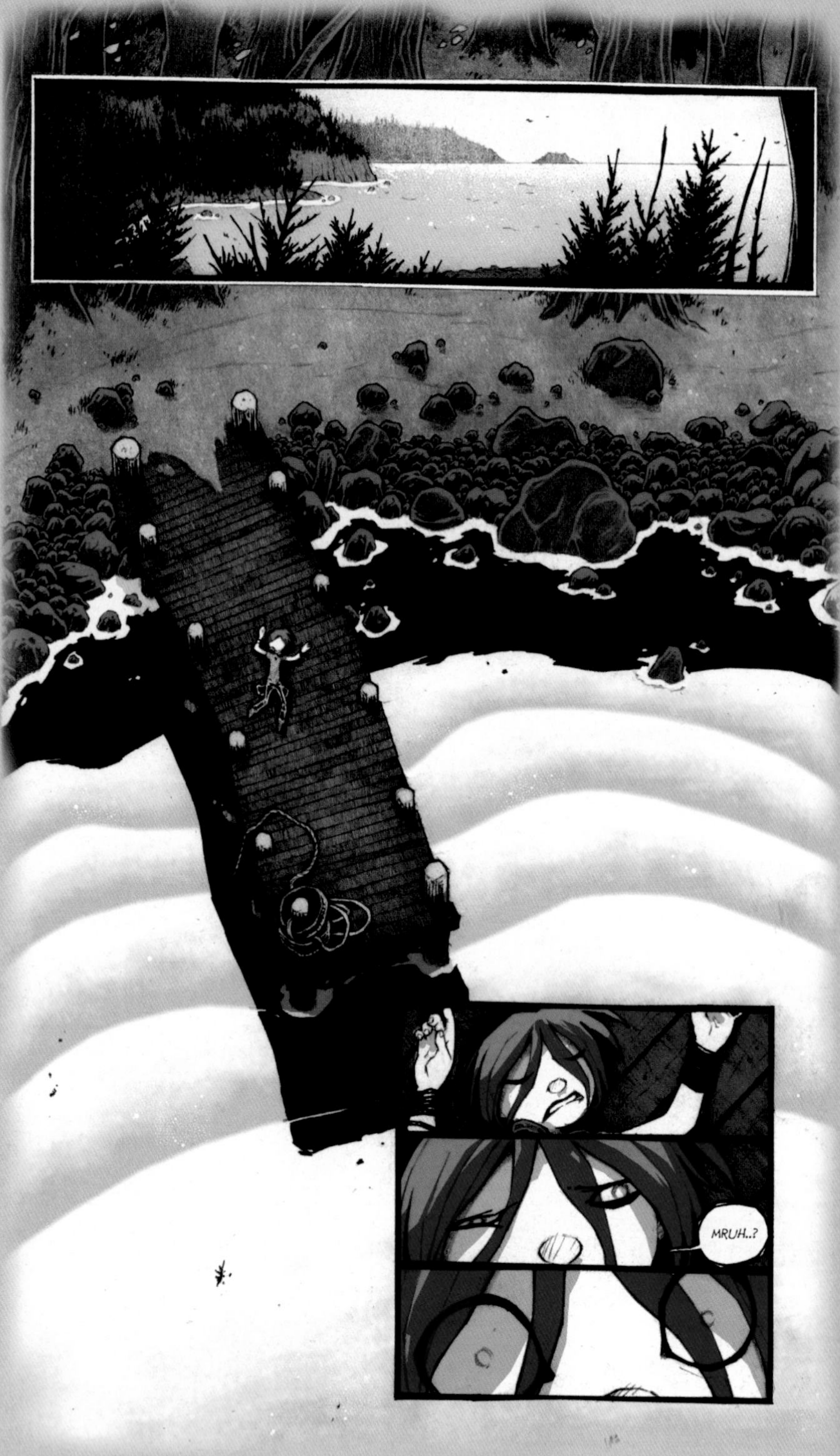
MRUH..?

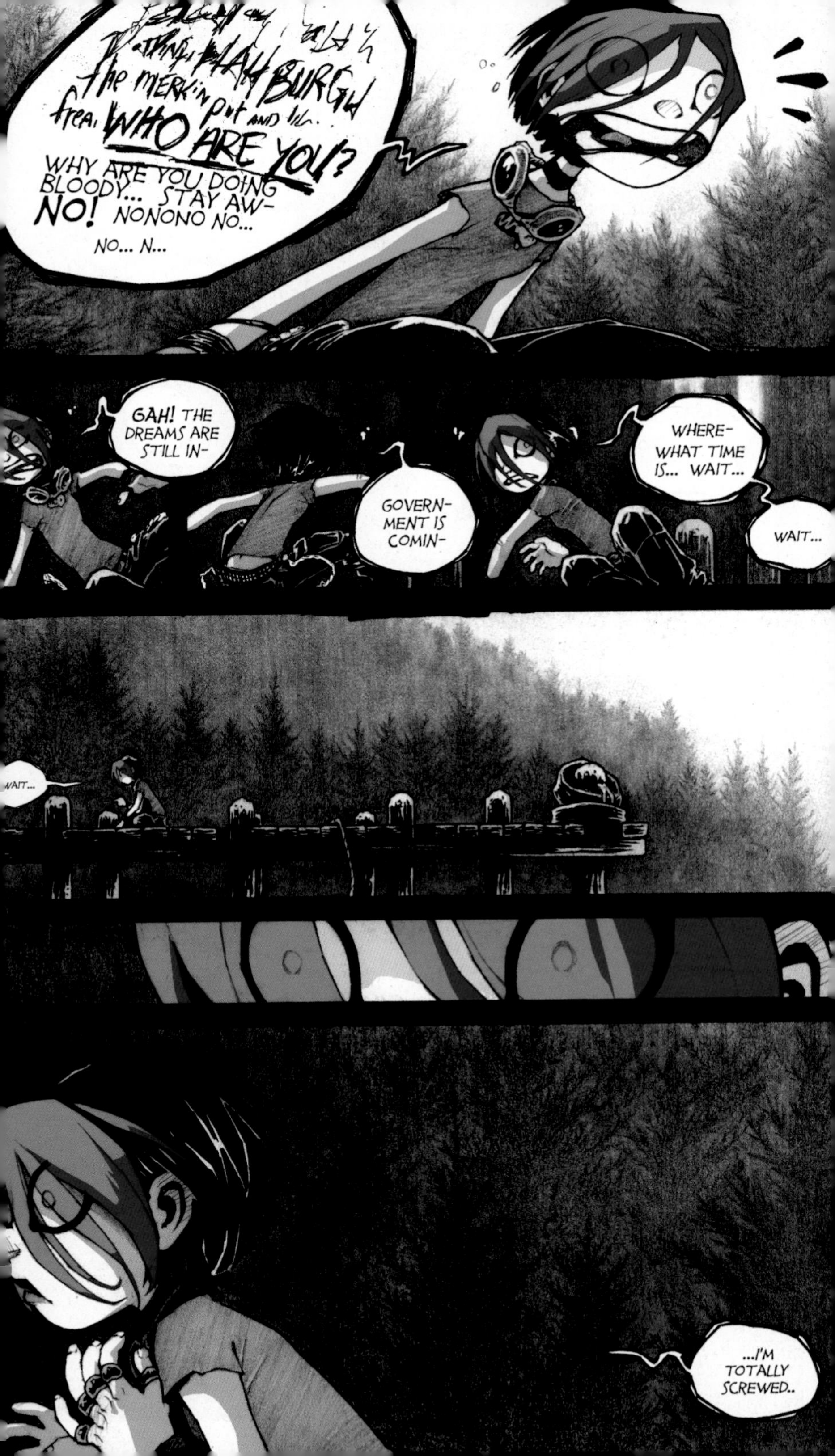
WHO ARE YOU!?
WHY ARE YOU DOING BLOODY... STAY AW- NO! NONONO NO... NO... N...
GAH! THE DREAMS ARE STILL IN-
GOVERNMENT IS COMIN-
WHERE- WHAT TIME IS... WAIT...
WAIT...
WAIT...
...I'M TOTALLY SCREWED..

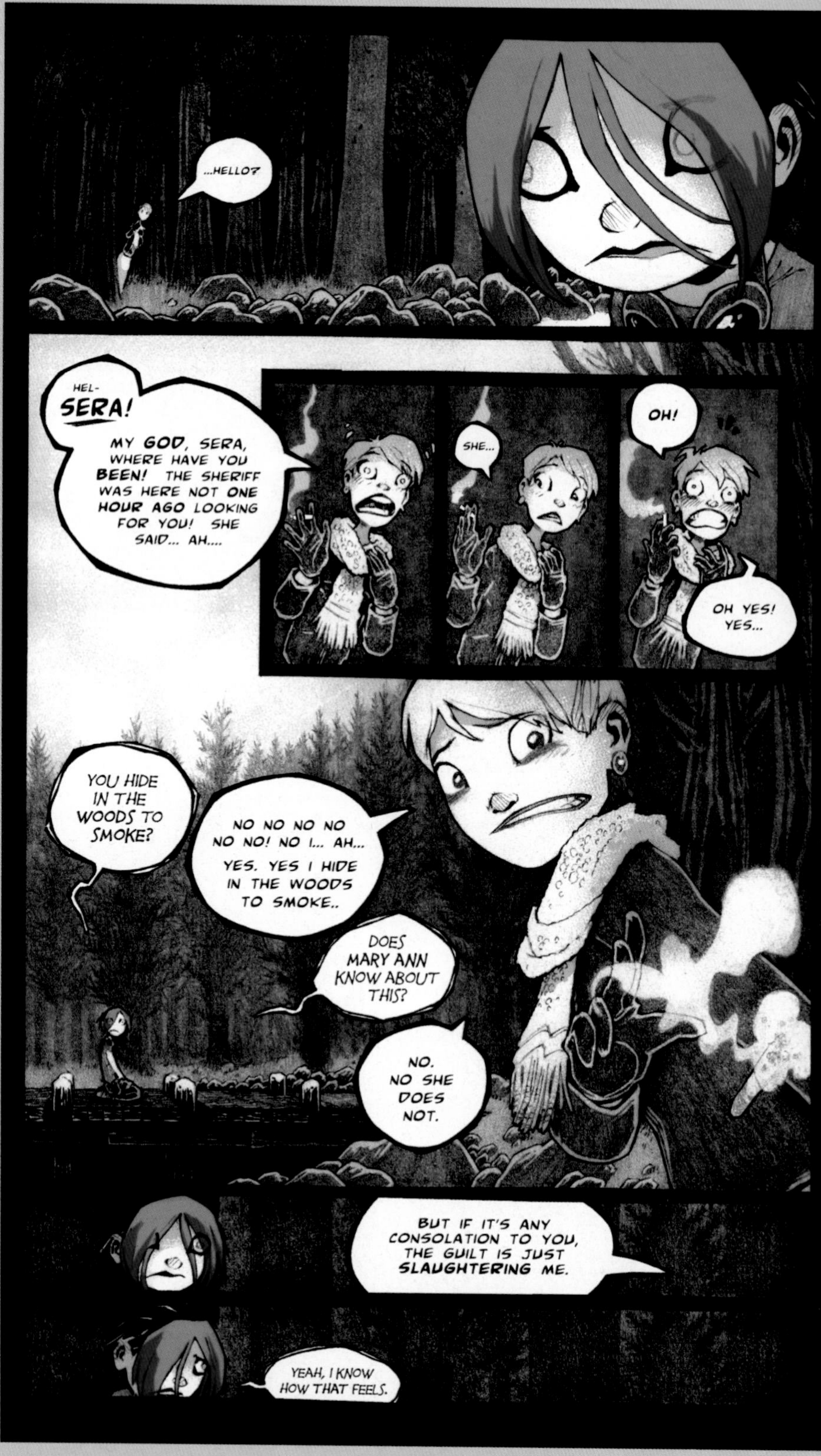
...HELLO?
HEL- SERA!
MY GOD, SERA, WHERE HAVE YOU BEEN! THE SHERIFF WAS HERE NOT ONE HOUR AGO LOOKING FOR YOU! SHE SAID... AH....
SHE...
OH!
OH YES! YES...
YOU HIDE IN THE WOODS TO SMOKE?
NO NO NO NO NO NO! NO I... AH...
YES. YES I HIDE IN THE WOODS TO SMOKE..
DOES MARY ANN KNOW ABOUT THIS?
NO. NO SHE DOES NOT.
BUT IF IT'S ANY CONSOLATION TO YOU, THE GUILT IS JUST SLAUGHTERING ME.
YEAH, I KNOW HOW THAT FEELS.

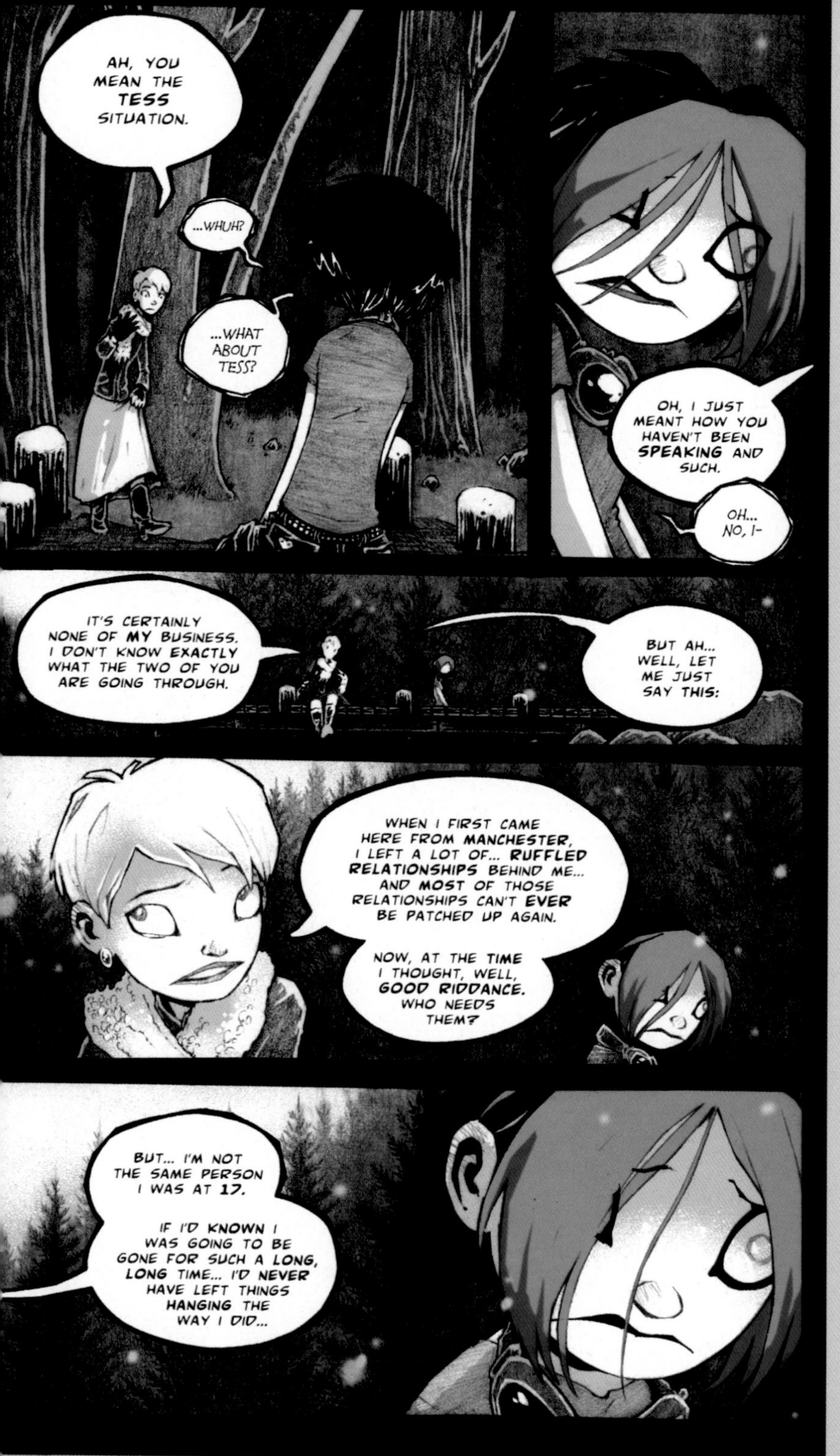
AH, YOU MEAN THE TESS SITUATION.
...WHUH?
...WHAT ABOUT TESS?
OH, I JUST MEANT HOW YOU HAVEN'T BEEN SPEAKING AND SUCH.
OH... NO, I-
IT'S CERTAINLY NONE OF MY BUSINESS. I DON'T KNOW EXACTLY WHAT THE TWO OF YOU ARE GOING THROUGH.
BUT AH... WELL, LET ME JUST SAY THIS:
WHEN I FIRST CAME HERE FROM MANCHESTER, I LEFT A LOT OF... RUFFLED RELATIONSHIPS BEHIND ME... AND MOST OF THOSE RELATIONSHIPS CAN'T EVER BE PATCHED UP AGAIN.
NOW, AT THE TIME I THOUGHT, WELL, GOOD RIDDANCE. WHO NEEDS THEM?
BUT... I'M NOT THE SAME PERSON I WAS AT 17.
IF I'D KNOWN I WAS GOING TO BE GONE FOR SUCH A LONG, LONG TIME... I'D NEVER HAVE LEFT THINGS HANGING THE WAY I DID...

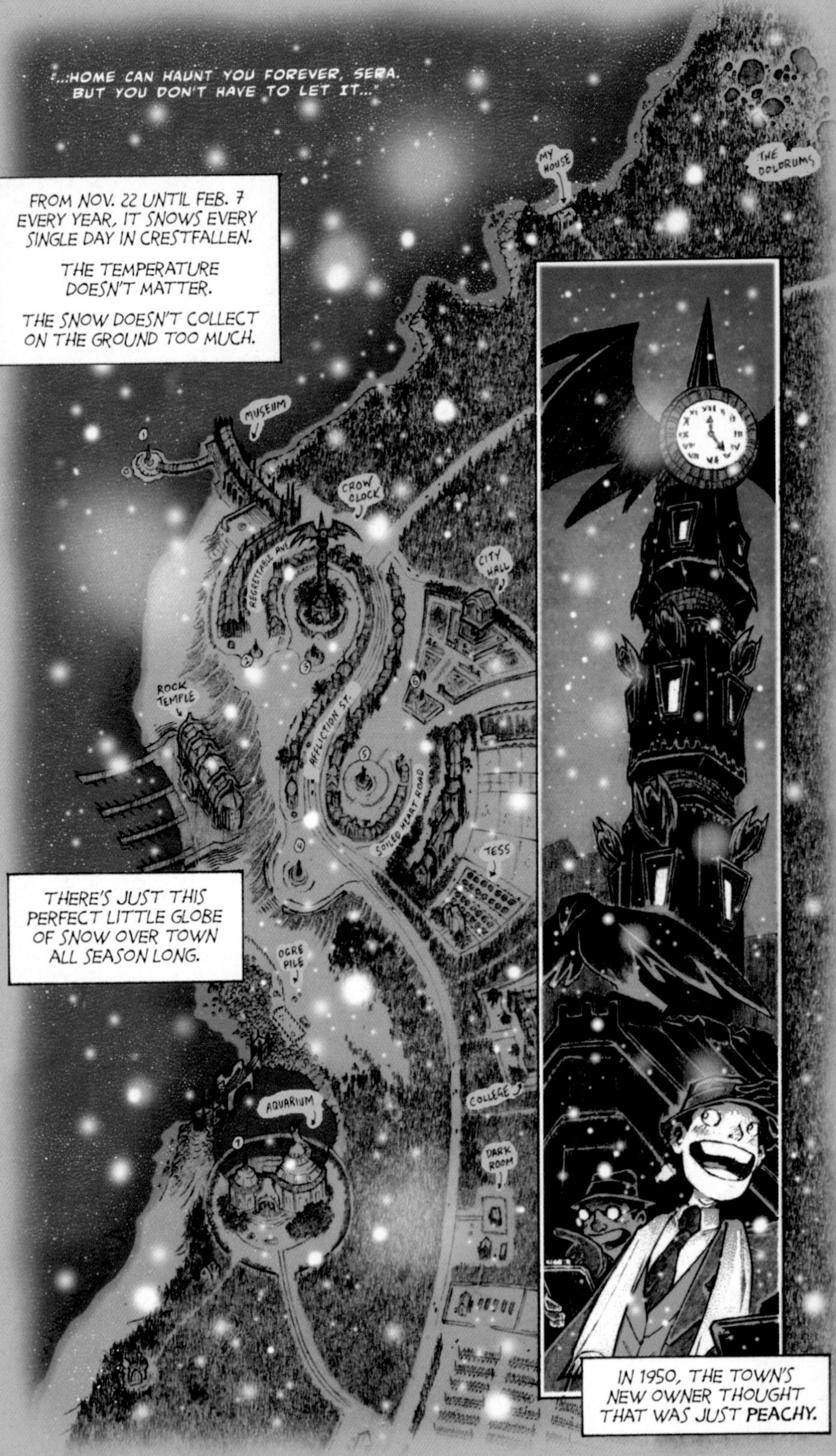
"...HOME CAN HAUNT YOU FOREVER, SERA. BUT YOU DON'T HAVE TO LET IT..."
FROM NOV. 22 UNTIL FEB. 7 EVERY YEAR, IT SNOWS EVERY SINGLE DAY IN CRESTFALLEN.
THE TEMPERATURE DOESN'T MATTER.
THE SNOW DOESN'T COLLECT ON THE GROUND TOO MUCH.
MY HOUSE
THE DOLDRUMS
MUSEUM
CROW CLOCK
REGRETTABLE AVE
CITY HALL
ROCK TEMPLE
AFFLICTION ST.
SOILED HEART ROAD
TESS
THERE'S JUST THIS PERFECT LITTLE GLOBE OF SNOW OVER TOWN ALL SEASON LONG.
OGRE PILE
AQUARIUM
COLLEGE
DARK ROOM
IN 1950, THE TOWN'S NEW OWNER THOUGHT THAT WAS JUST **PEACHY.**

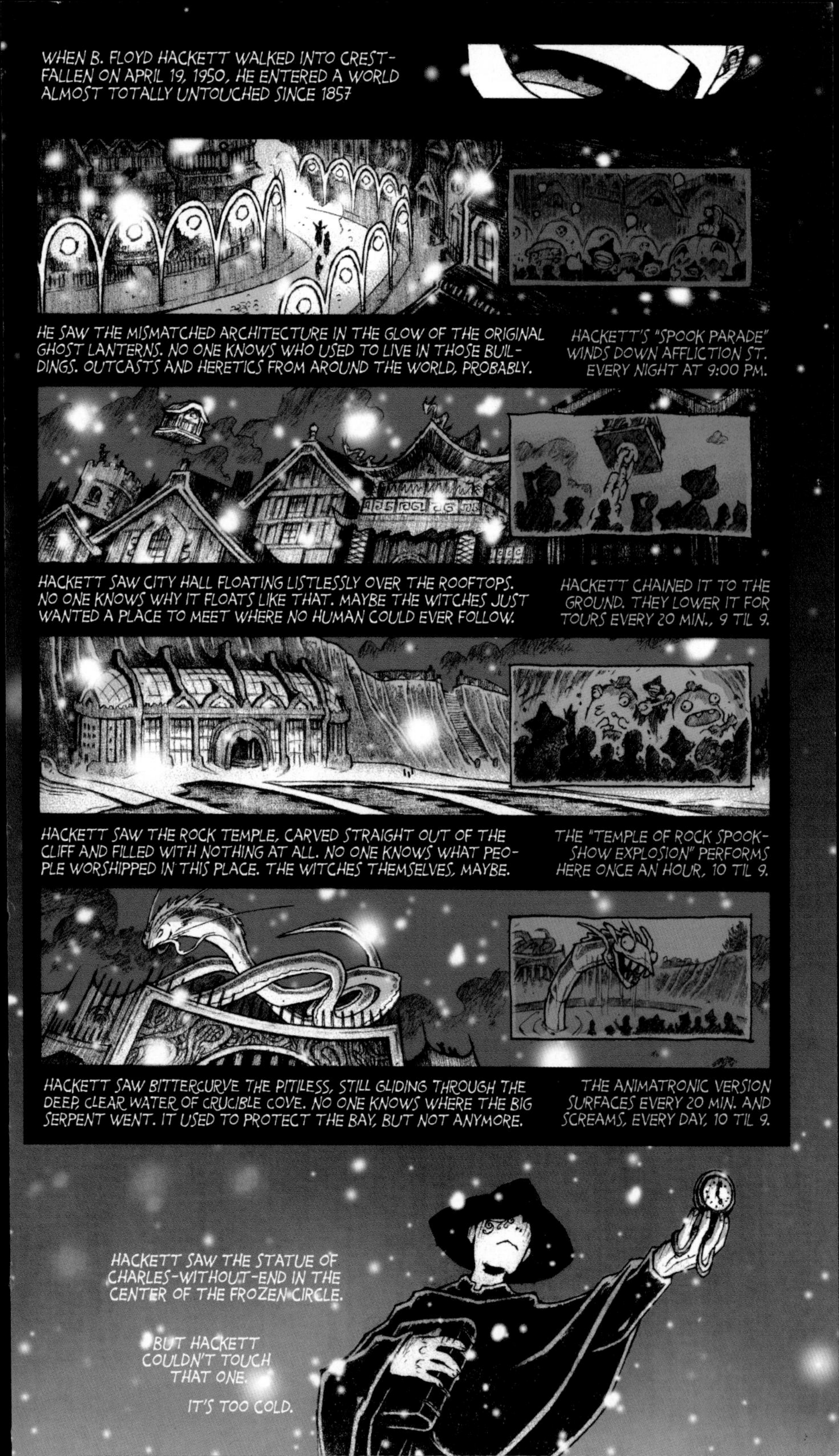
WHEN B. FLOYD HACKETT WALKED INTO CREST-FALLEN ON APRIL 19, 1950, HE ENTERED A WORLD ALMOST TOTALLY UNTOUCHED SINCE 1857
HE SAW THE MISMATCHED ARCHITECTURE IN THE GLOW OF THE ORIGINAL GHOST LANTERNS. NO ONE KNOWS WHO USED TO LIVE IN THOSE BUILDINGS. OUTCASTS AND HERETICS FROM AROUND THE WORLD, PROBABLY.
HACKETT'S "SPOOK PARADE" WINDS DOWN AFFLICTION ST. EVERY NIGHT AT 9:00 PM.
HACKETT SAW CITY HALL FLOATING LISTLESSLY OVER THE ROOFTOPS. NO ONE KNOWS WHY IT FLOATS LIKE THAT. MAYBE THE WITCHES JUST WANTED A PLACE TO MEET WHERE NO HUMAN COULD EVER FOLLOW.
HACKETT CHAINED IT TO THE GROUND. THEY LOWER IT FOR TOURS EVERY 20 MIN., 9 TIL 9.
HACKETT SAW THE ROCK TEMPLE, CARVED STRAIGHT OUT OF THE CLIFF AND FILLED WITH NOTHING AT ALL. NO ONE KNOWS WHAT PEOPLE WORSHIPPED IN THIS PLACE. THE WITCHES THEMSELVES, MAYBE.
THE "TEMPLE OF ROCK SPOOK-SHOW EXPLOSION" PERFORMS HERE ONCE AN HOUR, 10 TIL 9.
HACKETT SAW BITTERCURVE THE PITILESS, STILL GLIDING THROUGH THE DEEP, CLEAR WATER OF CRUCIBLE COVE. NO ONE KNOWS WHERE THE BIG SERPENT WENT. IT USED TO PROTECT THE BAY, BUT NOT ANYMORE.
THE ANIMATRONIC VERSION SURFACES EVERY 20 MIN. AND SCREAMS, EVERY DAY, 10 TIL 9.
HACKETT SAW THE STATUE OF CHARLES-WITHOUT-END IN THE CENTER OF THE FROZEN CIRCLE.
BUT HACKETT COULDN'T TOUCH THAT ONE.
IT'S TOO COLD.

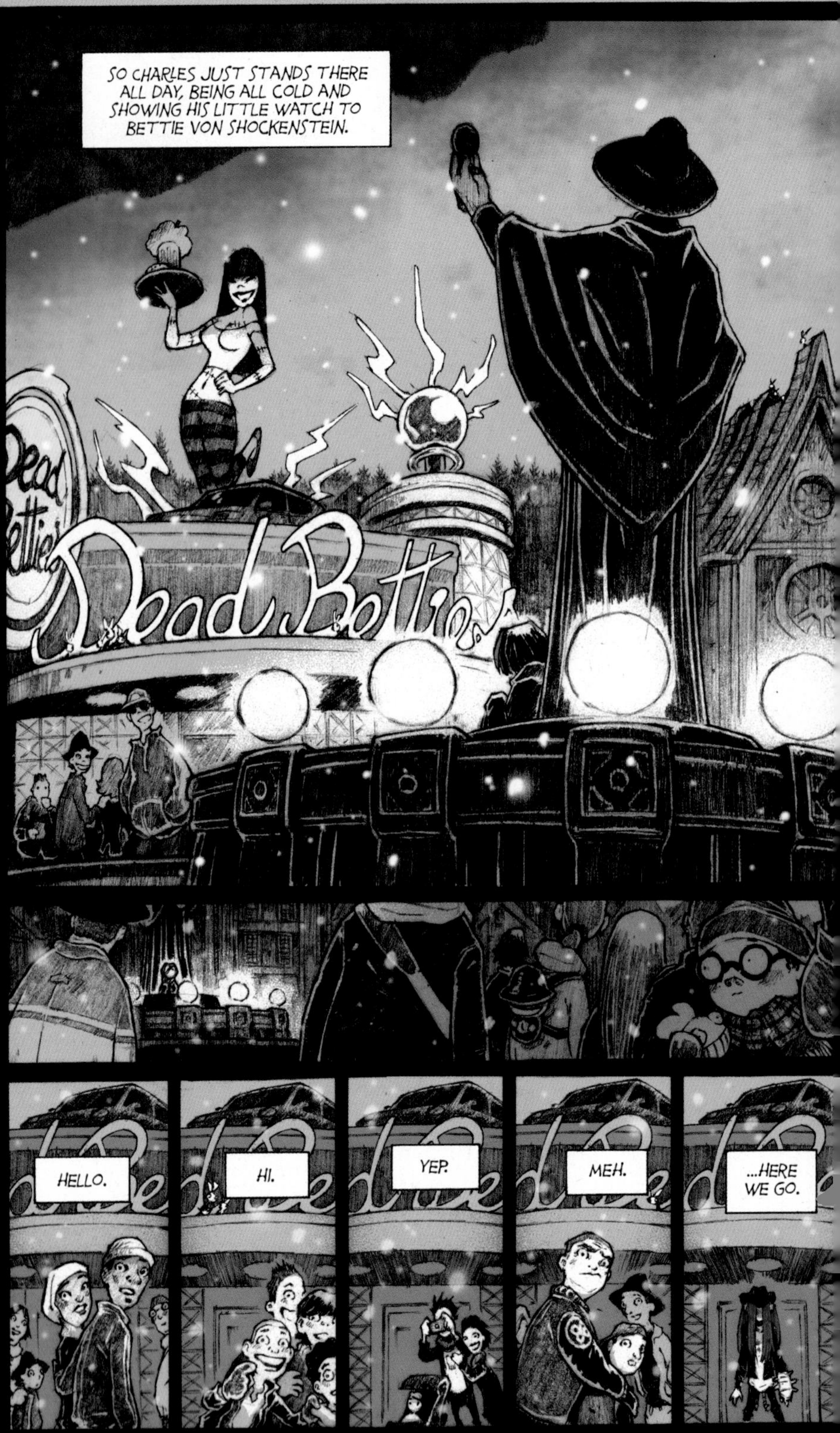
SO CHARLES JUST STANDS THERE ALL DAY, BEING ALL COLD AND SHOWING HIS LITTLE WATCH TO BETTIE VON SHOCKENSTEIN.
Dead Betties
Dead Betties
HELLO.
HI.
YEP.
MEH.
...HERE WE GO.

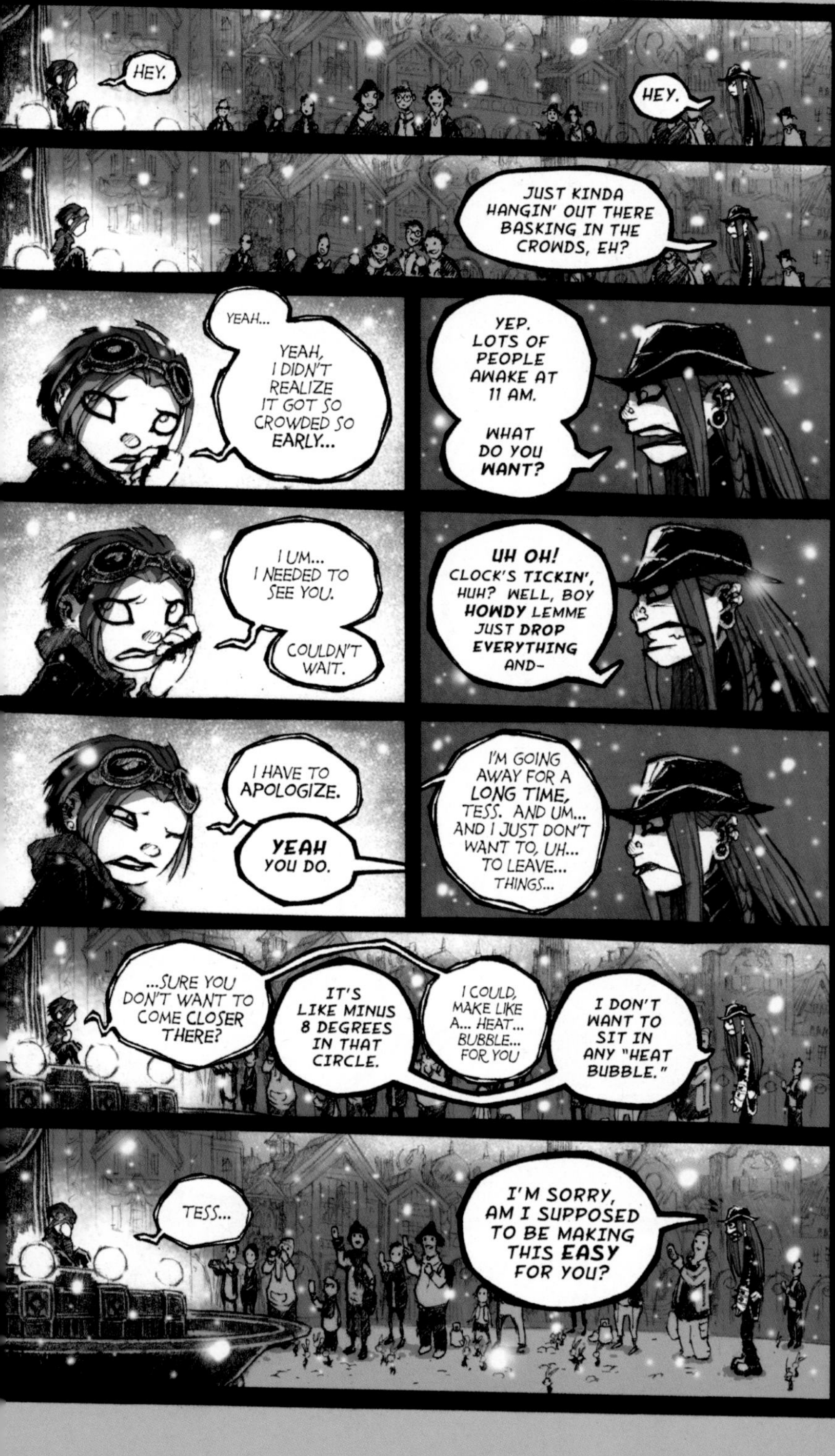
HEY.
HEY.
JUST KINDA HANGIN' OUT THERE BASKING IN THE CROWDS, EH?
YEAH...
YEAH, I DIDN'T REALIZE IT GOT SO CROWDED SO EARLY...
YEP. LOTS OF PEOPLE AWAKE AT 11 AM.
WHAT DO YOU WANT?
I UM... I NEEDED TO SEE YOU.
COULDN'T WAIT.
UH OH! CLOCK'S TICKIN', HUH? WELL, BOY HOWDY LEMME JUST DROP EVERYTHING AND-
I HAVE TO APOLOGIZE.
YEAH YOU DO.
I'M GOING AWAY FOR A LONG TIME, TESS. AND UM... AND I JUST DON'T WANT TO, UH... TO LEAVE... THINGS...
...SURE YOU DON'T WANT TO COME CLOSER THERE?
IT'S LIKE MINUS 8 DEGREES IN THAT CIRCLE.
I COULD, MAKE LIKE A... HEAT... BUBBLE... FOR YOU
I DON'T WANT TO SIT IN ANY "HEAT BUBBLE."
TESS...
I'M SORRY, AM I SUPPOSED TO BE MAKING THIS EASY FOR YOU?

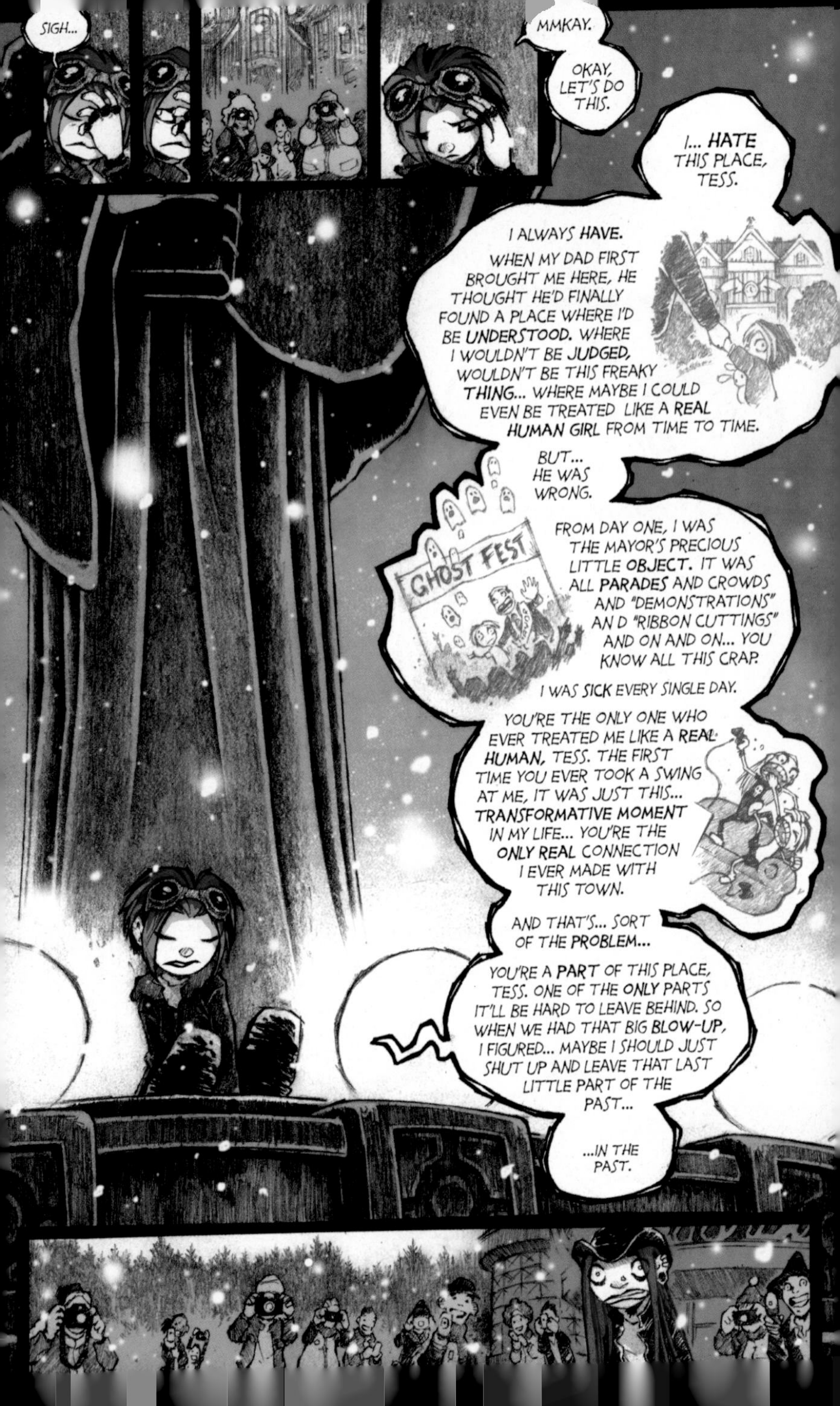
SIGH...
MMKAY.
OKAY, LET'S DO THIS.
I... HATE THIS PLACE, TESS.
I ALWAYS HAVE.
WHEN MY DAD FIRST BROUGHT ME HERE, HE THOUGHT HE'D FINALLY FOUND A PLACE WHERE I'D BE UNDERSTOOD. WHERE I WOULDN'T BE JUDGED, WOULDN'T BE THIS FREAKY THING... WHERE MAYBE I COULD EVEN BE TREATED LIKE A REAL HUMAN GIRL FROM TIME TO TIME.
BUT... HE WAS WRONG.
GHOST FEST
FROM DAY ONE, I WAS THE MAYOR'S PRECIOUS LITTLE OBJECT. IT WAS ALL PARADES AND CROWDS AND "DEMONSTRATIONS" AN D "RIBBON CUTTINGS" AND ON AND ON... YOU KNOW ALL THIS CRAP.
I WAS SICK EVERY SINGLE DAY.
YOU'RE THE ONLY ONE WHO EVER TREATED ME LIKE A REAL HUMAN, TESS. THE FIRST TIME YOU EVER TOOK A SWING AT ME, IT WAS JUST THIS... TRANSFORMATIVE MOMENT IN MY LIFE... YOU'RE THE ONLY REAL CONNECTION I EVER MADE WITH THIS TOWN.
AND THAT'S... SORT OF THE PROBLEM...
YOU'RE A PART OF THIS PLACE, TESS. ONE OF THE ONLY PARTS IT'LL BE HARD TO LEAVE BEHIND. SO WHEN WE HAD THAT BIG BLOW-UP, I FIGURED... MAYBE I SHOULD JUST SHUT UP AND LEAVE THAT LAST LITTLE PART OF THE PAST...
...IN THE PAST.

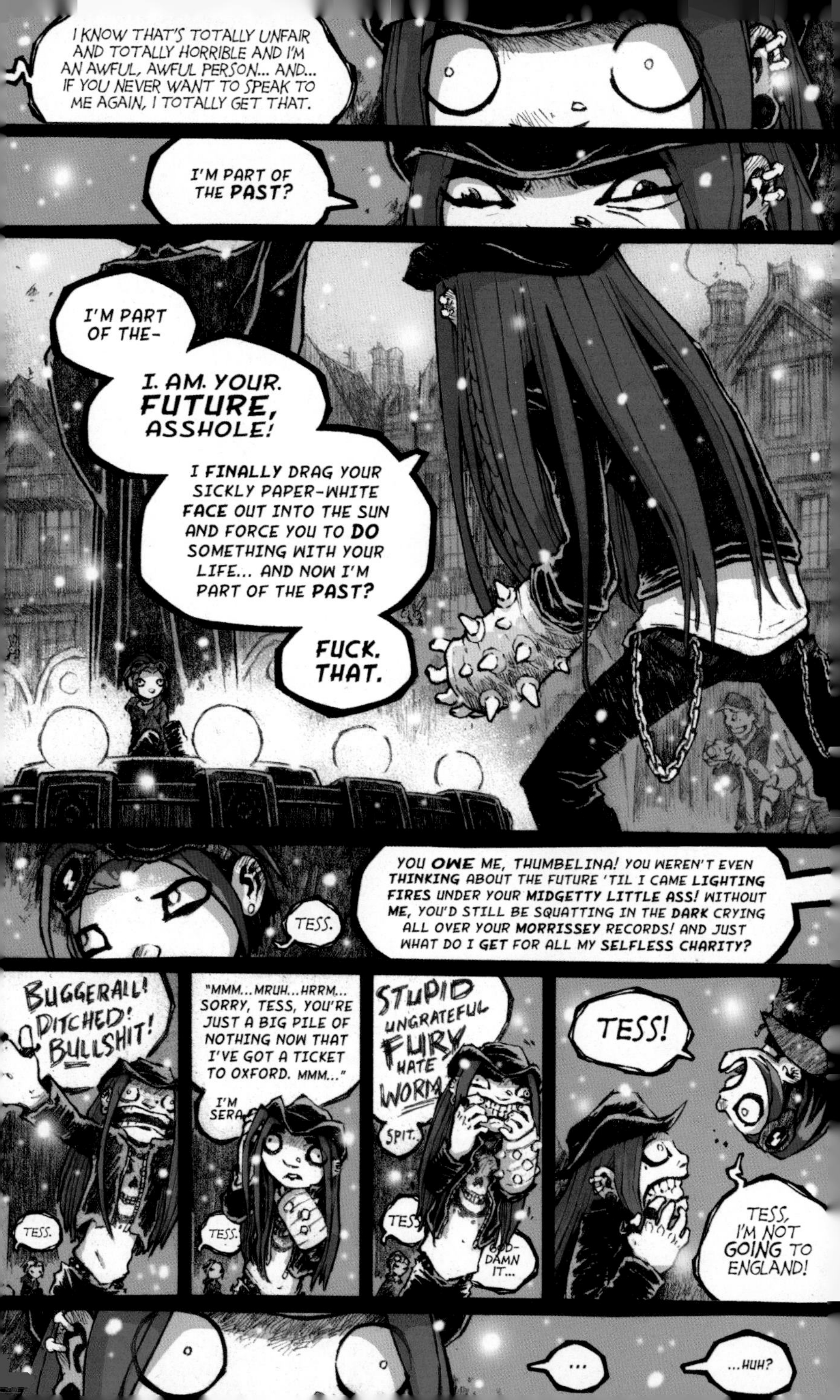
I KNOW THAT'S TOTALLY UNFAIR AND TOTALLY HORRIBLE AND I'M AN AWFUL, AWFUL PERSON... AND... IF YOU NEVER WANT TO SPEAK TO ME AGAIN, I TOTALLY GET THAT.
I'M PART OF THE PAST?
I'M PART OF THE-
I. AM. YOUR. FUTURE, ASSHOLE!
I FINALLY DRAG YOUR SICKLY PAPER-WHITE FACE OUT INTO THE SUN AND FORCE YOU TO DO SOMETHING WITH YOUR LIFE... AND NOW I'M PART OF THE PAST?
FUCK. THAT.
TESS.
YOU OWE ME, THUMBELINA! YOU WEREN'T EVEN THINKING ABOUT THE FUTURE 'TIL I CAME LIGHTING FIRES UNDER YOUR MIDGETTY LITTLE ASS! WITHOUT ME, YOU'D STILL BE SQUATTING IN THE DARK CRYING ALL OVER YOUR MORRISSEY RECORDS! AND JUST WHAT DO I GET FOR ALL MY SELFLESS CHARITY?
BUGGERALL! DITCHED! BULLSHIT!
TESS.
"MMM...MRUH...HRRM... SORRY, TESS, YOU'RE JUST A BIG PILE OF NOTHING NOW THAT I'VE GOT A TICKET TO OXFORD. MMM..."
I'M SERA
TESS.
STUPID UNGRATEFUL FURY HATE WORM
SPIT.
TESS
GOD-DAMN IT...
TESS!
TESS, I'M NOT GOING TO ENGLAND!
...
...HUH?

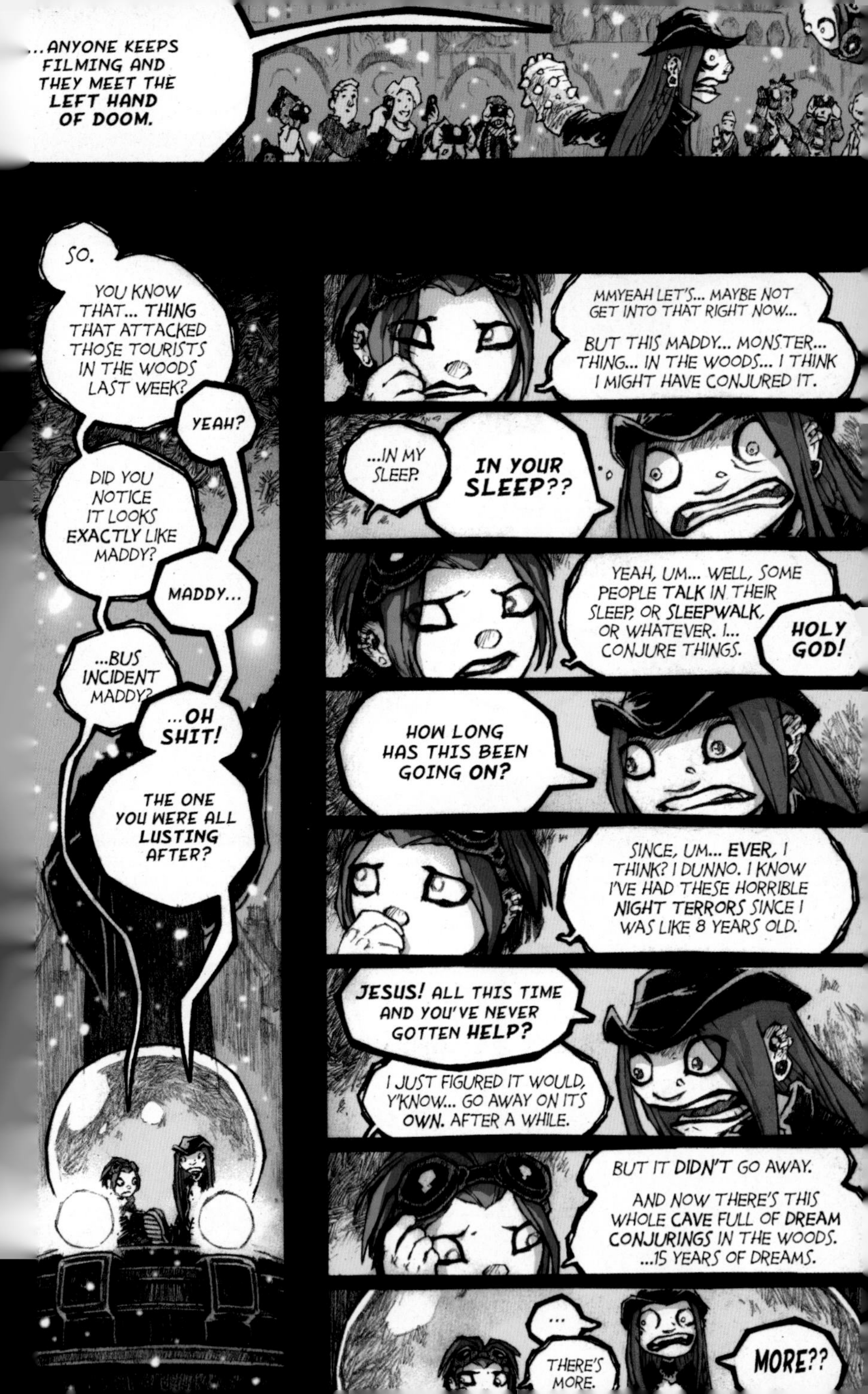
...ANYONE KEEPS FILMING AND THEY MEET THE LEFT HAND OF DOOM.
SO.
YOU KNOW THAT... THING THAT ATTACKED THOSE TOURISTS IN THE WOODS LAST WEEK?
YEAH?
DID YOU NOTICE IT LOOKS EXACTLY LIKE MADDY?
MADDY...
...BUS INCIDENT MADDY?
...OH SHIT!
THE ONE YOU WERE ALL LUSTING AFTER?
MMYEAH LET'S... MAYBE NOT GET INTO THAT RIGHT NOW...
BUT THIS MADDY... MONSTER... THING... IN THE WOODS... I THINK I MIGHT HAVE CONJURED IT.
...IN MY SLEEP.
IN YOUR SLEEP??
YEAH, UM... WELL, SOME PEOPLE TALK IN THEIR SLEEP, OR SLEEPWALK, OR WHATEVER. I... CONJURE THINGS.
HOLY GOD!
HOW LONG HAS THIS BEEN GOING ON?
SINCE, UM... EVER, I THINK? I DUNNO. I KNOW I'VE HAD THESE HORRIBLE NIGHT TERRORS SINCE I WAS LIKE 8 YEARS OLD.
JESUS! ALL THIS TIME AND YOU'VE NEVER GOTTEN HELP?
I JUST FIGURED IT WOULD, Y'KNOW... GO AWAY ON ITS OWN. AFTER A WHILE.
BUT IT DIDN'T GO AWAY.
AND NOW THERE'S THIS WHOLE CAVE FULL OF DREAM CONJURINGS IN THE WOODS. ...15 YEARS OF DREAMS.
...
THERE'S MORE.
MORE??

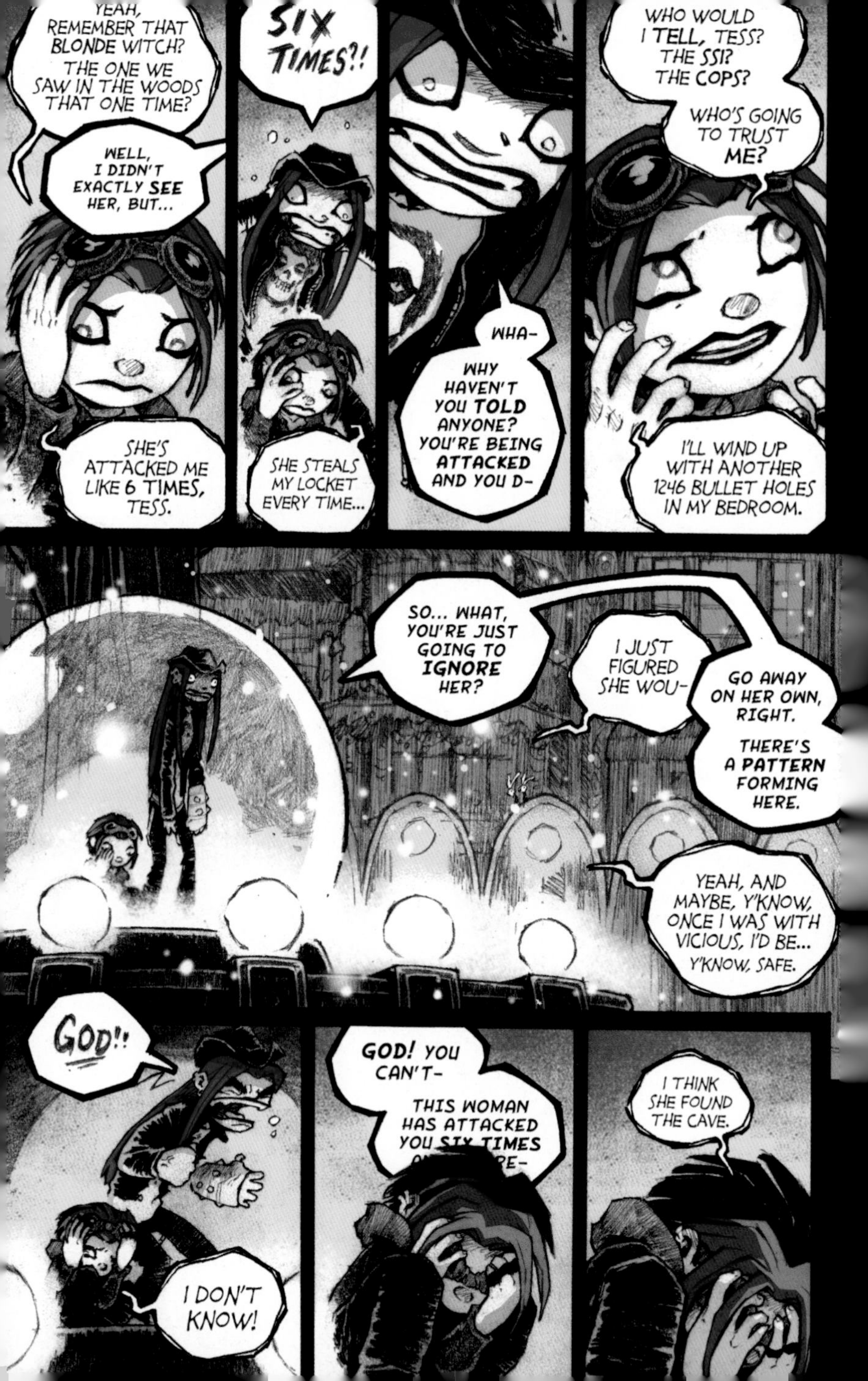
YEAH, REMEMBER THAT BLONDE WITCH? THE ONE WE SAW IN THE WOODS THAT ONE TIME?
WELL, I DIDN'T EXACTLY SEE HER, BUT...
SHE'S ATTACKED ME LIKE 6 TIMES, TESS.
SIX TIMES?!
SHE STEALS MY LOCKET EVERY TIME...
WHA-
WHY HAVEN'T YOU TOLD ANYONE? YOU'RE BEING ATTACKED AND YOU D-
WHO WOULD I TELL, TESS? THE SSI? THE COPS?
WHO'S GOING TO TRUST ME?
I'LL WIND UP WITH ANOTHER 1246 BULLET HOLES IN MY BEDROOM.
SO... WHAT, YOU'RE JUST GOING TO IGNORE HER?
I JUST FIGURED SHE WOU-
GO AWAY ON HER OWN, RIGHT.
THERE'S A PATTERN FORMING HERE.
YEAH, AND MAYBE, Y'KNOW, ONCE I WAS WITH VICIOUS, I'D BE... Y'KNOW, SAFE.
GOD!!
I DON'T KNOW!
GOD! YOU CAN'T-
THIS WOMAN HAS ATTACKED YOU SIX TIMES
I THINK SHE FOUND THE CAVE.

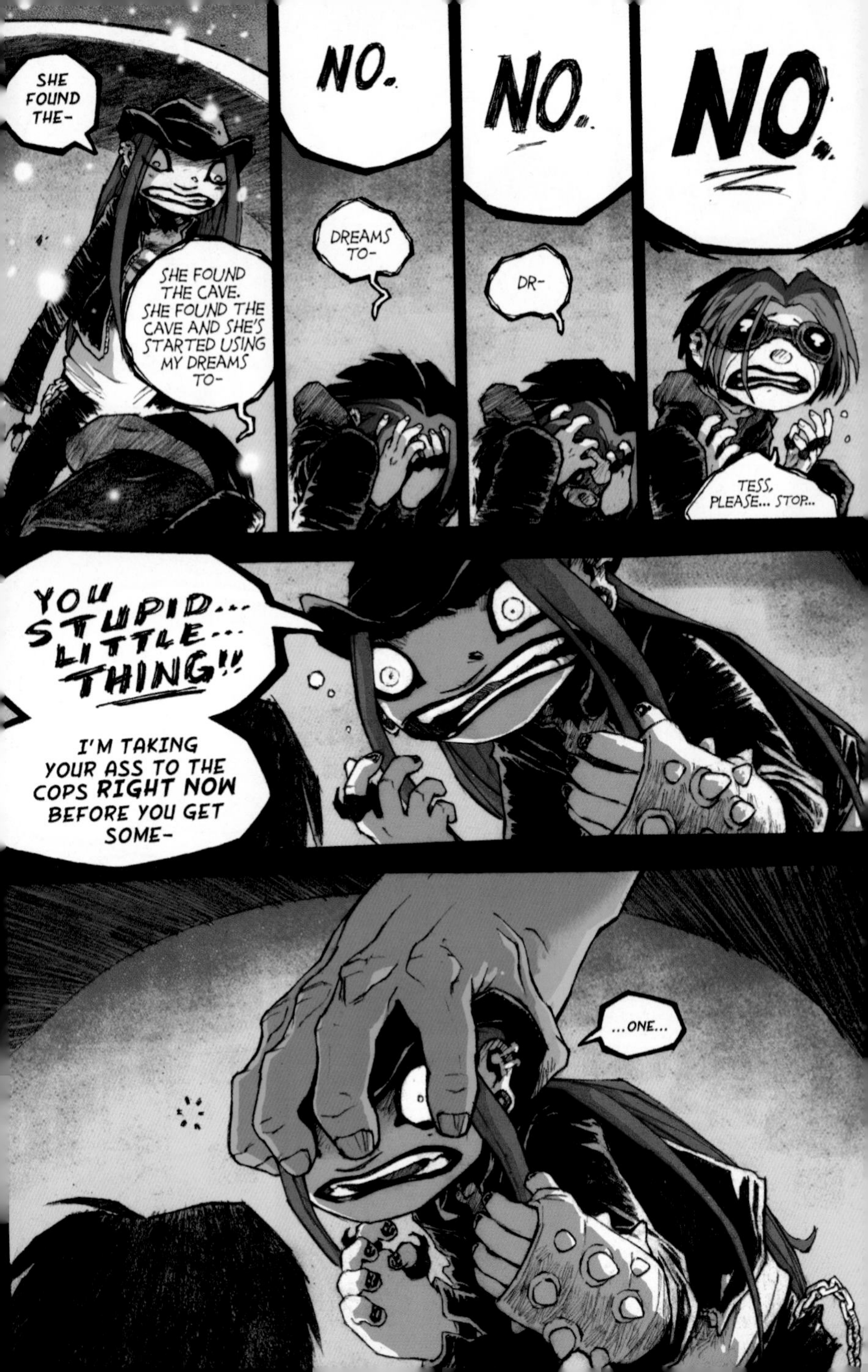
SHE FOUND THE-
SHE FOUND THE CAVE. SHE FOUND THE CAVE AND SHE'S STARTED USING MY DREAMS TO-
NO.
DREAMS TO-
NO.
DR-
NO.
TESS, PLEASE... STOP...
YOU STUPID... LITTLE... THING!!
I'M TAKING YOUR ASS TO THE COPS RIGHT NOW BEFORE YOU GET SOME-
...ONE...

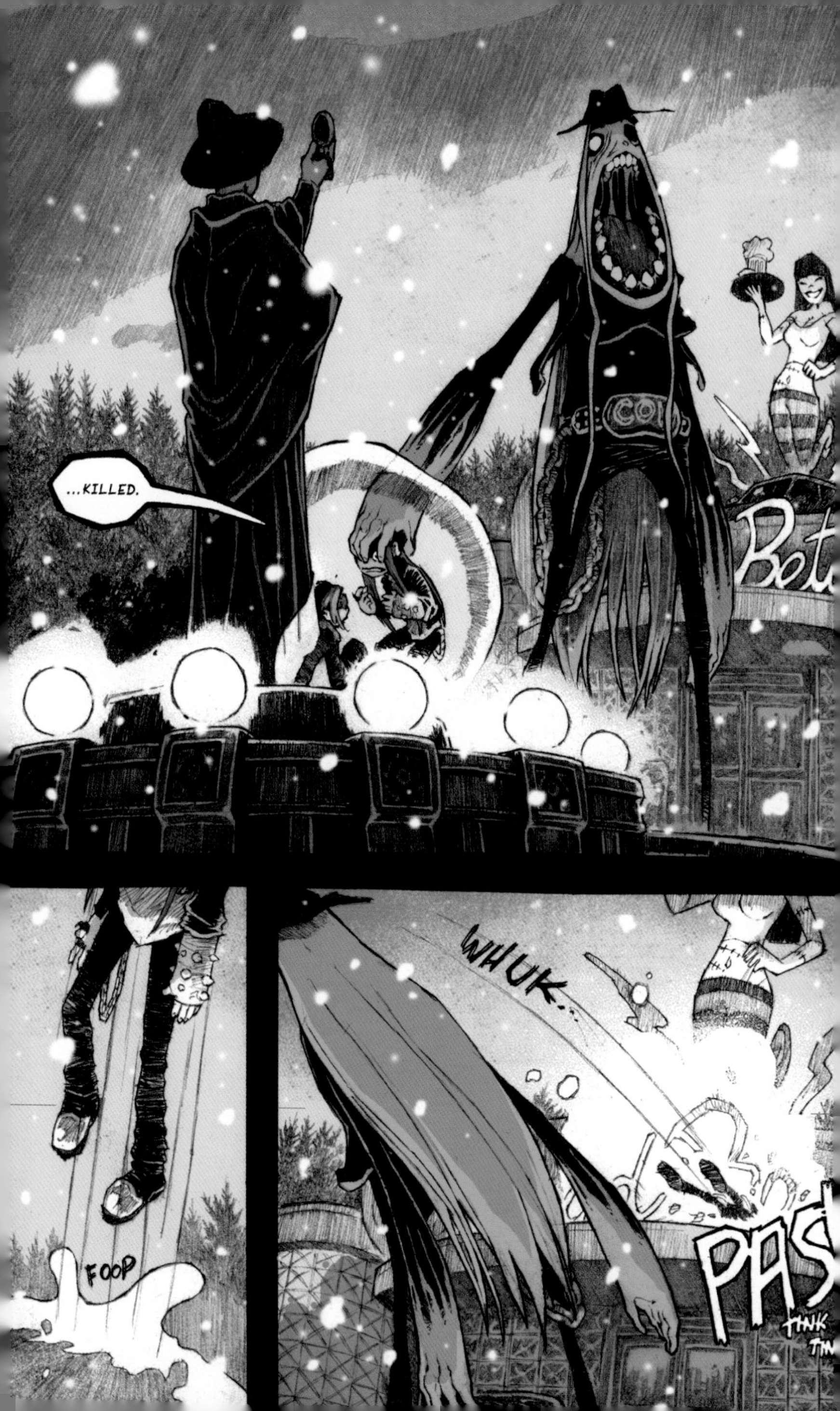
...KILLED.
WHUK...
FOOP

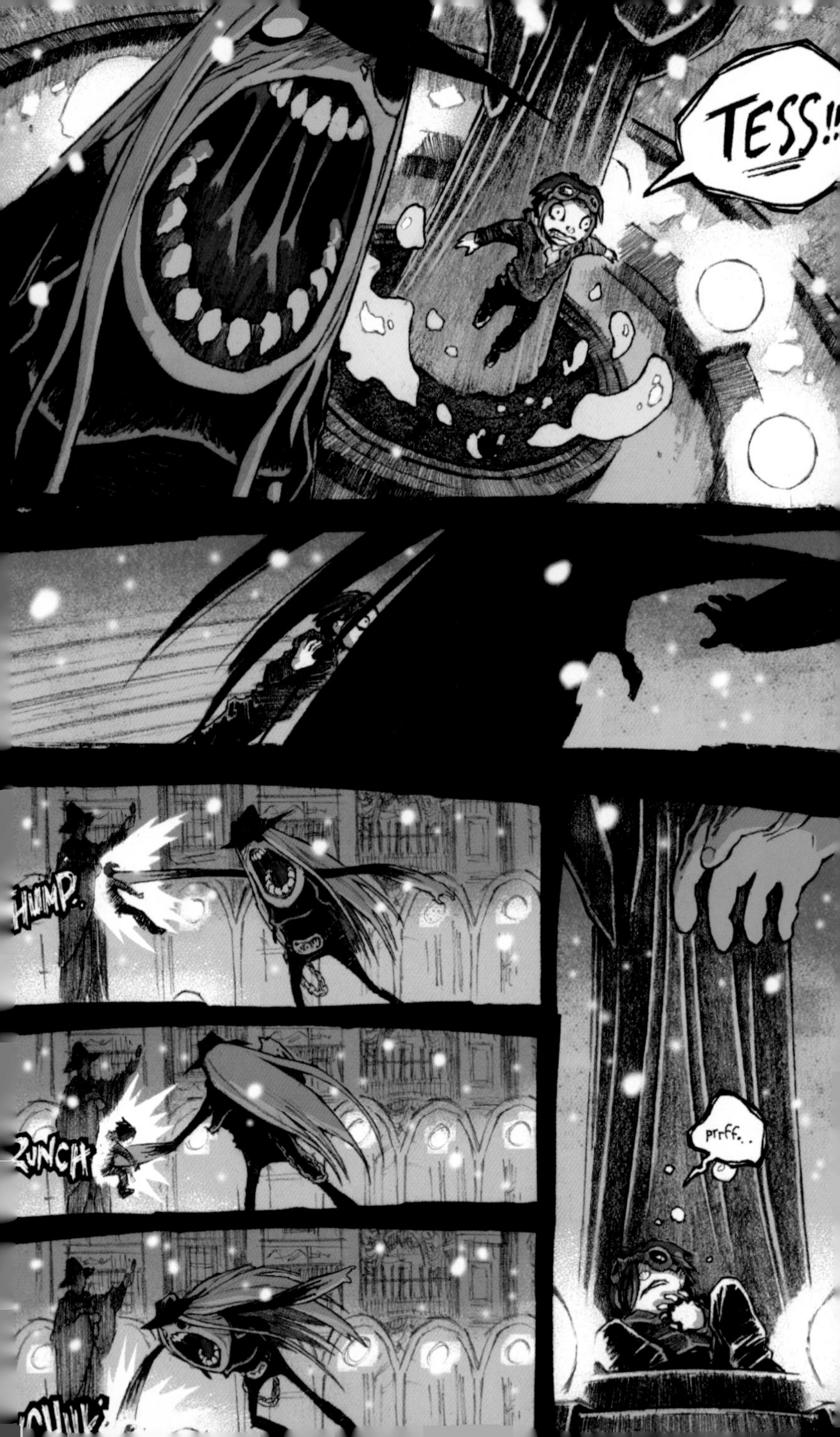
TESS!!
HUMP.
ZUNCH
prrff...

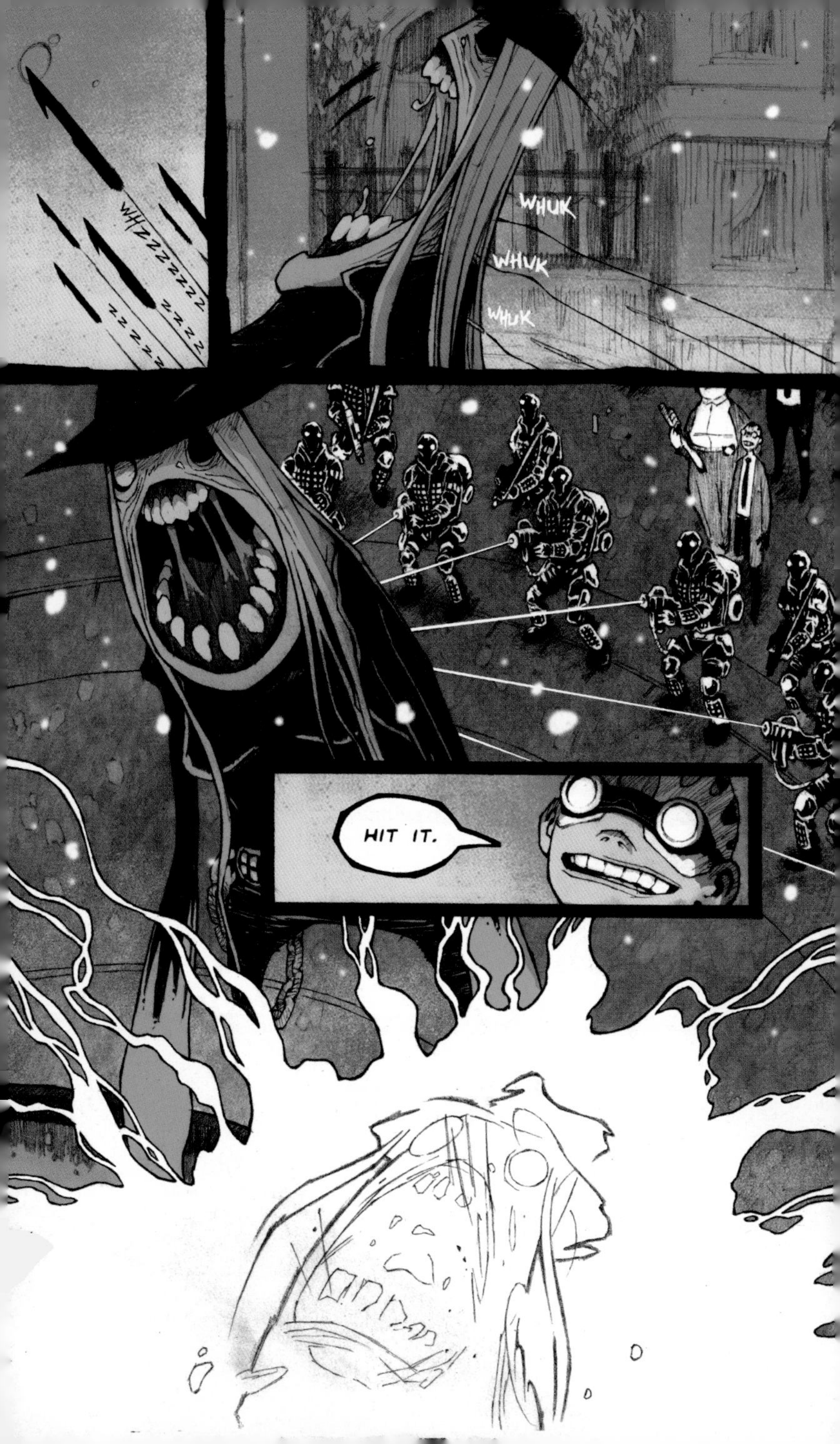
WHZZZZZZZZ ZZZZ ZZZZ
WHUK
WHUK
WHUK
HIT IT.

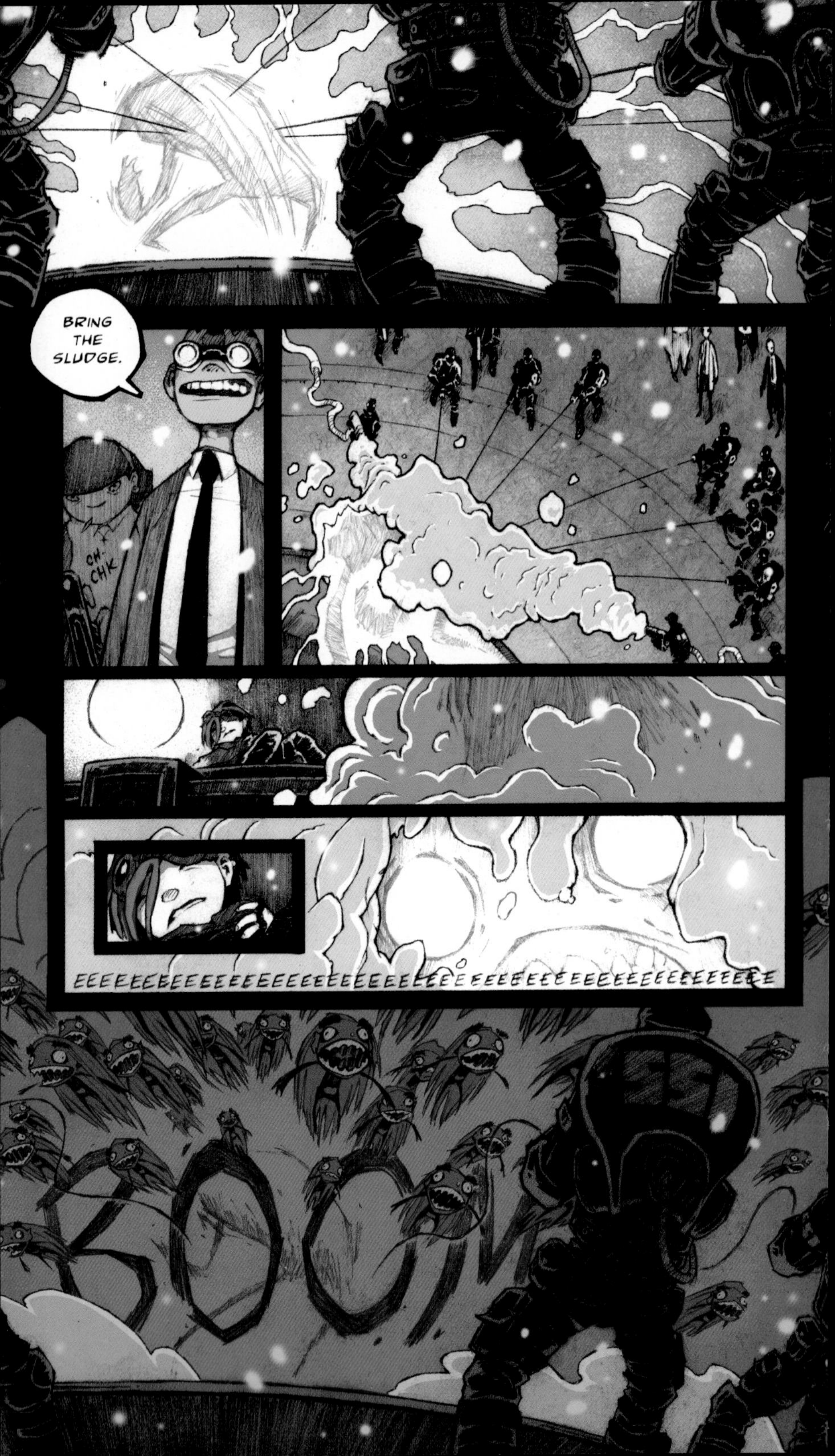
BRING THE SLUDGE.
CH-CHK
EEEEEEEEEEEEEEEEEEEEEEEEEEEEEEEEEEEEEEEEEEEEEEEEEEEE
BOOOM

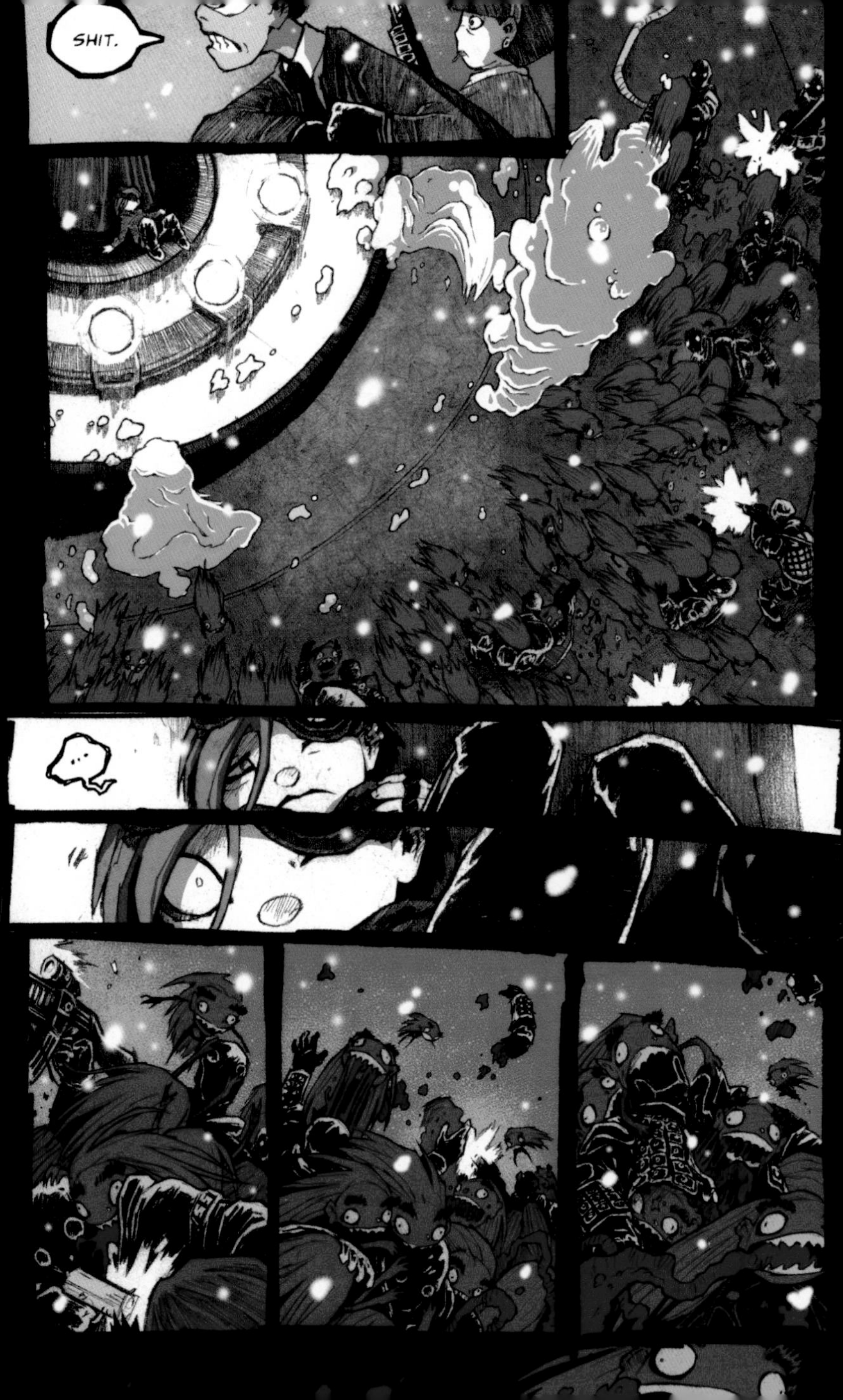
SHIT.
...

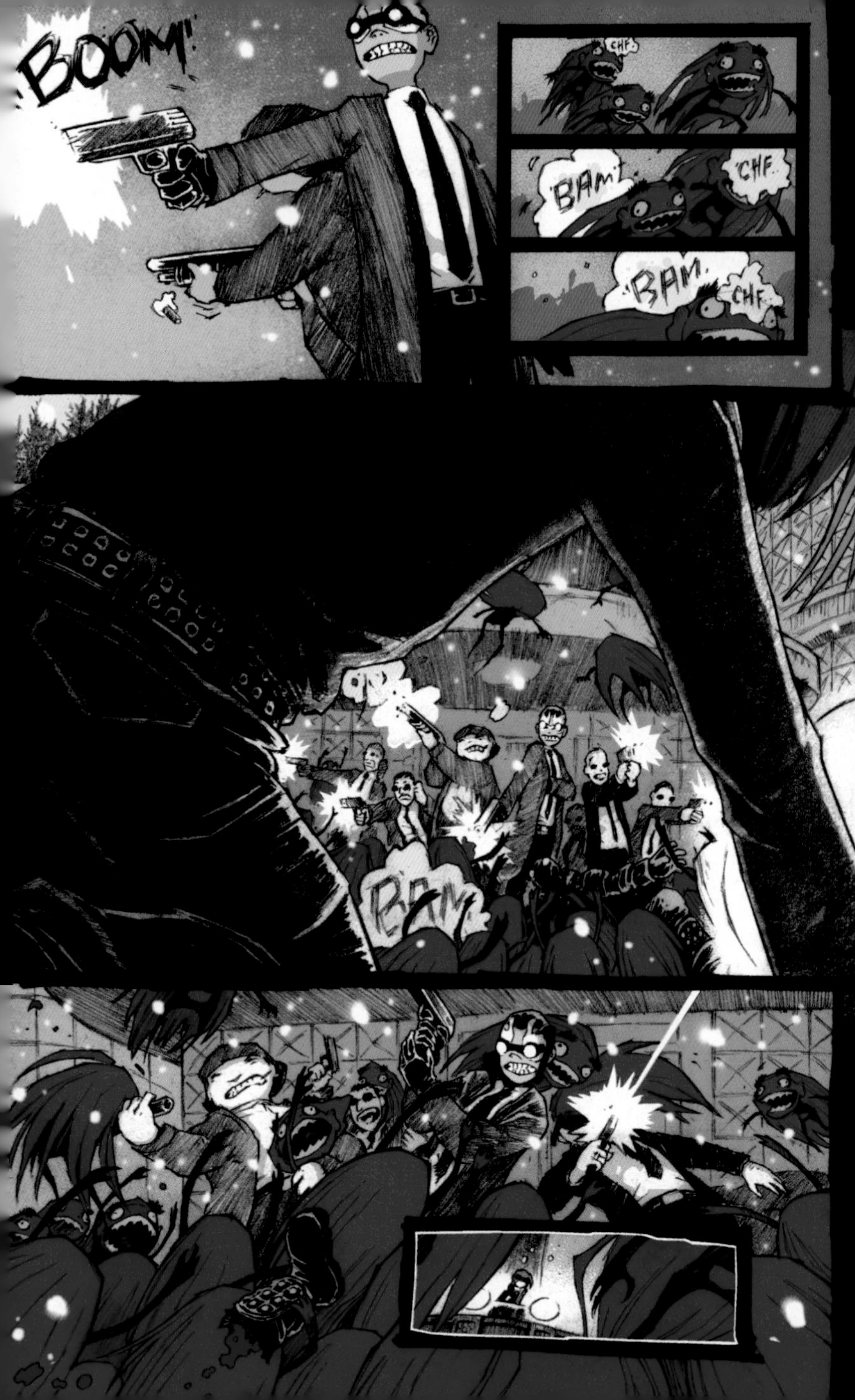
BOOM!
CHF
BAM!
CHF
BAM
CHF
BAM

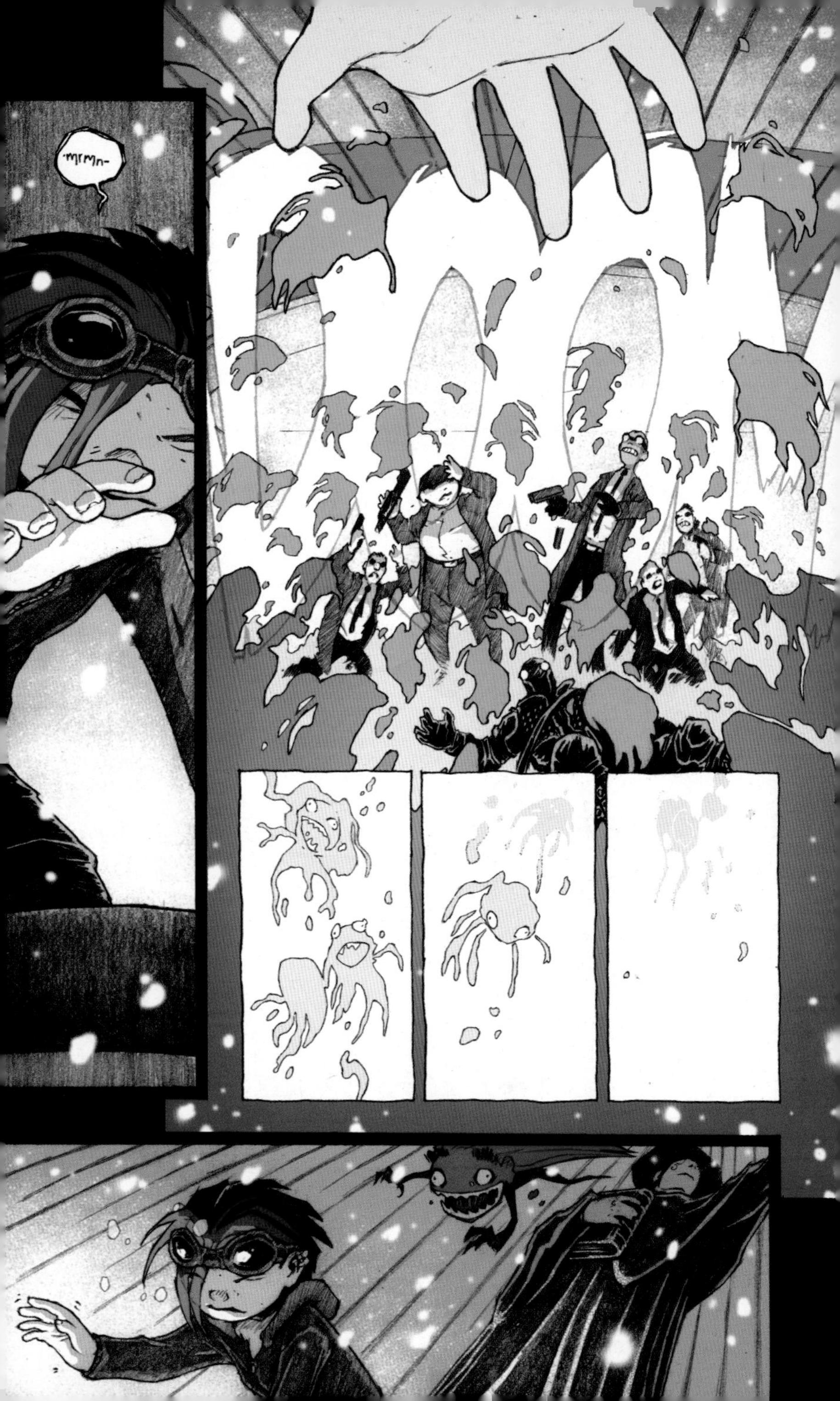
-mrmn-

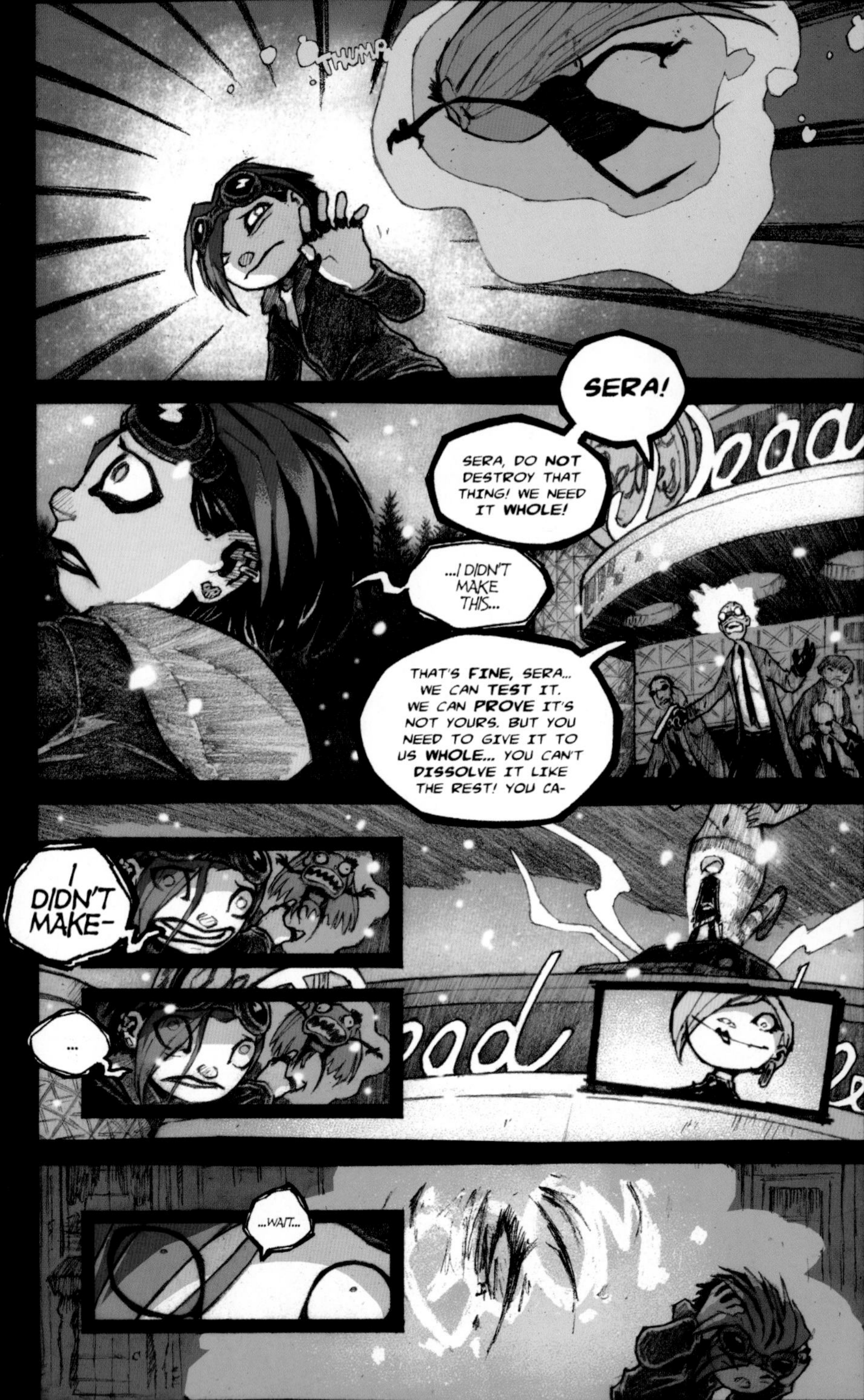
THUMP
SERA!
SERA, DO NOT DESTROY THAT THING! WE NEED IT WHOLE!
...I DIDN'T MAKE THIS...
THAT'S FINE, SERA... WE CAN TEST IT. WE CAN PROVE IT'S NOT YOURS. BUT YOU NEED TO GIVE IT TO US WHOLE... YOU CAN'T DISSOLVE IT LIKE THE REST! YOU CA-
I DIDN'T MAKE-
...
...WAIT...

CHAOS IN CRESTFALLEN

AGE ANALYSIS CONFIRMS THE CREATURE'S "SPELLCAST" NATUR

-ATEUR VIDEO OF THE 20-FOOT "GREEN BEHEMOTH" EXITING THE WOODS DIRECTLY BEHIND CITY HALL. THE CREATURE MADE ITS WAY SOUTHW-

THE MAKING OF A MONSTER

-RESEMBLANCE TO THE LARGE RED-HAIRED MAN SEEN IN THIS *EXCLUSIVE* AMATEUR VIDEO ARGUING WITH SERENITY ROSE JUST MINUTES BEFORE THE-

EXCLUSIVE

-ESCRIBED BY ONLOOKERS AS A QUOTE UNQUOTE "LOVER'S SPAT," EXPERTS ARE NOW SCOURING THE PUBLIC RECORD IN SEARCH OF-

CRESTFALLEN MASSACRE

DRIES "BURST LIKE OVERSTUFFED BLOOD SAUSAGE"... CIVILIAN CASUALTIES YET :
15 -18.5 PIL -8.40 MOTH -187.5 KUT -182 JPL -58 NIN -2.5 ART -9.0 GAO =0.1

-AGENTS LOST THE CREATURE DEEP IN THE *"DOLDRUMS"* AREA OF THE INCONSOLABLE WOODS, BUT MANAGED TO TRACK IT VIA HELICOPTER-MOUNTED SENS-

BOX NEWS

-CLAIM MS. ROSE WAS TOTALLY **UNABLE** TO GAIN CONTROL OF HER CREATIONS UNTIL **AFTER** THE **BRUTAL** SLAUGHTER OF 8 SSI AGENTS, RAISING SERI-

CHAOS IN CRESTFALLEN

TION TEAMS FROM TWIN PINES ARRIVED AT APPROX. 3 PM PACI

-ARE TOLD SSI AND LOCAL AUTHORITIES **IMMEDIATELY** TOOK ROSE INTO CUSTODY, BUT HER EXACT LOCATION AND **MENTAL STATE** ARE, AT THIS HOUR...

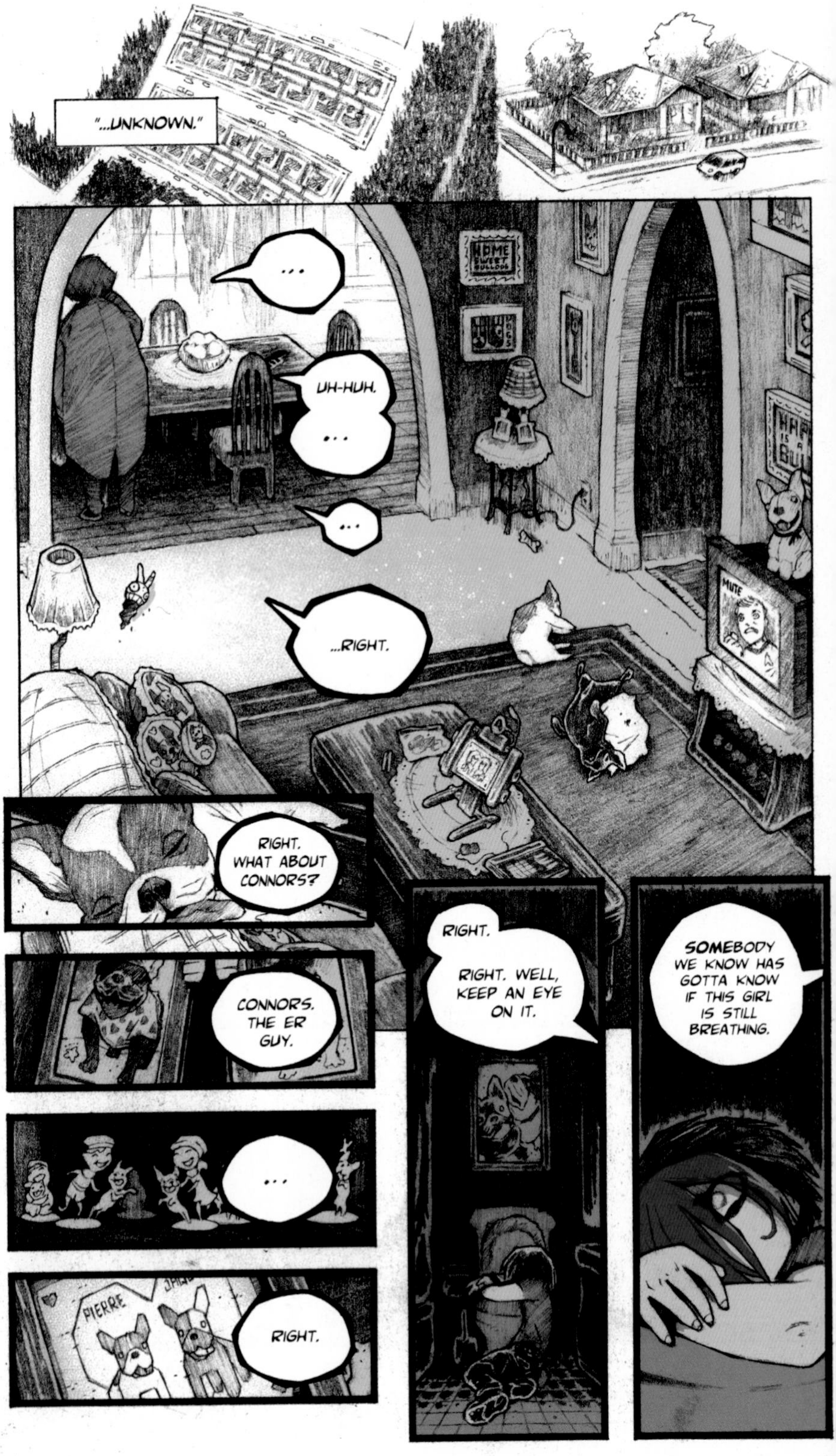
"...UNKNOWN."
...
UH-HUH.
...
...
...RIGHT.
RIGHT. WHAT ABOUT CONNORS?
CONNORS. THE ER GUY.
...
RIGHT.
RIGHT.
RIGHT. WELL, KEEP AN EYE ON IT.
SOMEBODY WE KNOW HAS GOTTA KNOW IF THIS GIRL IS STILL BREATHING.

BEEP

...ANY NEWS?

NAH.

MERRICK'S GOT THE WHOLE HOSPITAL LOCKED DOWN PRETTY TIGHT. BUT NO WORRIES.

I STILL KNOW PLENTY OF PEOPLE WHO—

DON'T BOTHER.

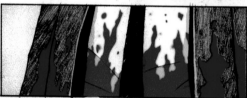

THERE'S THIS LITTLE BUTTON BY THE DOOR. YOU PRESS IT, MAKES A LITTLE DING-A-DING, MAY-BE I COME AND SEE WHO, AH...

...

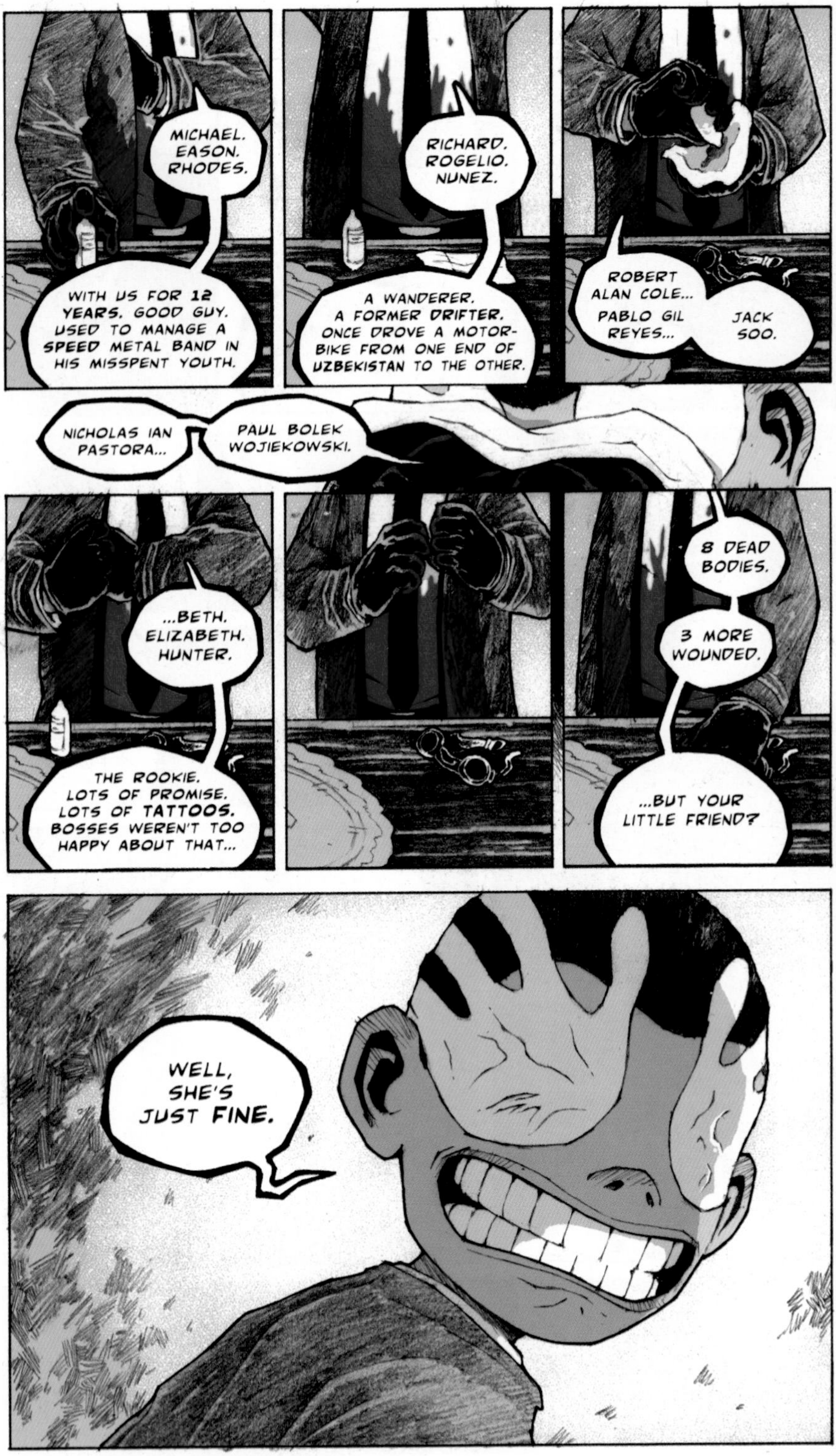

MICHAEL. EASON. RHODES.
WITH US FOR 12 YEARS. GOOD GUY. USED TO MANAGE A SPEED METAL BAND IN HIS MISSPENT YOUTH.
RICHARD. ROGELIO. NUNEZ.
A WANDERER. A FORMER DRIFTER. ONCE DROVE A MOTOR-BIKE FROM ONE END OF UZBEKISTAN TO THE OTHER.
ROBERT ALAN COLE... PABLO GIL REYES...
JACK SOO.
NICHOLAS IAN PASTORA...
PAUL BOLEK WOJIEKOWSKI.
...BETH. ELIZABETH. HUNTER.
THE ROOKIE. LOTS OF PROMISE. LOTS OF TATTOOS. BOSSES WEREN'T TOO HAPPY ABOUT THAT...
8 DEAD BODIES.
3 MORE WOUNDED.
...BUT YOUR LITTLE FRIEND?
WELL, SHE'S JUST FINE.

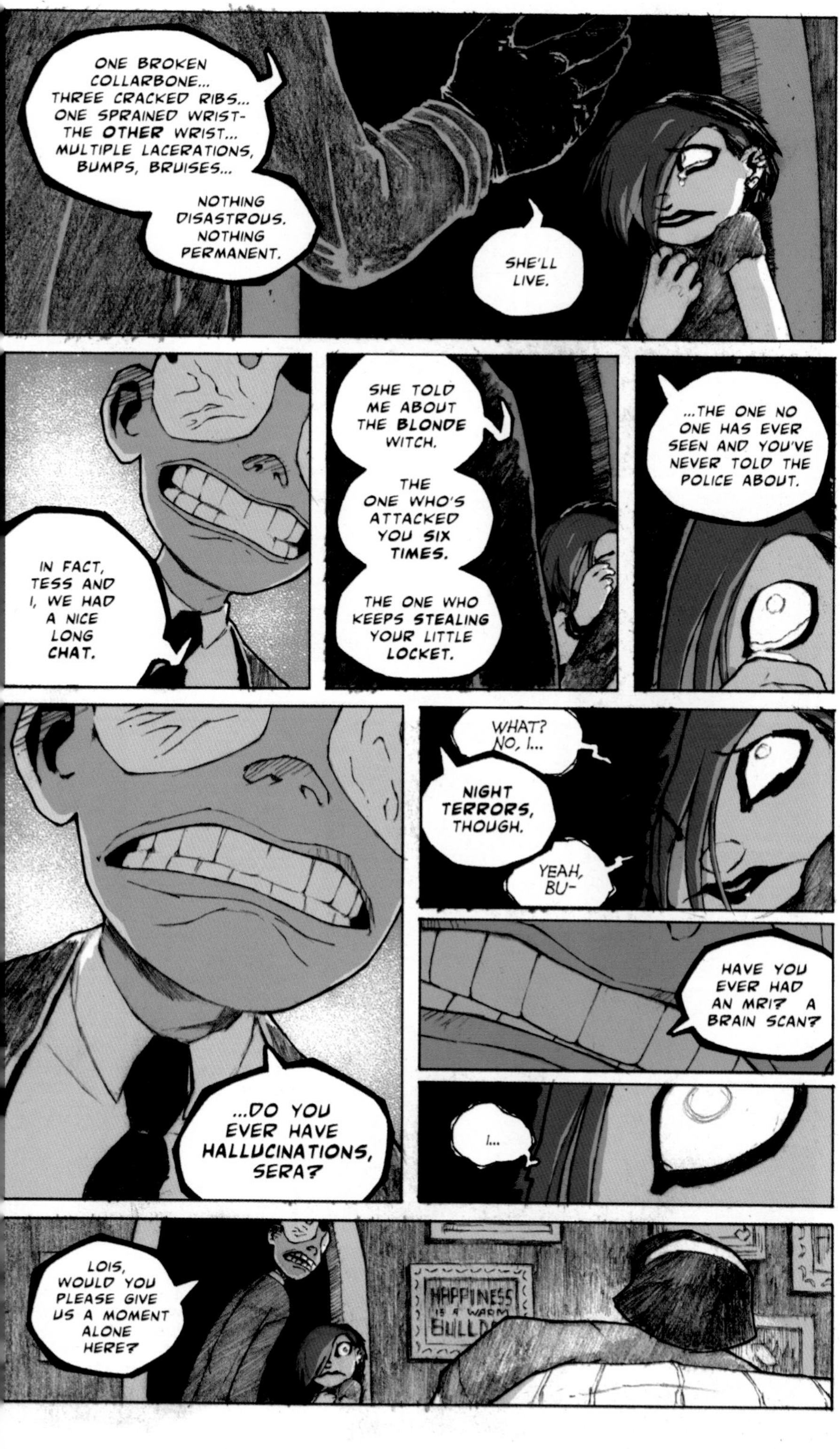
ONE BROKEN COLLARBONE... THREE CRACKED RIBS... ONE SPRAINED WRIST- THE **OTHER** WRIST... MULTIPLE LACERATIONS, BUMPS, BRUISES...
NOTHING DISASTROUS. NOTHING PERMANENT.
SHE'LL LIVE.
IN FACT, TESS AND I, WE HAD A NICE LONG CHAT.
SHE TOLD ME ABOUT THE **BLONDE** WITCH.
THE ONE WHO'S ATTACKED YOU **SIX TIMES.**
THE ONE WHO KEEPS **STEALING** YOUR LITTLE LOCKET.
...THE ONE NO ONE HAS EVER SEEN AND YOU'VE NEVER TOLD THE POLICE ABOUT.
WHAT? NO, I...
NIGHT TERRORS, THOUGH.
YEAH, BU-
HAVE YOU EVER HAD AN MRI? A BRAIN SCAN?
...DO YOU EVER HAVE **HALLUCINATIONS,** SERA?
I...
LOIS, WOULD YOU PLEASE GIVE US A MOMENT ALONE HERE?
HAPPINESS IS A WARM

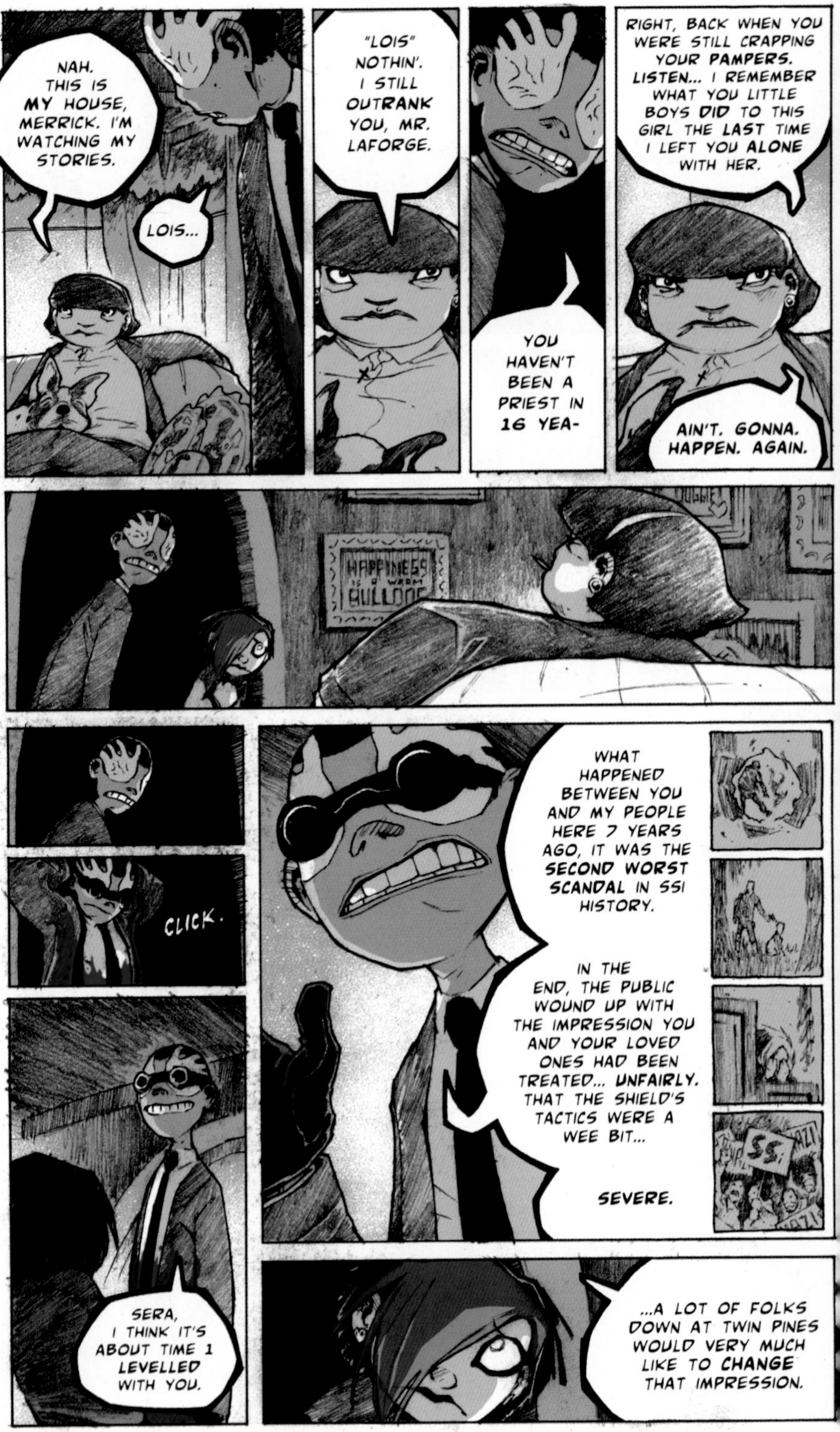

NAH. THIS IS MY HOUSE, MERRICK. I'M WATCHING MY STORIES.
LOIS...
"LOIS" NOTHIN'. I STILL OUTRANK YOU, MR. LAFORGE.
YOU HAVEN'T BEEN A PRIEST IN 16 YEA-
RIGHT, BACK WHEN YOU WERE STILL CRAPPING YOUR PAMPERS. LISTEN... I REMEMBER WHAT YOU LITTLE BOYS DID TO THIS GIRL THE LAST TIME I LEFT YOU ALONE WITH HER.
AIN'T. GONNA. HAPPEN. AGAIN.
HAPPINESS IS A WARM BULLDOG
CLICK.
SERA, I THINK IT'S ABOUT TIME I LEVELLED WITH YOU.
WHAT HAPPENED BETWEEN YOU AND MY PEOPLE HERE 7 YEARS AGO, IT WAS THE SECOND WORST SCANDAL IN SSI HISTORY.
IN THE END, THE PUBLIC WOUND UP WITH THE IMPRESSION YOU AND YOUR LOVED ONES HAD BEEN TREATED... UNFAIRLY. THAT THE SHIELD'S TACTICS WERE A WEE BIT...
SEVERE.
...A LOT OF FOLKS DOWN AT TWIN PINES WOULD VERY MUCH LIKE TO CHANGE THAT IMPRESSION.

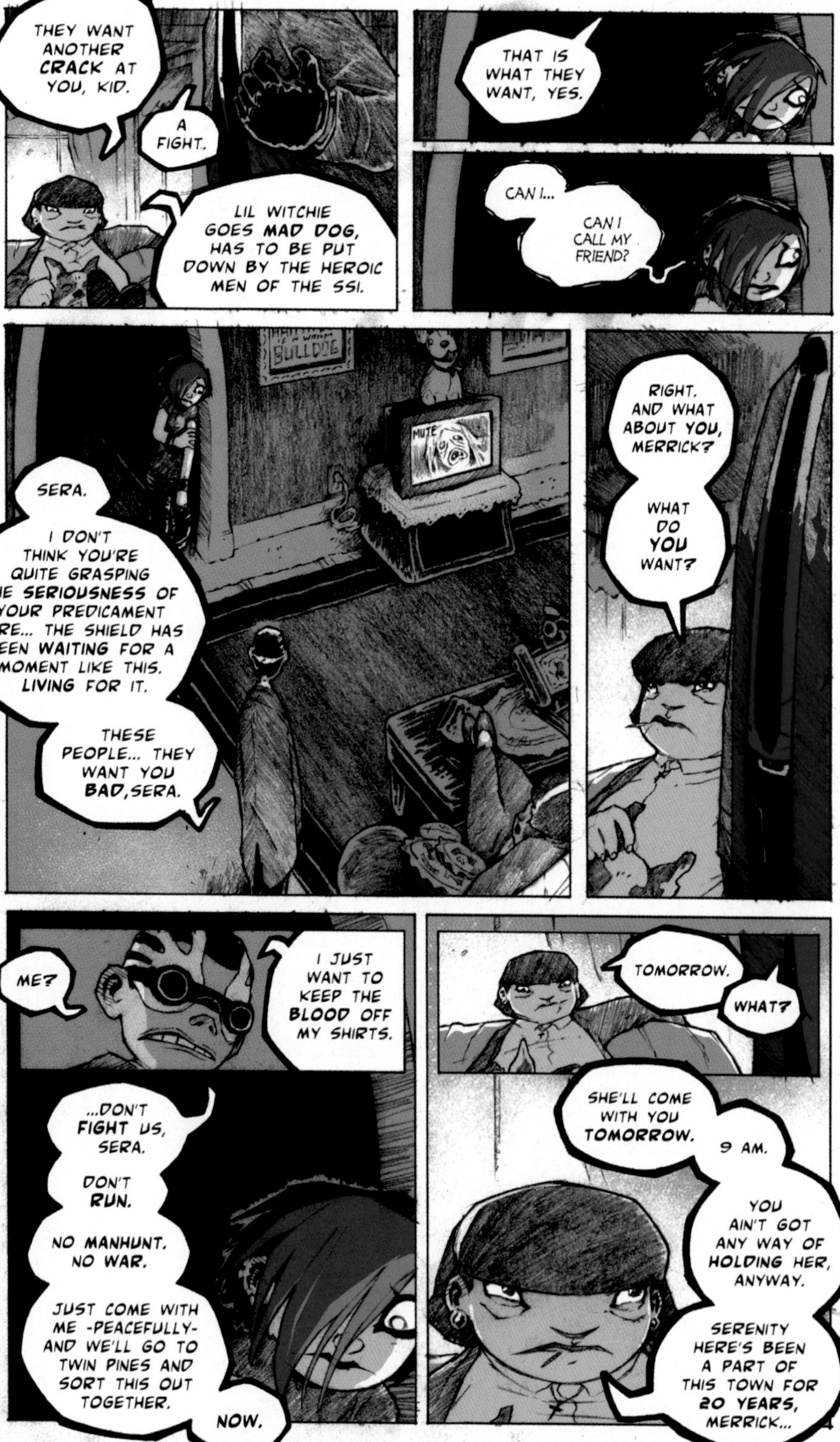
THEY WANT ANOTHER CRACK AT YOU, KID.
A FIGHT.
LIL WITCHIE GOES MAD DOG, HAS TO BE PUT DOWN BY THE HEROIC MEN OF THE SSI.
THAT IS WHAT THEY WANT, YES.
CAN I...
CAN I CALL MY FRIEND?
MUTE
SERA.
I DON'T THINK YOU'RE QUITE GRASPING THE SERIOUSNESS OF YOUR PREDICAMENT ERE... THE SHIELD HAS BEEN WAITING FOR A MOMENT LIKE THIS. LIVING FOR IT.
THESE PEOPLE... THEY WANT YOU BAD, SERA.
RIGHT. AND WHAT ABOUT YOU, MERRICK?
WHAT DO YOU WANT?
ME?
I JUST WANT TO KEEP THE BLOOD OFF MY SHIRTS.
...DON'T FIGHT US, SERA.
DON'T RUN.
NO MANHUNT. NO WAR.
JUST COME WITH ME -PEACEFULLY- AND WE'LL GO TO TWIN PINES AND SORT THIS OUT TOGETHER.
NOW.
TOMORROW.
WHAT?
SHE'LL COME WITH YOU TOMORROW.
9 AM.
YOU AIN'T GOT ANY WAY OF HOLDING HER, ANYWAY.
SERENITY HERE'S BEEN A PART OF THIS TOWN FOR 20 YEARS, MERRICK...

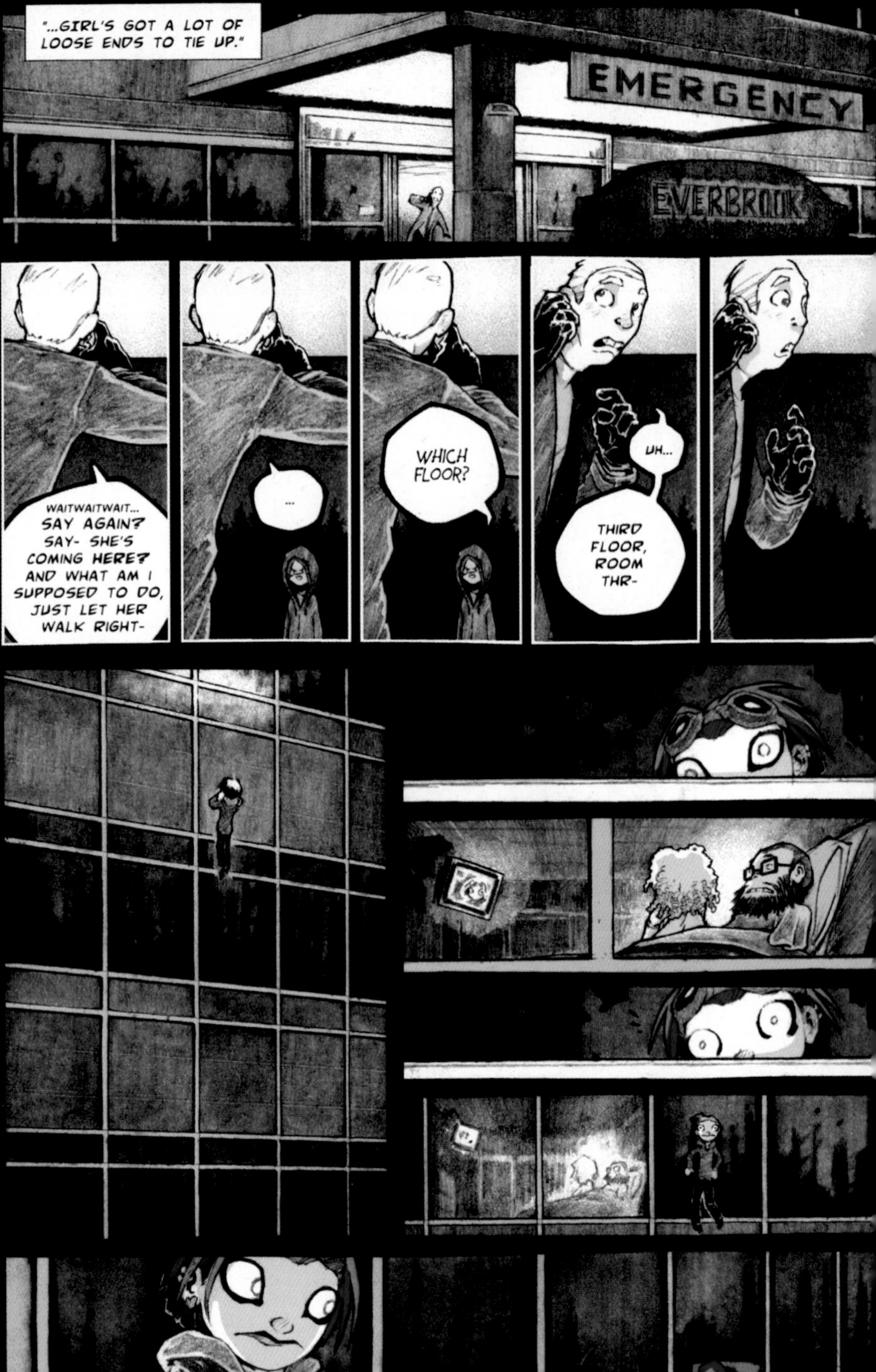
"...GIRL'S GOT A LOT OF LOOSE ENDS TO TIE UP."
EMERGENCY
EVERBROOK
WAITWAITWAIT... SAY AGAIN? SAY- SHE'S COMING HERE? AND WHAT AM I SUPPOSED TO DO, JUST LET HER WALK RIGHT-
...
WHICH FLOOR?
UH...
THIRD FLOOR, ROOM THR-

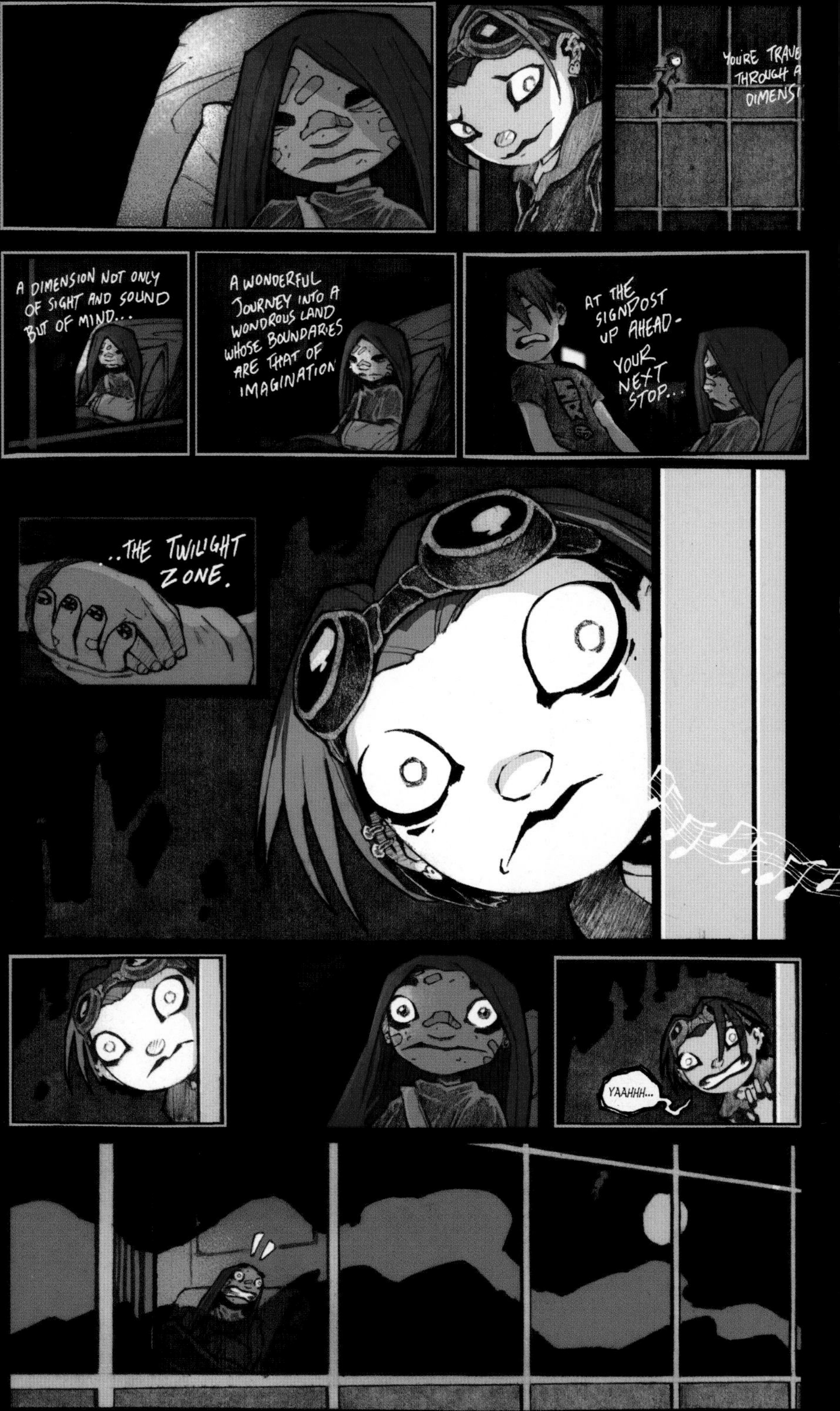
YOU'RE TRAVE
THROUGH A
DIMENS
A DIMENSION NOT ONLY OF SIGHT AND SOUND BUT OF MIND...
A WONDERFUL JOURNEY INTO A WONDROUS LAND WHOSE BOUNDARIES ARE THAT OF IMAGINATION
AT THE SIGNPOST UP AHEAD-
YOUR NEXT STOP...
..THE TWILIGHT ZONE.
YAAHHH...

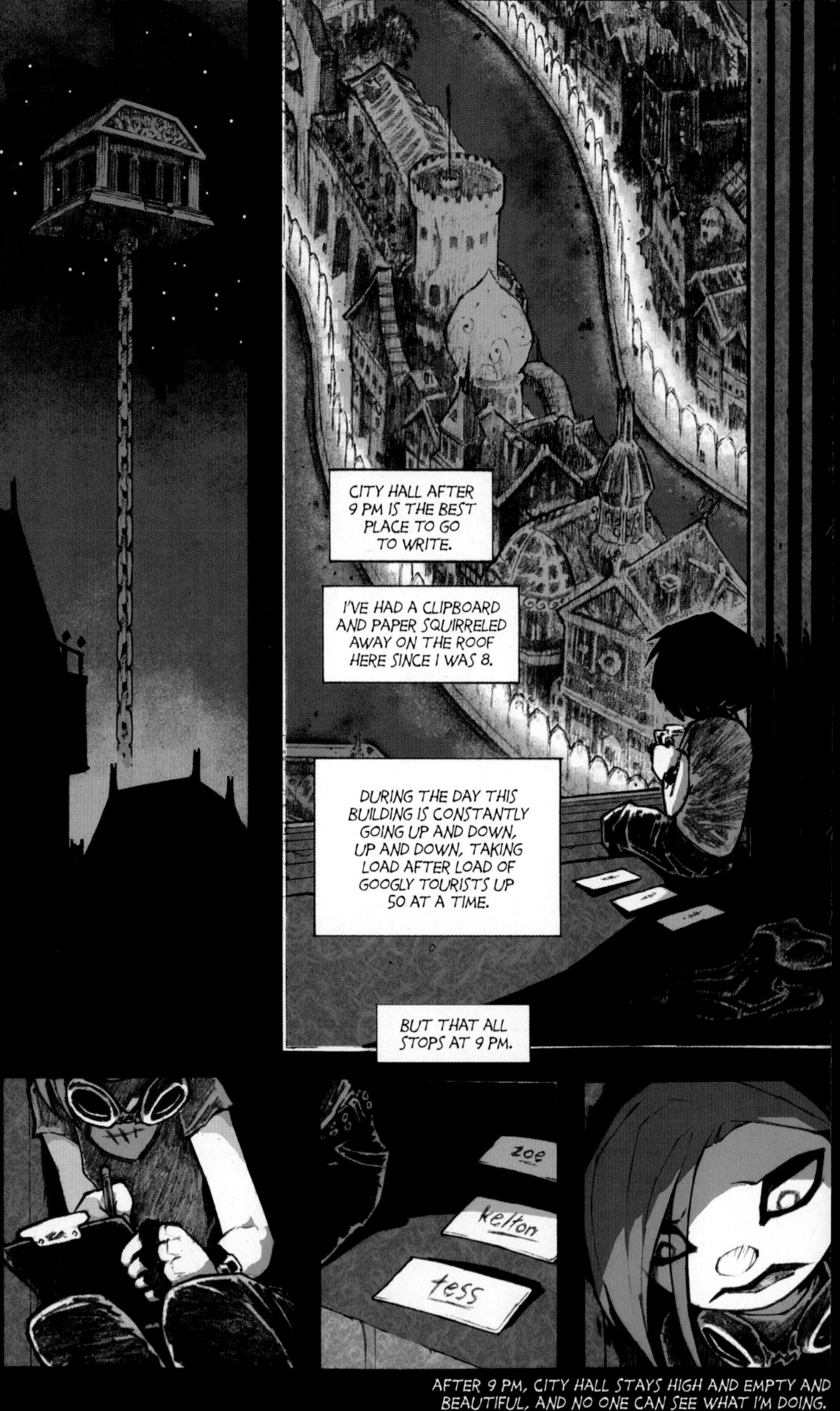

CITY HALL AFTER 9 PM IS THE BEST PLACE TO GO TO WRITE.
I'VE HAD A CLIPBOARD AND PAPER SQUIRRELED AWAY ON THE ROOF HERE SINCE I WAS 8.
DURING THE DAY THIS BUILDING IS CONSTANTLY GOING UP AND DOWN, UP AND DOWN, TAKING LOAD AFTER LOAD OF GOOGLY TOURISTS UP 50 AT A TIME.
BUT THAT ALL STOPS AT 9 PM.
zoe
kelton
tess
AFTER 9 PM, CITY HALL STAYS HIGH AND EMPTY AND BEAUTIFUL, AND NO ONE CAN SEE WHAT I'M DOING.

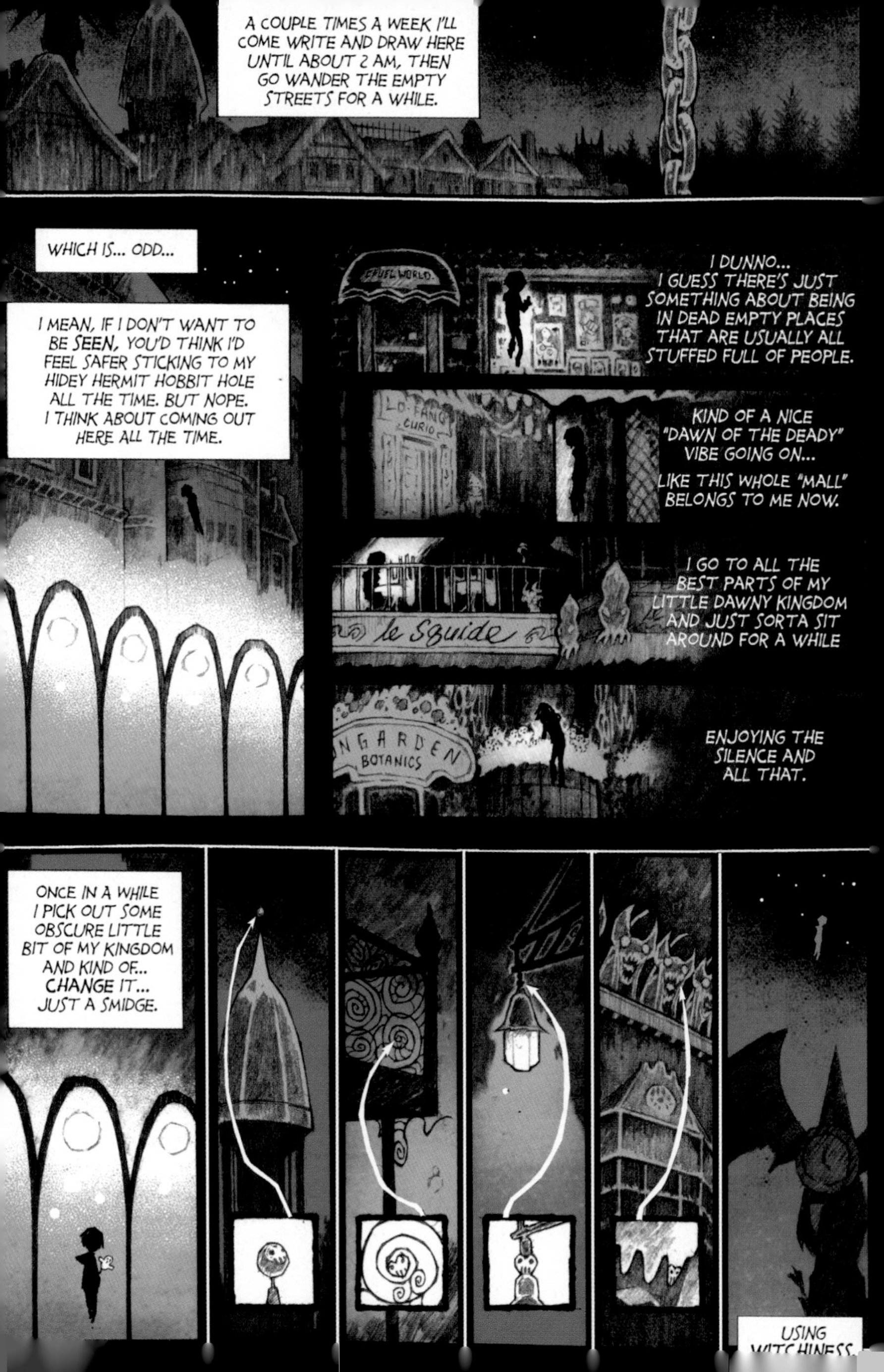
A COUPLE TIMES A WEEK I'LL COME WRITE AND DRAW HERE UNTIL ABOUT 2 AM, THEN GO WANDER THE EMPTY STREETS FOR A WHILE.
WHICH IS... ODD...
I MEAN, IF I DON'T WANT TO BE **SEEN**, YOU'D THINK I'D FEEL SAFER STICKING TO MY HIDEY HERMIT HOBBIT HOLE ALL THE TIME. BUT NOPE. I THINK ABOUT COMING OUT HERE ALL THE TIME.
CRUEL WORLD
I DUNNO... I GUESS THERE'S JUST SOMETHING ABOUT BEING IN DEAD EMPTY PLACES THAT ARE USUALLY ALL STUFFED FULL OF PEOPLE.
LO-FANG CURIO
KIND OF A NICE "DAWN OF THE DEADY" VIBE GOING ON...
LIKE THIS WHOLE "MALL" BELONGS TO ME NOW.
le Squide
I GO TO ALL THE BEST PARTS OF MY LITTLE DAWNY KINGDOM AND JUST SORTA SIT AROUND FOR A WHILE
NGARDEN BOTANICS
ENJOYING THE SILENCE AND ALL THAT.
ONCE IN A WHILE I PICK OUT SOME OBSCURE LITTLE BIT OF MY KINGDOM AND KIND OF... **CHANGE** IT... JUST A SMIDGE.
USING

WHEN I WAS YOUNGER (AND FEELING ESPECIALLY ADVENTUROUS), I'D GO WANDERING OFF THE SAFELY BEATEN PATH...

IN MORE DANGEROUS DIRECTIONS...

LIKE INTO HACKETTOWN, FOR INSTANCE, THE BIG CHUNK OF CRESTFALLEN THEY DUG UP IN THE 50'S TO PLANT NEW BUNGALOWS FOR EMPLOYEES.

SNEAKING AROUND THE BURBS ALWAYS SEEMED SO NAUGHTY AND WRONG...

...I MEAN, WHAT IF SOMEONE SAW ME?

CAUTION!

EEK!

RUBIKOV

SAME THING WITH THE UNIVERSITY.

I'D GO THERE AND MAKE THIS WEIRD LITTLE GAME OF AVOIDING THE NIGHT WATCHMEN AND SNATCHING COOL BOOKS FROM THE LIBRARY. IN 10 YEARS ONLY ONE GUARD EVER NOTICED WHAT I WAS DOING.

SPASTIC RAZCALZ

POO PIRATE!

kelton

SPASTIC RAZCALZ

THE DARK

EVERY SO OFTEN THE GUY WOULD LEAVE THESE TINY RUM BALL COOKIES FOR ME IN THE CLOCK TOWER.

I REALLY APPRECIATED THAT.

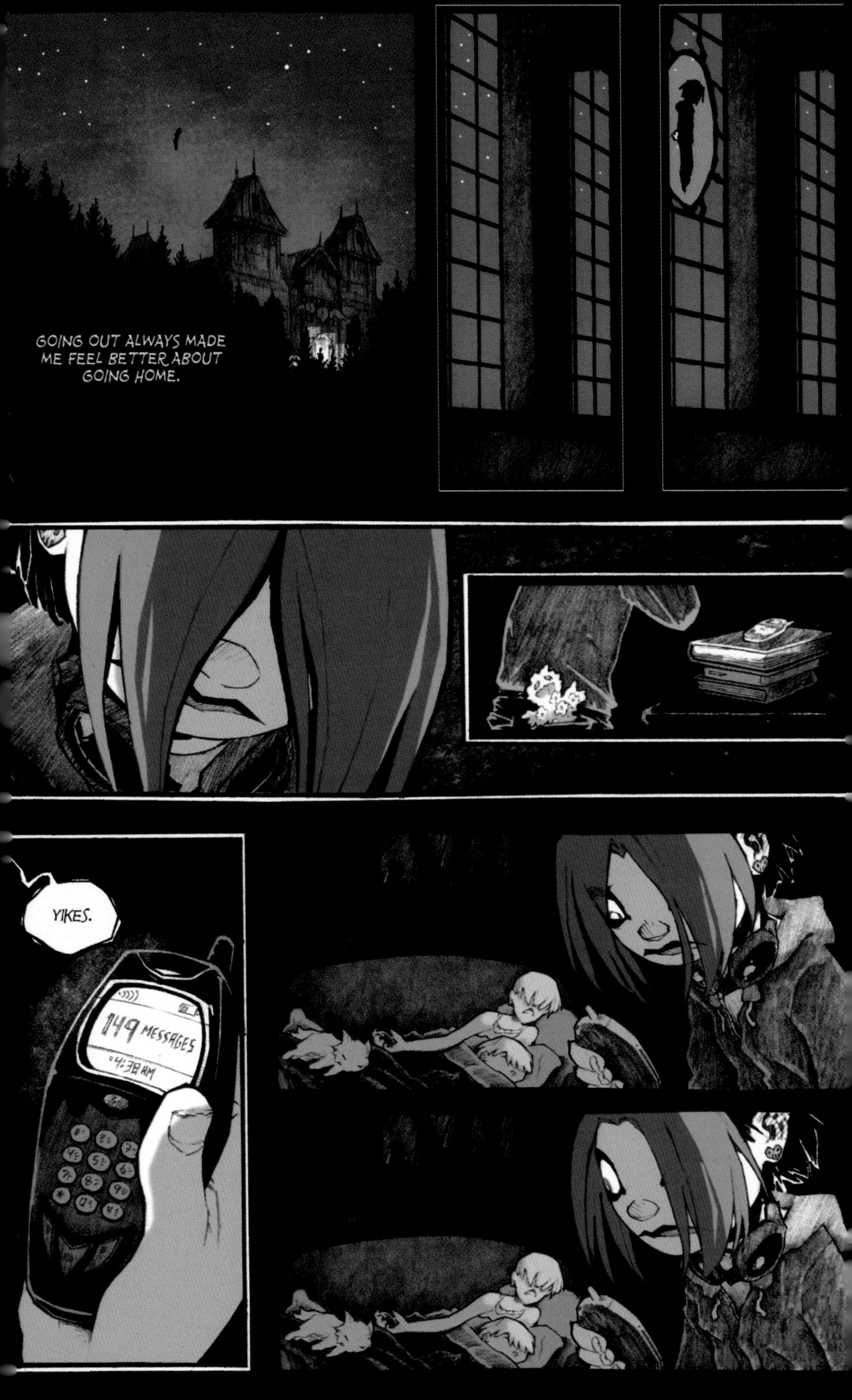
GOING OUT ALWAYS MADE ME FEEL BETTER ABOUT GOING HOME.
YIKES.
049 MESSAGES
4:38 AM

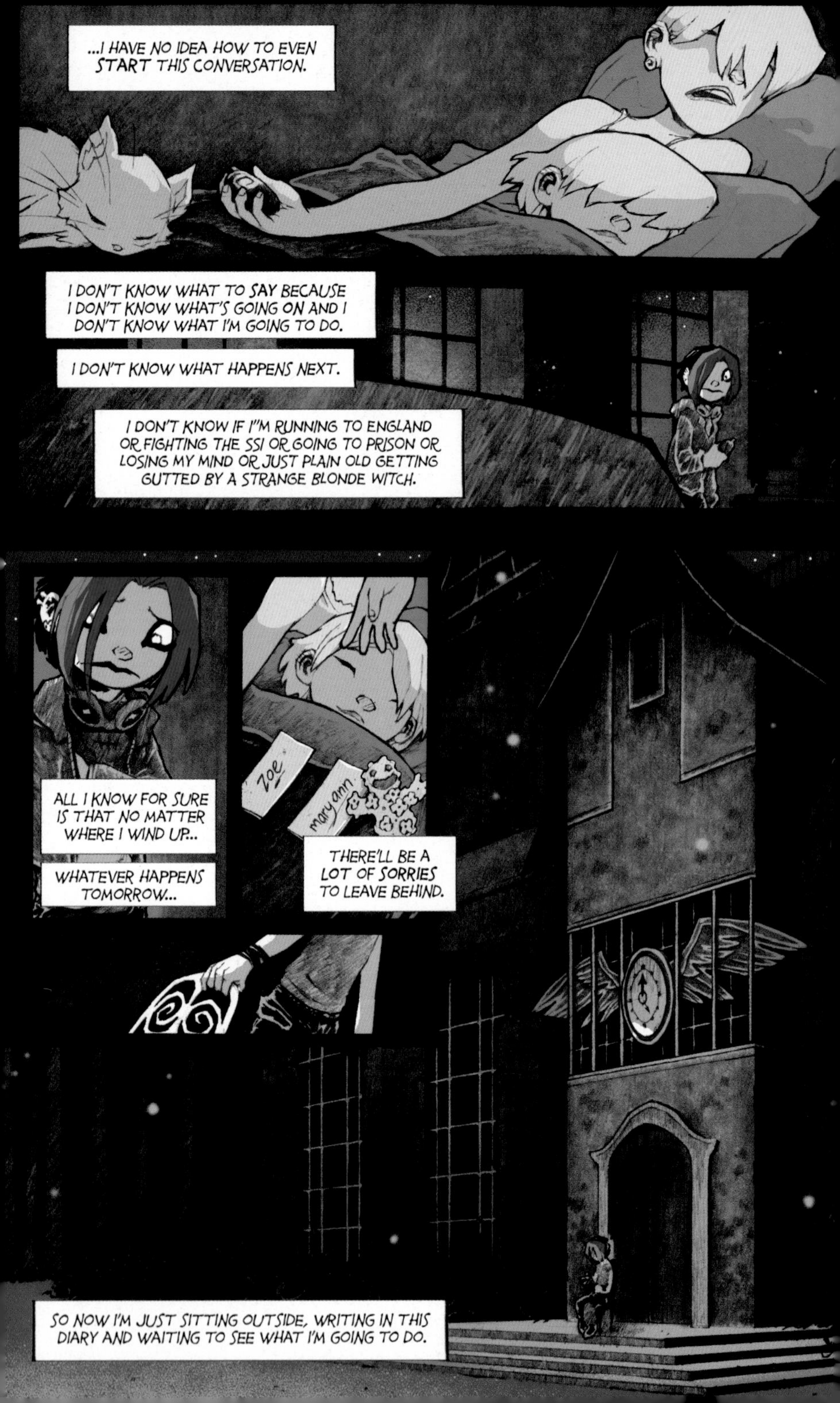
...I HAVE NO IDEA HOW TO EVEN START THIS CONVERSATION.
I DON'T KNOW WHAT TO SAY BECAUSE I DON'T KNOW WHAT'S GOING ON AND I DON'T KNOW WHAT I'M GOING TO DO.
I DON'T KNOW WHAT HAPPENS NEXT.
I DON'T KNOW IF I'M RUNNING TO ENGLAND OR FIGHTING THE SSI OR GOING TO PRISON OR LOSING MY MIND OR JUST PLAIN OLD GETTING GUTTED BY A STRANGE BLONDE WITCH.
ALL I KNOW FOR SURE IS THAT NO MATTER WHERE I WIND UP...
WHATEVER HAPPENS TOMORROW...
Zoe
mary ann
THERE'LL BE A LOT OF SORRIES TO LEAVE BEHIND.
SO NOW I'M JUST SITTING OUTSIDE, WRITING IN THIS DIARY AND WAITING TO SEE WHAT I'M GOING TO DO.

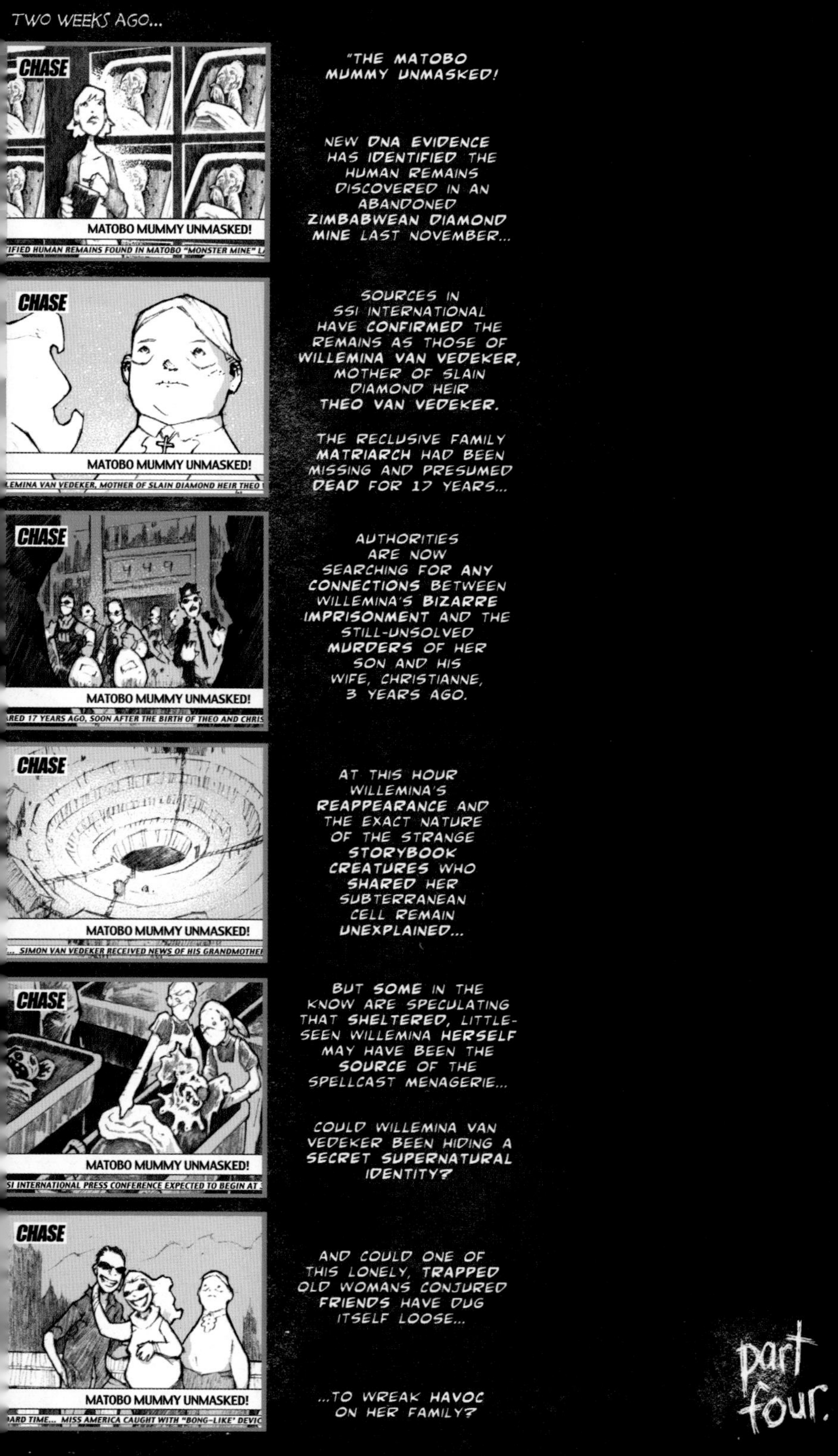
TWO WEEKS AGO...
CHASE
MATOBO MUMMY UNMASKED!
IFIED HUMAN REMAINS FOUND IN MATOBO "MONSTER MINE" L
"THE MATOBO MUMMY UNMASKED!
NEW DNA EVIDENCE HAS IDENTIFIED THE HUMAN REMAINS DISCOVERED IN AN ABANDONED ZIMBABWEAN DIAMOND MINE LAST NOVEMBER...
CHASE
MATOBO MUMMY UNMASKED!
LEMINA VAN VEDEKER, MOTHER OF SLAIN DIAMOND HEIR THEO
SOURCES IN SSI INTERNATIONAL HAVE CONFIRMED THE REMAINS AS THOSE OF WILLEMINA VAN VEDEKER, MOTHER OF SLAIN DIAMOND HEIR THEO VAN VEDEKER.
THE RECLUSIVE FAMILY MATRIARCH HAD BEEN MISSING AND PRESUMED DEAD FOR 17 YEARS...
CHASE
MATOBO MUMMY UNMASKED!
ARED 17 YEARS AGO, SOON AFTER THE BIRTH OF THEO AND CHRIS
AUTHORITIES ARE NOW SEARCHING FOR ANY CONNECTIONS BETWEEN WILLEMINA'S BIZARRE IMPRISONMENT AND THE STILL-UNSOLVED MURDERS OF HER SON AND HIS WIFE, CHRISTIANNE, 3 YEARS AGO.
CHASE
MATOBO MUMMY UNMASKED!
... SIMON VAN VEDEKER RECEIVED NEWS OF HIS GRANDMOTHER
AT THIS HOUR WILLEMINA'S REAPPEARANCE AND THE EXACT NATURE OF THE STRANGE STORYBOOK CREATURES WHO SHARED HER SUBTERRANEAN CELL REMAIN UNEXPLAINED...
CHASE
MATOBO MUMMY UNMASKED!
SI INTERNATIONAL PRESS CONFERENCE EXPECTED TO BEGIN AT
BUT SOME IN THE KNOW ARE SPECULATING THAT SHELTERED, LITTLE-SEEN WILLEMINA HERSELF MAY HAVE BEEN THE SOURCE OF THE SPELLCAST MENAGERIE...
COULD WILLEMINA VAN VEDEKER BEEN HIDING A SECRET SUPERNATURAL IDENTITY?
CHASE
MATOBO MUMMY UNMASKED!
ARD TIME... MISS AMERICA CAUGHT WITH "BONG-LIKE" DEVIC
AND COULD ONE OF THIS LONELY, TRAPPED OLD WOMANS CONJURED FRIENDS HAVE DUG ITSELF LOOSE...
...TO WREAK HAVOC ON HER FAMILY?
part four.

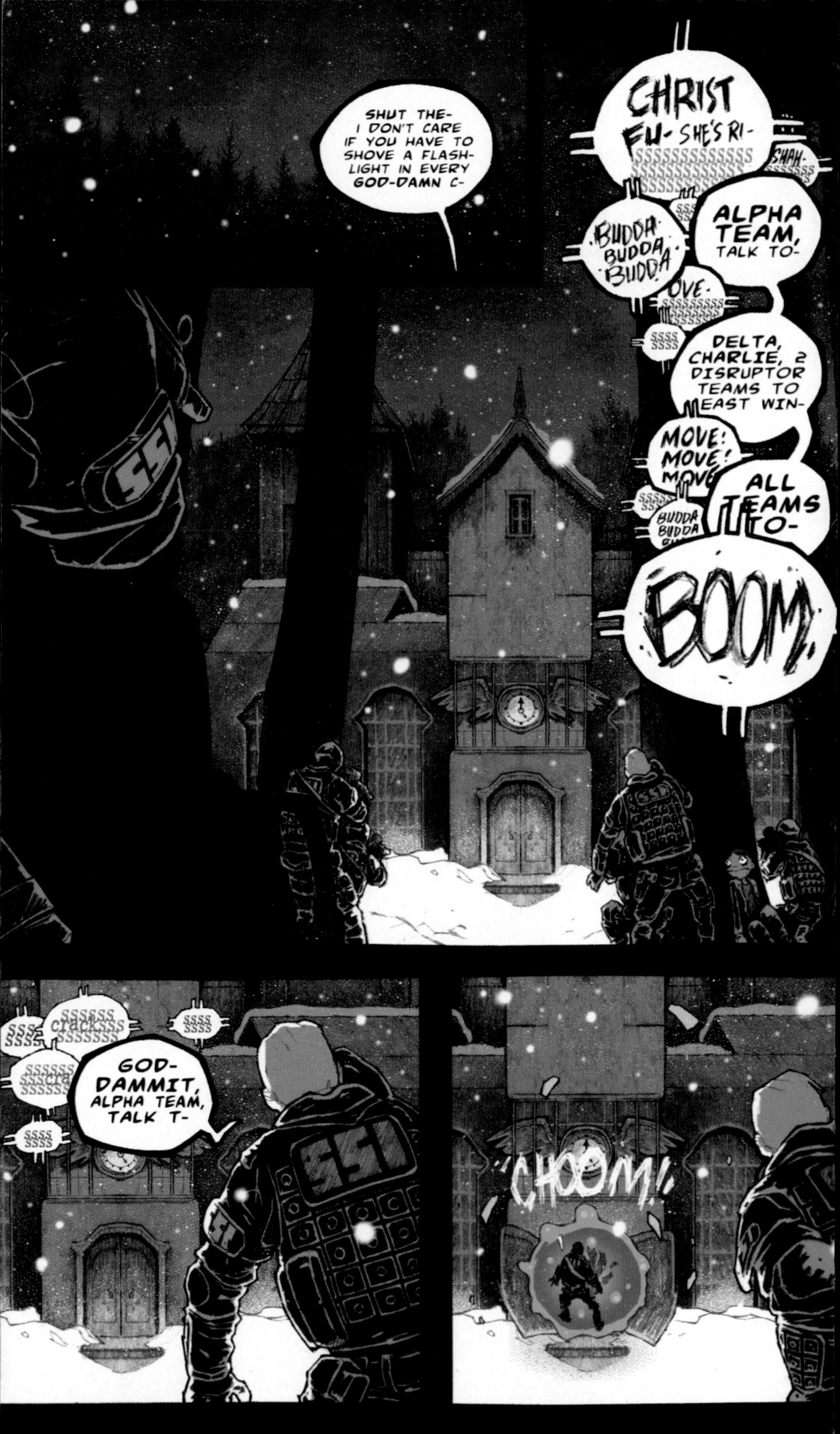
SHUT THE- I DON'T CARE IF YOU HAVE TO SHOVE A FLASHLIGHT IN EVERY GOD-DAMN C-
CHRIST FU- SHE'S RI-
SHAH-
BUDDA BUDDA BUDDA
ALPHA TEAM, TALK TO-
OVE-
DELTA, CHARLIE, 2 DISRUPTOR TEAMS TO EAST WIN-
MOVE! MOVE! MOVE
BUDDA BUDDA
ALL TEAMS TO-
BOOM
crack
crac
GOD-DAMMIT, ALPHA TEAM, TALK T-
CHOOM!!

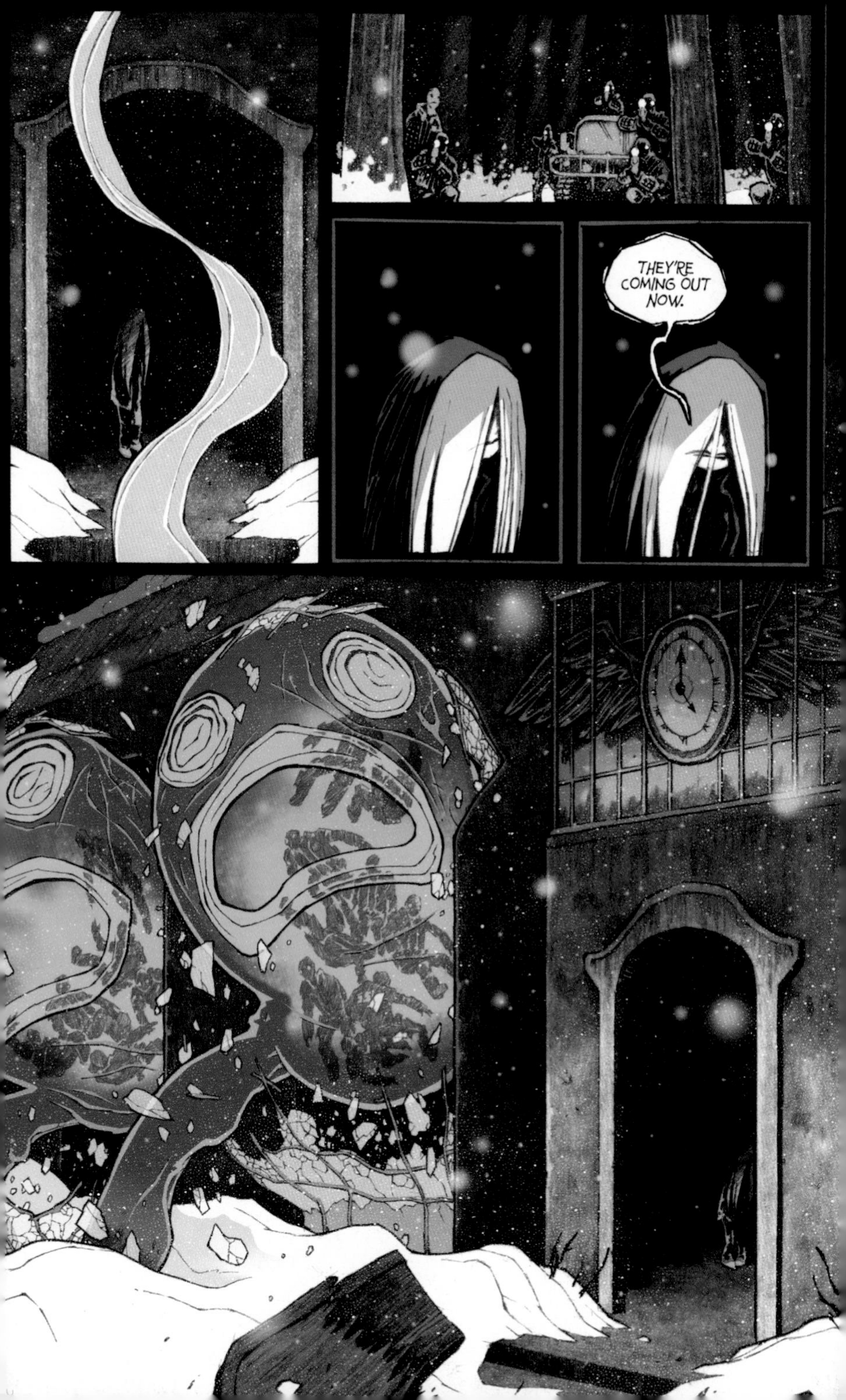
THEY'RE COMING OUT NOW.

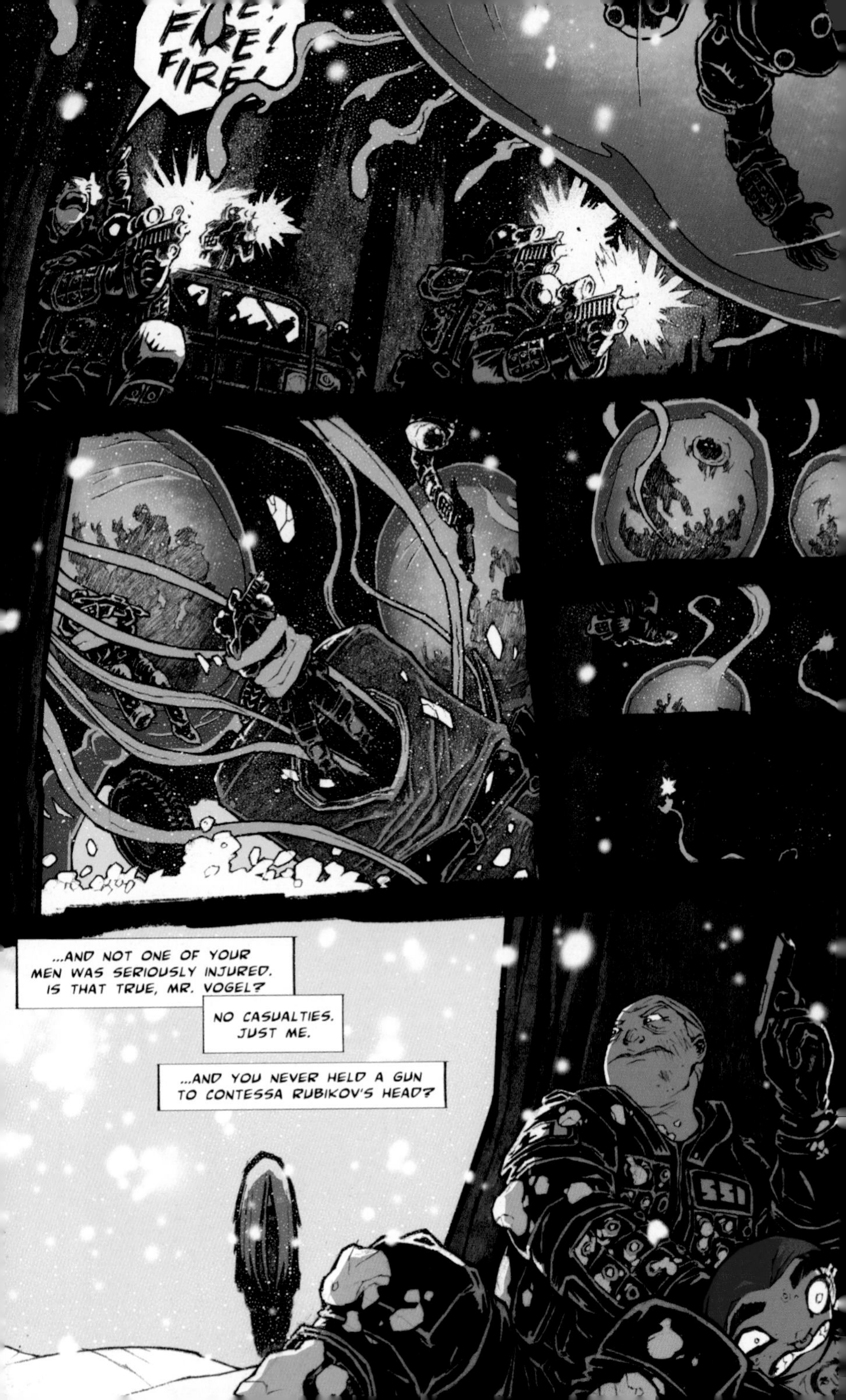
FIRE!
FIRE!
...AND NOT ONE OF YOUR MEN WAS SERIOUSLY INJURED. IS THAT TRUE, MR. VOGEL?
NO CASUALTIES. JUST ME.
...AND YOU NEVER HELD A GUN TO CONTESSA RUBIKOV'S HEAD?
SSI

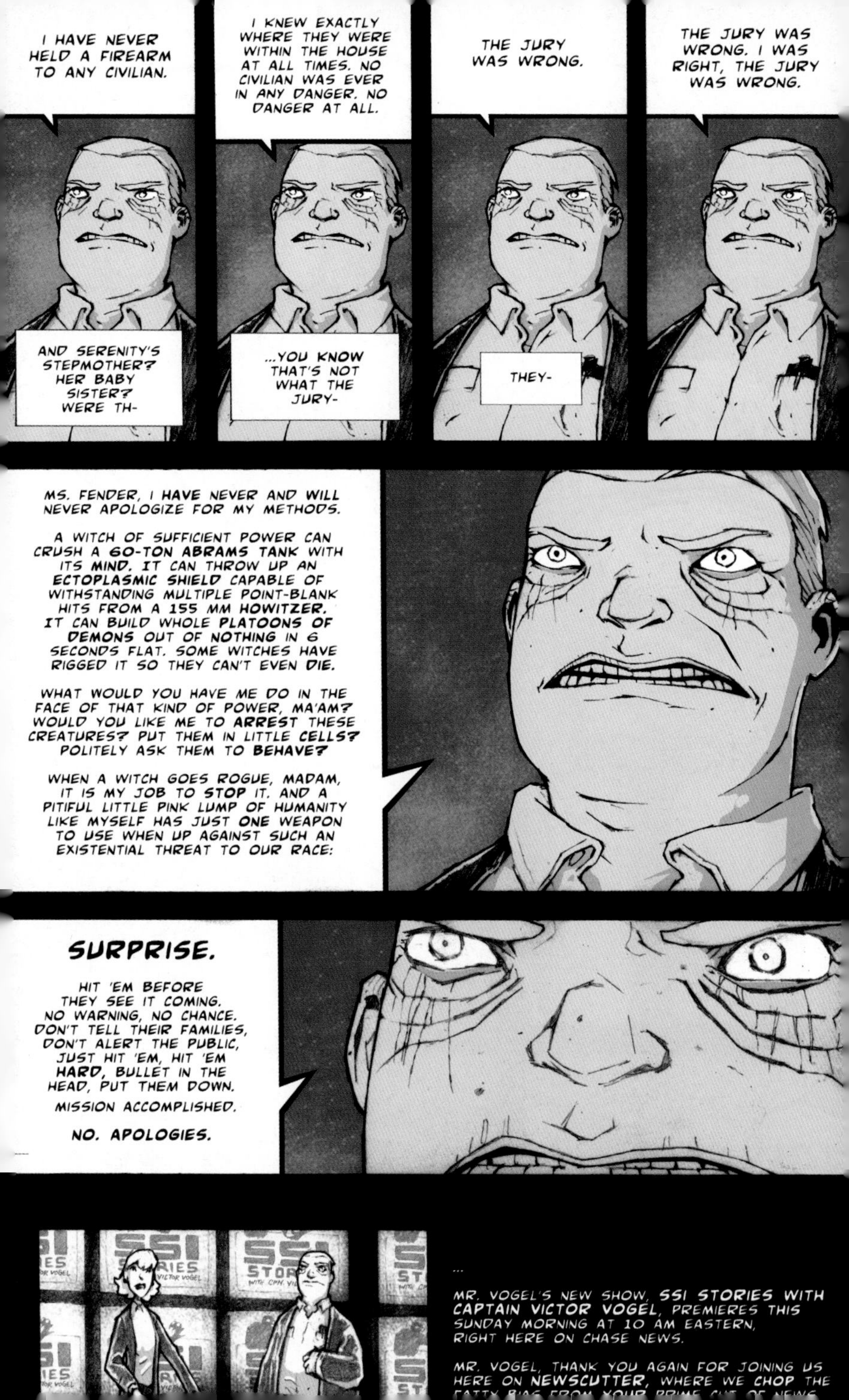

I HAVE NEVER HELD A FIREARM TO ANY CIVILIAN.
AND SERENITY'S STEPMOTHER? HER BABY SISTER? WERE TH-
I KNEW EXACTLY WHERE THEY WERE WITHIN THE HOUSE AT ALL TIMES. NO CIVILIAN WAS EVER IN ANY DANGER. NO DANGER AT ALL.
...YOU KNOW THAT'S NOT WHAT THE JURY-
THE JURY WAS WRONG.
THEY-
THE JURY WAS WRONG. I WAS RIGHT, THE JURY WAS WRONG.
MS. FENDER, I HAVE NEVER AND WILL NEVER APOLOGIZE FOR MY METHODS.
A WITCH OF SUFFICIENT POWER CAN CRUSH A 60-TON ABRAMS TANK WITH ITS MIND. IT CAN THROW UP AN ECTOPLASMIC SHIELD CAPABLE OF WITHSTANDING MULTIPLE POINT-BLANK HITS FROM A 155 MM HOWITZER. IT CAN BUILD WHOLE PLATOONS OF DEMONS OUT OF NOTHING IN 6 SECONDS FLAT. SOME WITCHES HAVE RIGGED IT SO THEY CAN'T EVEN DIE.
WHAT WOULD YOU HAVE ME DO IN THE FACE OF THAT KIND OF POWER, MA'AM? WOULD YOU LIKE ME TO ARREST THESE CREATURES? PUT THEM IN LITTLE CELLS? POLITELY ASK THEM TO BEHAVE?
WHEN A WITCH GOES ROGUE, MADAM, IT IS MY JOB TO STOP IT. AND A PITIFUL LITTLE PINK LUMP OF HUMANITY LIKE MYSELF HAS JUST ONE WEAPON TO USE WHEN UP AGAINST SUCH AN EXISTENTIAL THREAT TO OUR RACE:
SURPRISE.
HIT 'EM BEFORE THEY SEE IT COMING. NO WARNING, NO CHANCE. DON'T TELL THEIR FAMILIES, DON'T ALERT THE PUBLIC, JUST HIT 'EM, HIT 'EM HARD, BULLET IN THE HEAD, PUT THEM DOWN.
MISSION ACCOMPLISHED.
NO. APOLOGIES.
SSI STORIES
VICTOR VOGEL
...
MR. VOGEL'S NEW SHOW, SSI STORIES WITH CAPTAIN VICTOR VOGEL, PREMIERES THIS SUNDAY MORNING AT 10 AM EASTERN, RIGHT HERE ON CHASE NEWS.
MR. VOGEL, THANK YOU AGAIN FOR JOINING US HERE ON NEWSCUTTER, WHERE WE CHOP THE

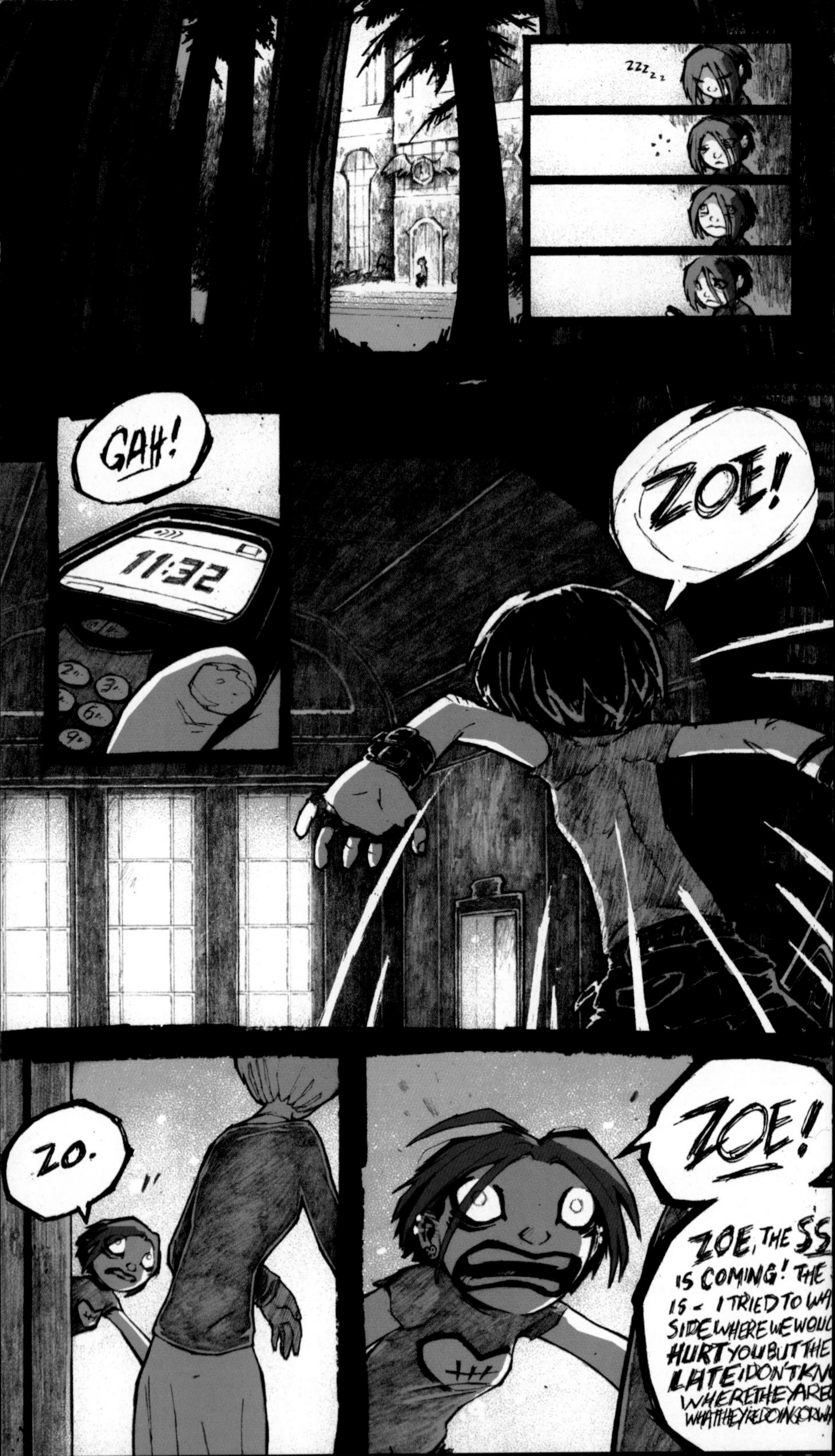
zzzzz
GAH!
11:32
ZOE!
ZO.
ZOE!
ZOE, THE SS
IS COMING! THE
IS - I TRIED TO WA
SIDE WHERE WE WOUL
HURT YOU BUT THE
LATE I DON'T KN
WHERE THEY ARE
WHAT THEY'RE DOING OR WH

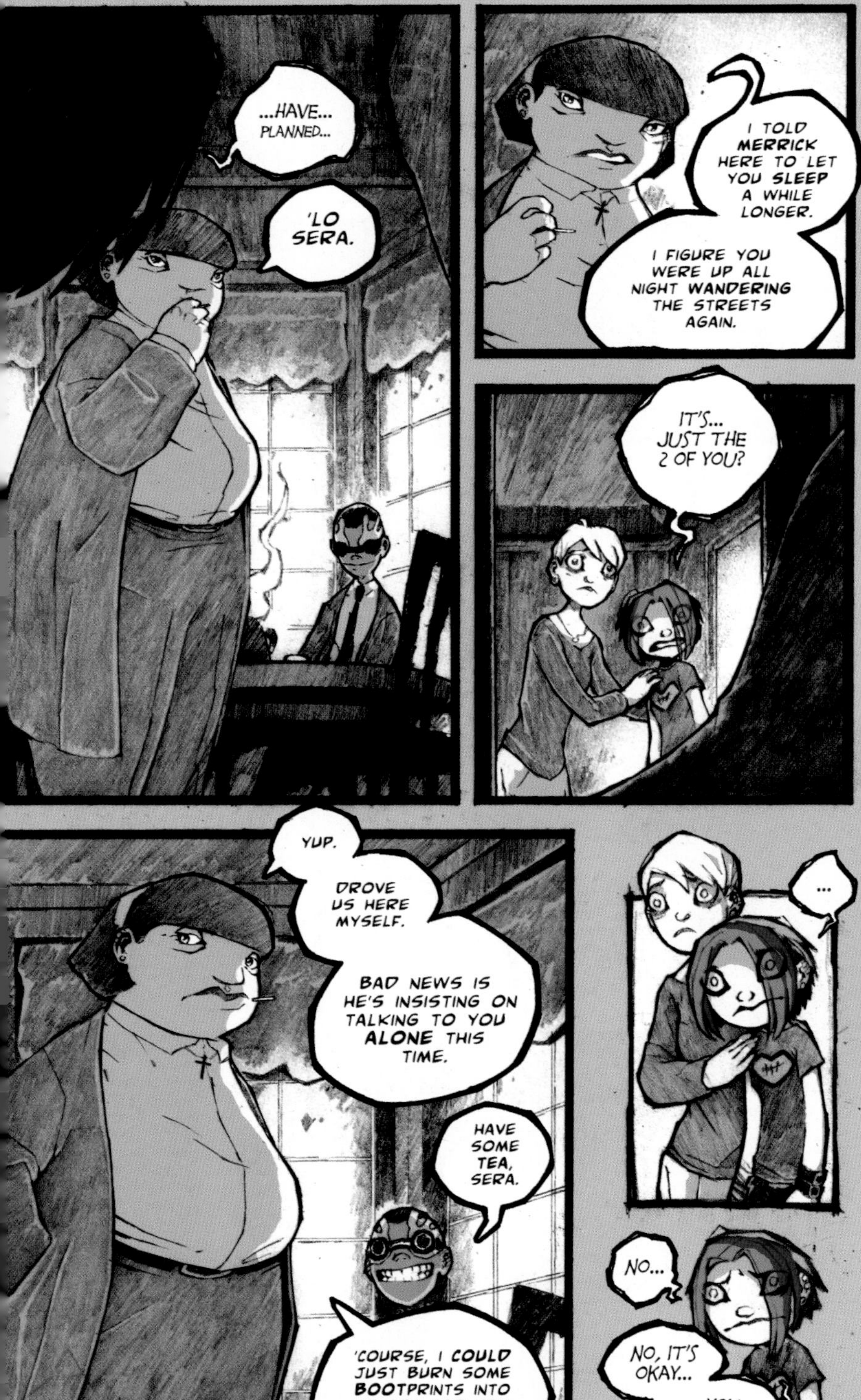

...HAVE... PLANNED...
'LO SERA.
I TOLD MERRICK HERE TO LET YOU SLEEP A WHILE LONGER.
I FIGURE YOU WERE UP ALL NIGHT WANDERING THE STREETS AGAIN.
IT'S... JUST THE 2 OF YOU?
YUP.
DROVE US HERE MYSELF.
BAD NEWS IS HE'S INSISTING ON TALKING TO YOU ALONE THIS TIME.
HAVE SOME TEA, SERA.
'COURSE, I COULD JUST BURN SOME BOOTPRINTS INTO HIS ASS FOR YOU. I WOULD BE VERY WILLING TO DO THAT.
...
NO...
NO, IT'S OKAY...
...YOU SHOULD LEAVE US ALONE.

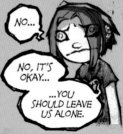

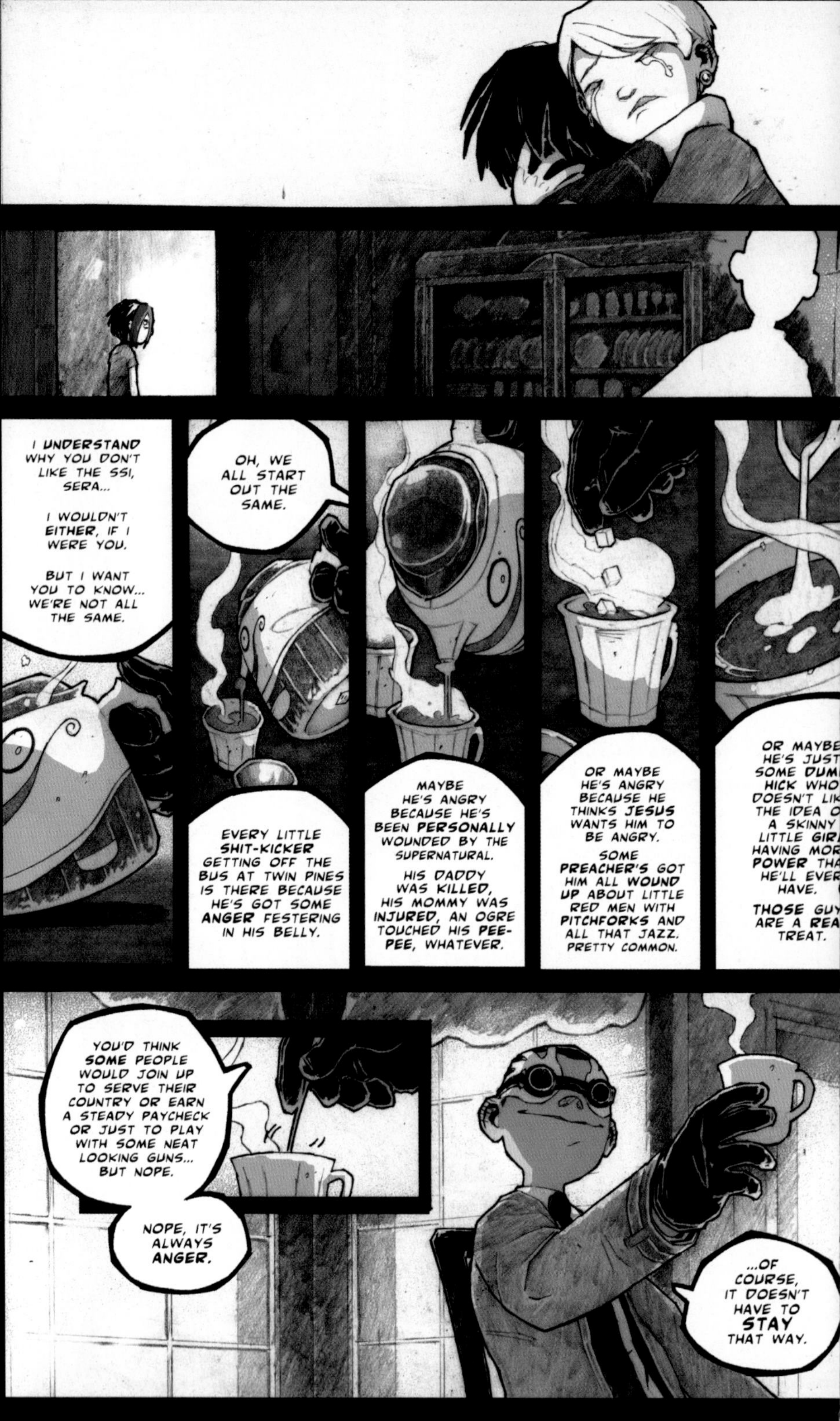

I UNDERSTAND WHY YOU DON'T LIKE THE SSI, SERA...
I WOULDN'T EITHER, IF I WERE YOU.
BUT I WANT YOU TO KNOW... WE'RE NOT ALL THE SAME.
OH, WE ALL START OUT THE SAME.
EVERY LITTLE SHIT-KICKER GETTING OFF THE BUS AT TWIN PINES IS THERE BECAUSE HE'S GOT SOME ANGER FESTERING IN HIS BELLY.
MAYBE HE'S ANGRY BECAUSE HE'S BEEN PERSONALLY WOUNDED BY THE SUPERNATURAL.
HIS DADDY WAS KILLED, HIS MOMMY WAS INJURED, AN OGRE TOUCHED HIS PEE-PEE, WHATEVER.
OR MAYBE HE'S ANGRY BECAUSE HE THINKS JESUS WANTS HIM TO BE ANGRY.
SOME PREACHER'S GOT HIM ALL WOUND UP ABOUT LITTLE RED MEN WITH PITCHFORKS AND ALL THAT JAZZ. PRETTY COMMON.
OR MAYBE HE'S JUST SOME DUMB HICK WHO DOESN'T LIKE THE IDEA OF A SKINNY LITTLE GIRL HAVING MORE POWER THAN HE'LL EVER HAVE.
THOSE GUYS ARE A REAL TREAT.
YOU'D THINK SOME PEOPLE WOULD JOIN UP TO SERVE THEIR COUNTRY OR EARN A STEADY PAYCHECK OR JUST TO PLAY WITH SOME NEAT LOOKING GUNS... BUT NOPE.
NOPE, IT'S ALWAYS ANGER.
...OF COURSE, IT DOESN'T HAVE TO STAY THAT WAY.

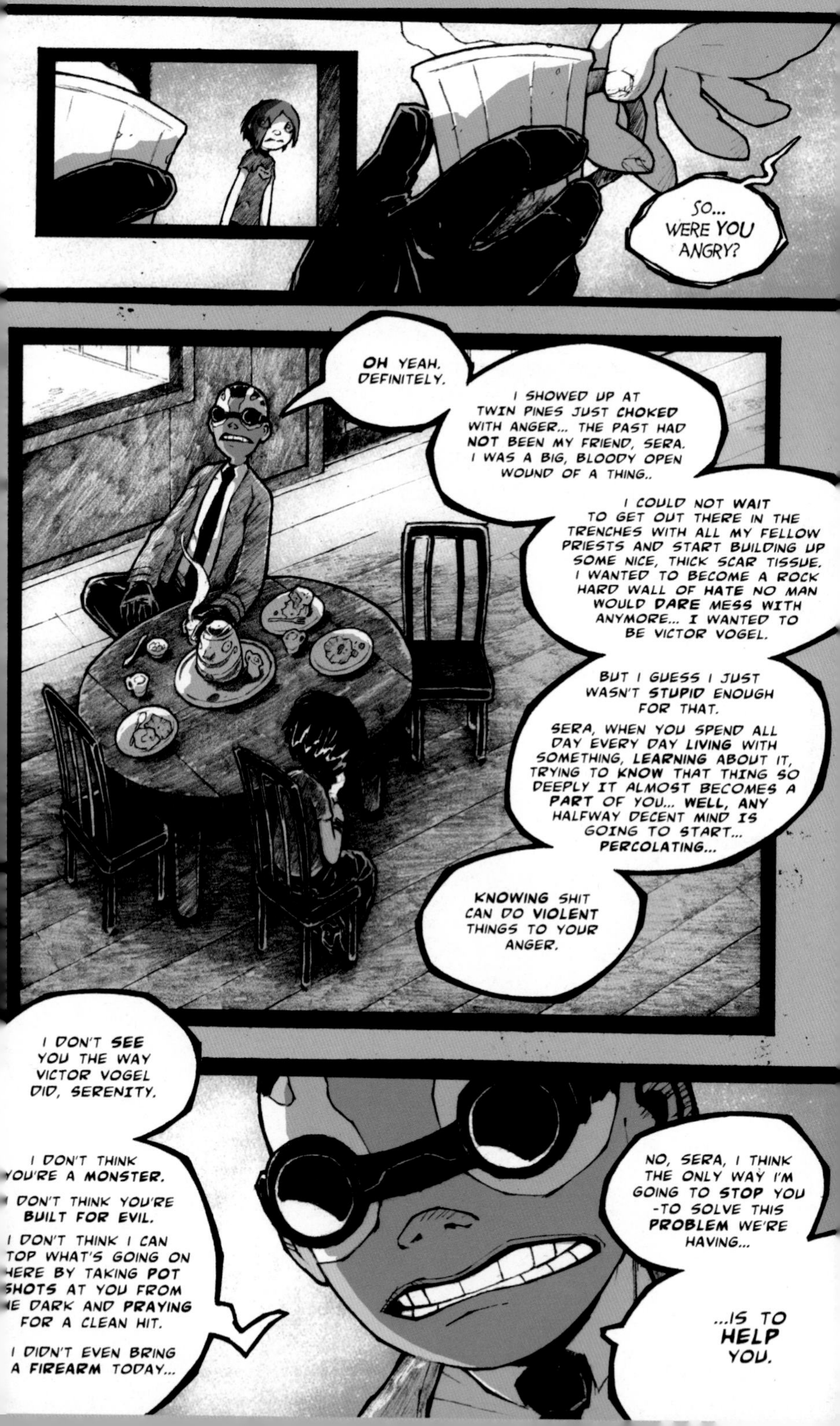

SO... WERE YOU ANGRY?
OH YEAH. DEFINITELY.
I SHOWED UP AT TWIN PINES JUST CHOKED WITH ANGER... THE PAST HAD NOT BEEN MY FRIEND, SERA. I WAS A BIG, BLOODY OPEN WOUND OF A THING..
I COULD NOT WAIT TO GET OUT THERE IN THE TRENCHES WITH ALL MY FELLOW PRIESTS AND START BUILDING UP SOME NICE, THICK SCAR TISSUE. I WANTED TO BECOME A ROCK HARD WALL OF HATE NO MAN WOULD DARE MESS WITH ANYMORE... I WANTED TO BE VICTOR VOGEL.
BUT I GUESS I JUST WASN'T STUPID ENOUGH FOR THAT.
SERA, WHEN YOU SPEND ALL DAY EVERY DAY LIVING WITH SOMETHING, LEARNING ABOUT IT, TRYING TO KNOW THAT THING SO DEEPLY IT ALMOST BECOMES A PART OF YOU... WELL, ANY HALFWAY DECENT MIND IS GOING TO START... PERCOLATING...
KNOWING SHIT CAN DO VIOLENT THINGS TO YOUR ANGER.
I DON'T SEE YOU THE WAY VICTOR VOGEL DID, SERENITY.
I DON'T THINK YOU'RE A MONSTER.
DON'T THINK YOU'RE BUILT FOR EVIL.
I DON'T THINK I CAN TOP WHAT'S GOING ON HERE BY TAKING POT SHOTS AT YOU FROM E DARK AND PRAYING FOR A CLEAN HIT.
I DIDN'T EVEN BRING A FIREARM TODAY...
NO, SERA, I THINK THE ONLY WAY I'M GOING TO STOP YOU -TO SOLVE THIS PROBLEM WE'RE HAVING...
...IS TO HELP YOU.

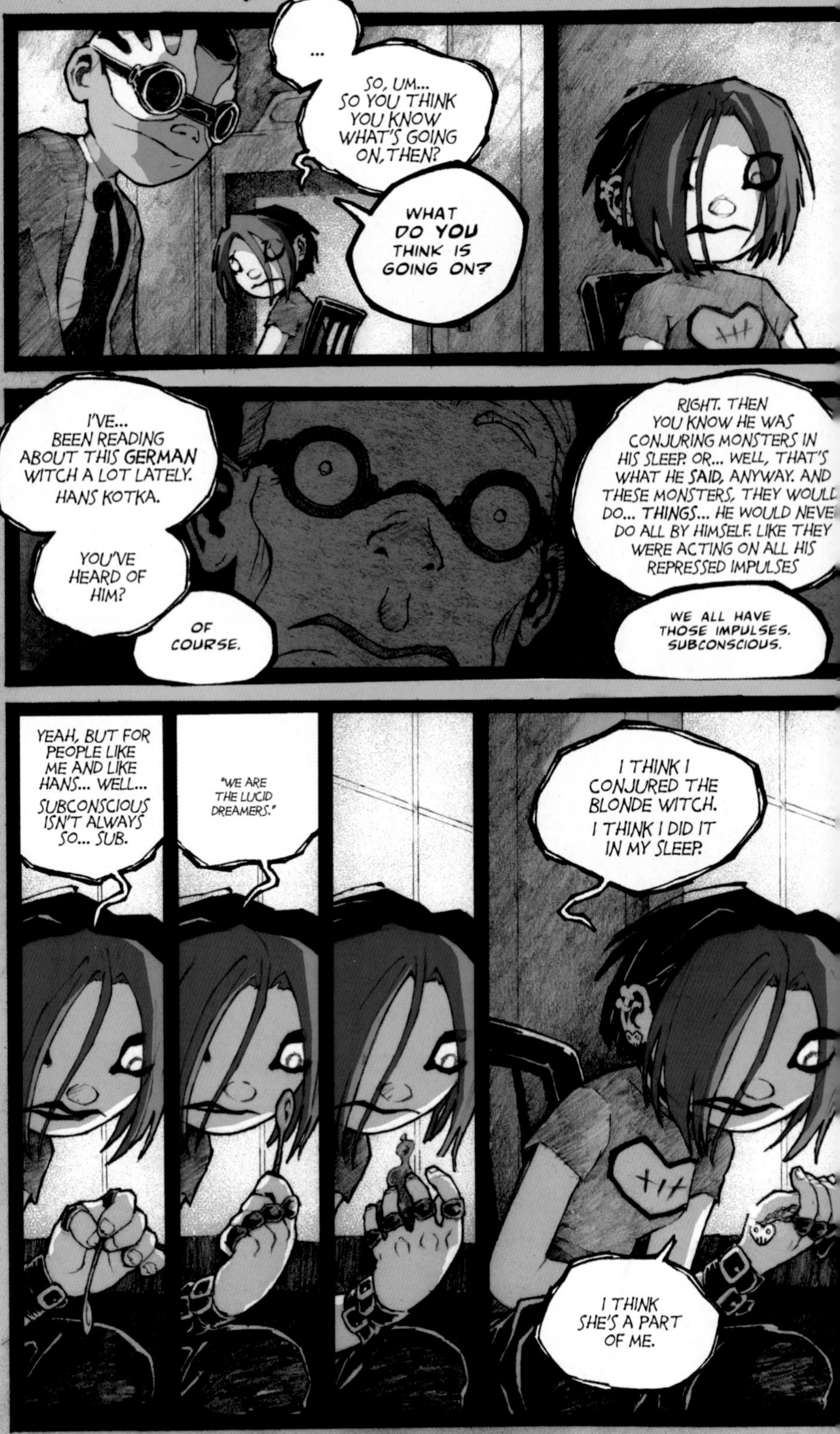
...
SO, UM... SO YOU THINK YOU KNOW WHAT'S GOING ON, THEN?
WHAT DO YOU THINK IS GOING ON?
I'VE... BEEN READING ABOUT THIS GERMAN WITCH A LOT LATELY. HANS KOTKA.
YOU'VE HEARD OF HIM?
OF COURSE.
RIGHT. THEN YOU KNOW HE WAS CONJURING MONSTERS IN HIS SLEEP. OR... WELL, THAT'S WHAT HE SAID, ANYWAY. AND THESE MONSTERS, THEY WOULD DO... THINGS... HE WOULD NEVER DO ALL BY HIMSELF. LIKE THEY WERE ACTING ON ALL HIS REPRESSED IMPULSES
WE ALL HAVE THOSE IMPULSES. SUBCONSCIOUS.
YEAH, BUT FOR PEOPLE LIKE ME AND LIKE HANS... WELL... SUBCONSCIOUS ISN'T ALWAYS SO... SUB.
"WE ARE THE LUCID DREAMERS."
I THINK I CONJURED THE BLONDE WITCH. I THINK I DID IT IN MY SLEEP.
I THINK SHE'S A PART OF ME.

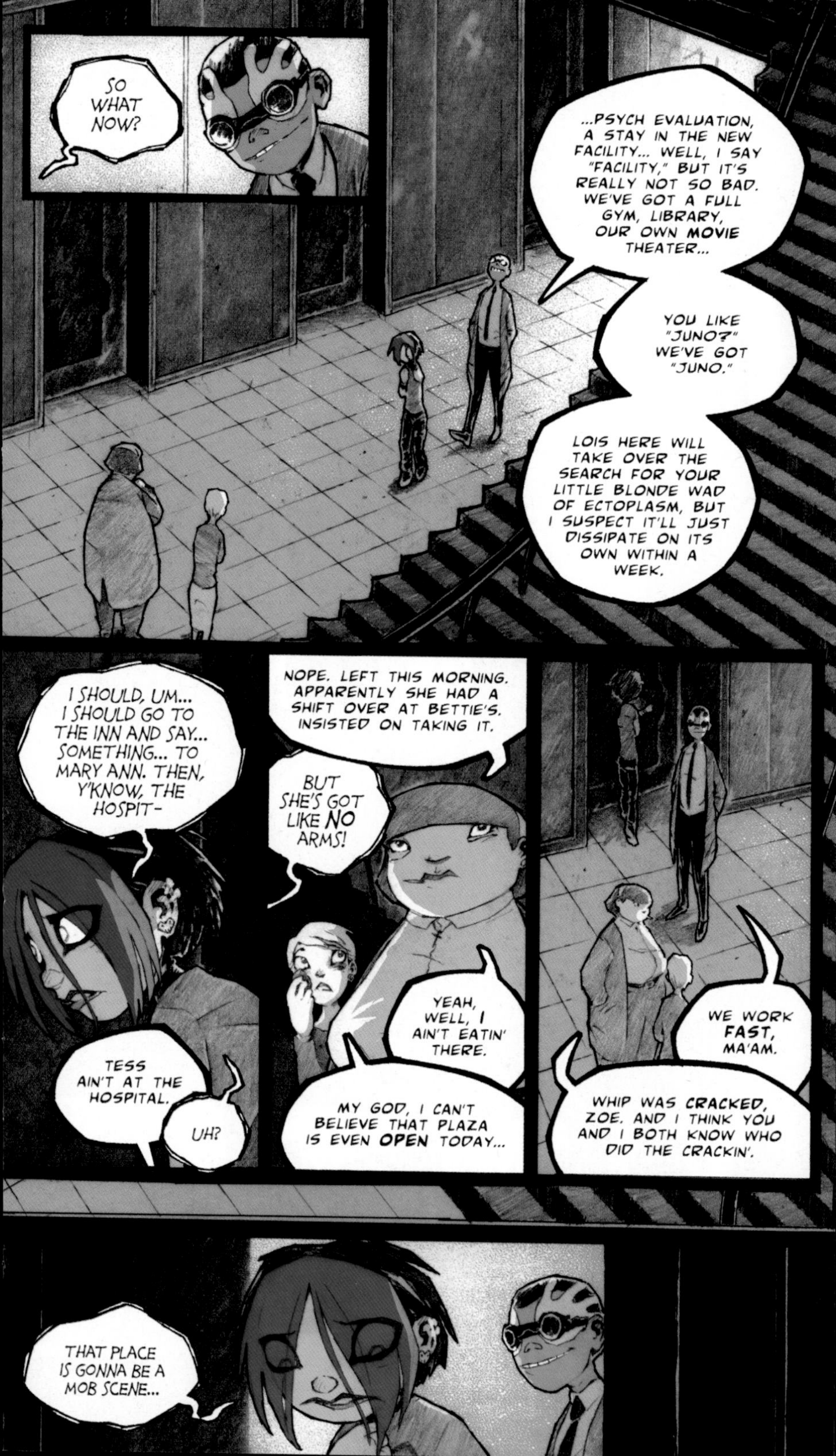
SO WHAT NOW?
...PSYCH EVALUATION, A STAY IN THE NEW FACILITY... WELL, I SAY "FACILITY," BUT IT'S REALLY NOT SO BAD. WE'VE GOT A FULL GYM, LIBRARY, OUR OWN MOVIE THEATER...
YOU LIKE "JUNO?" WE'VE GOT "JUNO."
LOIS HERE WILL TAKE OVER THE SEARCH FOR YOUR LITTLE BLONDE WAD OF ECTOPLASM, BUT I SUSPECT IT'LL JUST DISSIPATE ON ITS OWN WITHIN A WEEK.
I SHOULD, UM... I SHOULD GO TO THE INN AND SAY... SOMETHING... TO MARY ANN. THEN, Y'KNOW, THE HOSPIT-
TESS AIN'T AT THE HOSPITAL.
UH?
NOPE. LEFT THIS MORNING. APPARENTLY SHE HAD A SHIFT OVER AT BETTIE'S. INSISTED ON TAKING IT.
BUT SHE'S GOT LIKE NO ARMS!
YEAH, WELL, I AIN'T EATIN' THERE.
MY GOD, I CAN'T BELIEVE THAT PLAZA IS EVEN OPEN TODAY...
WE WORK FAST, MA'AM.
WHIP WAS CRACKED, ZOE. AND I THINK YOU AND I BOTH KNOW WHO DID THE CRACKIN'.
THAT PLACE IS GONNA BE A MOB SCENE...

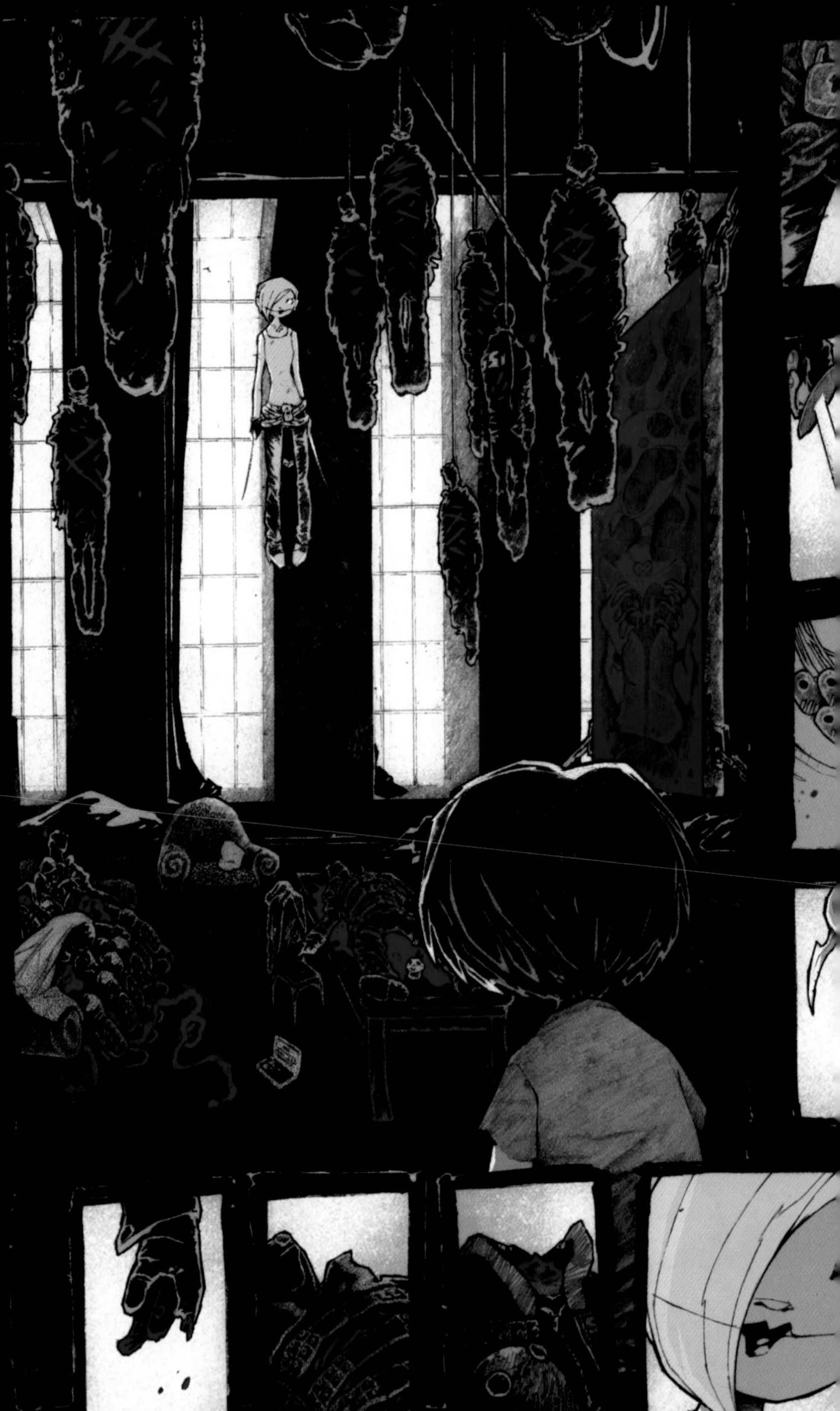

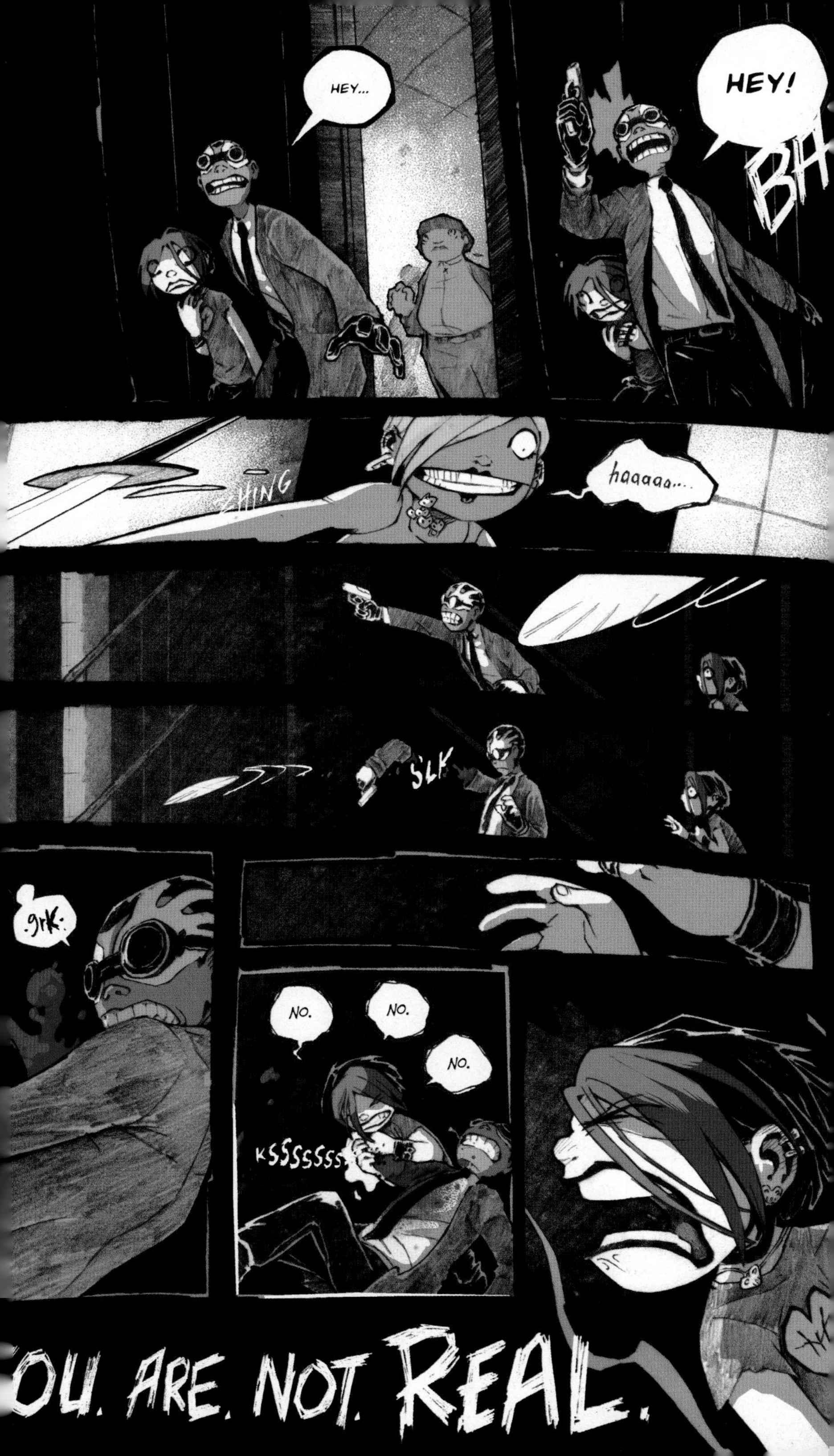
HEY...
HEY!
BA
CHING
haaaaa....
SLK
.grK.
NO.
NO.
NO.
KSSSSSSS
OU. ARE. NOT. REAL.

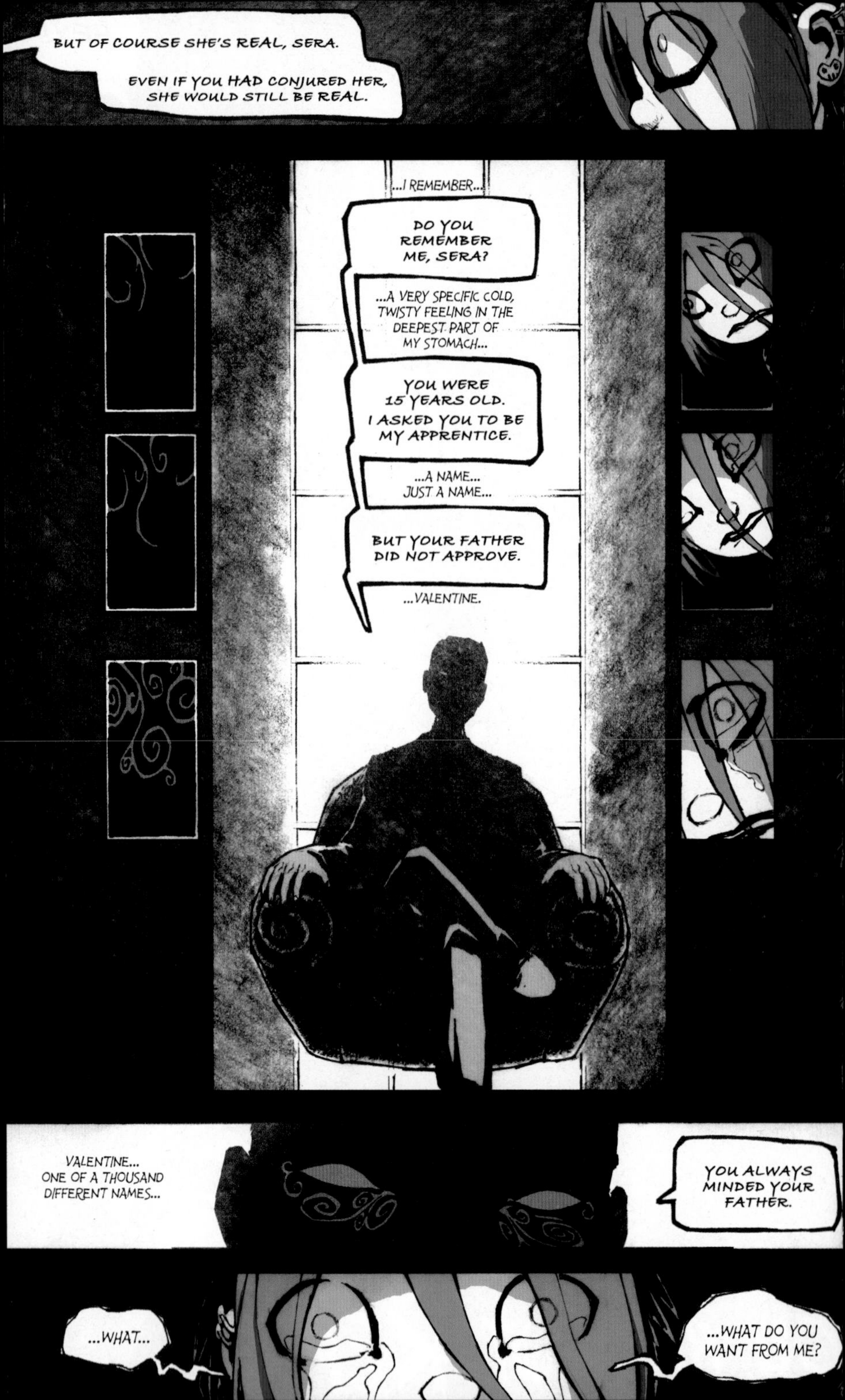
BUT OF COURSE SHE'S REAL, SERA.
EVEN IF YOU HAD CONJURED HER, SHE WOULD STILL BE REAL.
...I REMEMBER...
DO YOU REMEMBER ME, SERA?
...A VERY SPECIFIC COLD, TWISTY FEELING IN THE DEEPEST PART OF MY STOMACH...
YOU WERE 15 YEARS OLD.
I ASKED YOU TO BE MY APPRENTICE.
...A NAME... JUST A NAME...
BUT YOUR FATHER DID NOT APPROVE.
...VALENTINE.
VALENTINE... ONE OF A THOUSAND DIFFERENT NAMES...
YOU ALWAYS MINDED YOUR FATHER.
...WHAT...
...WHAT DO YOU WANT FROM ME?

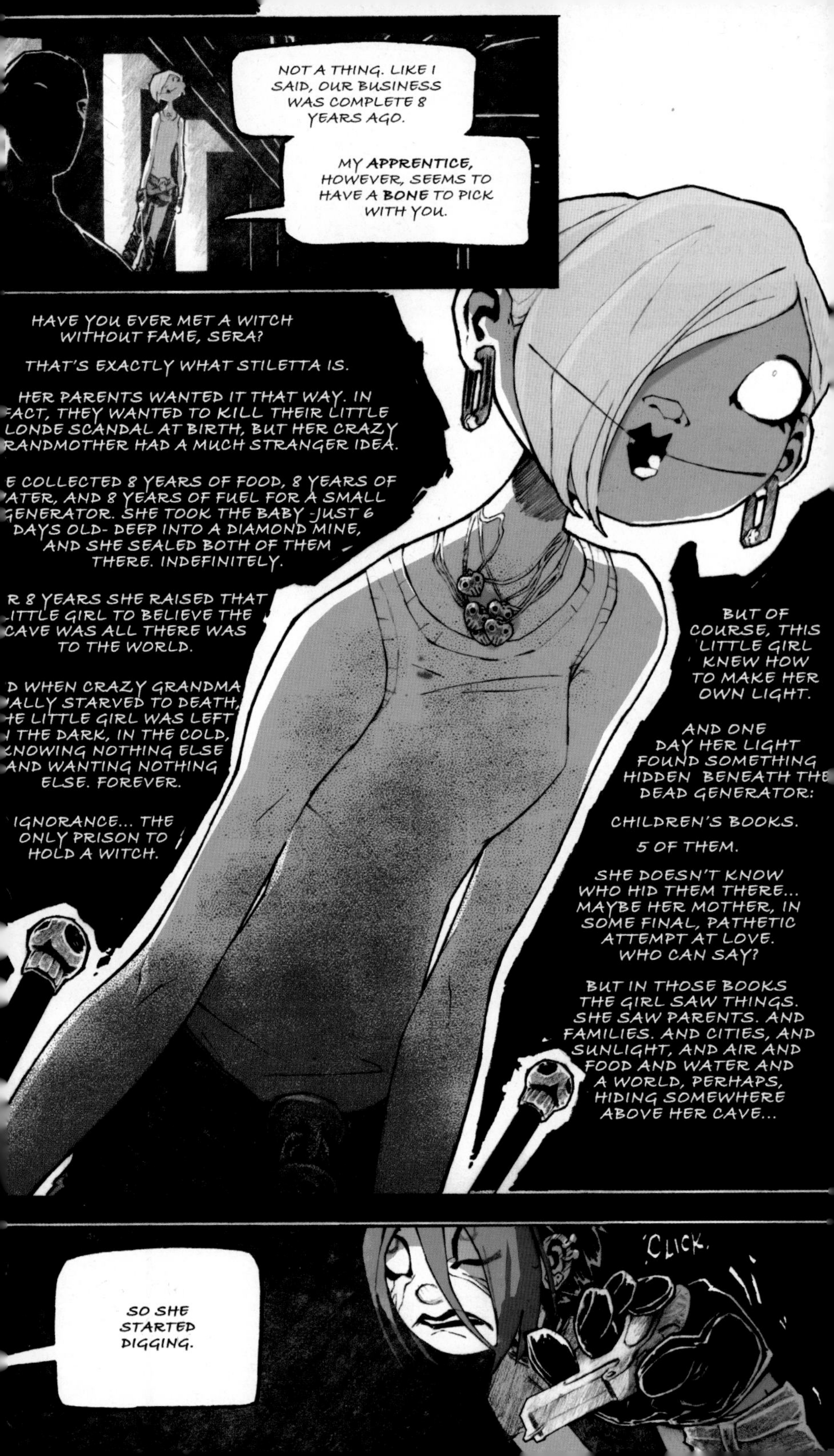
NOT A THING. LIKE I SAID, OUR BUSINESS WAS COMPLETE 8 YEARS AGO.
MY APPRENTICE, HOWEVER, SEEMS TO HAVE A BONE TO PICK WITH YOU.
HAVE YOU EVER MET A WITCH WITHOUT FAME, SERA?
THAT'S EXACTLY WHAT STILETTA IS.
HER PARENTS WANTED IT THAT WAY. IN ACT, THEY WANTED TO KILL THEIR LITTLE LONDE SCANDAL AT BIRTH, BUT HER CRAZY RANDMOTHER HAD A MUCH STRANGER IDEA.
E COLLECTED 8 YEARS OF FOOD, 8 YEARS OF ATER, AND 8 YEARS OF FUEL FOR A SMALL GENERATOR. SHE TOOK THE BABY -JUST 6 DAYS OLD- DEEP INTO A DIAMOND MINE, AND SHE SEALED BOTH OF THEM THERE. INDEFINITELY.
R 8 YEARS SHE RAISED THAT ITTLE GIRL TO BELIEVE THE CAVE WAS ALL THERE WAS TO THE WORLD.
D WHEN CRAZY GRANDMA ALLY STARVED TO DEATH, E LITTLE GIRL WAS LEFT THE DARK, IN THE COLD, NOWING NOTHING ELSE AND WANTING NOTHING ELSE. FOREVER.
IGNORANCE... THE ONLY PRISON TO HOLD A WITCH.
BUT OF COURSE, THIS LITTLE GIRL KNEW HOW TO MAKE HER OWN LIGHT.
AND ONE DAY HER LIGHT FOUND SOMETHING HIDDEN BENEATH THE DEAD GENERATOR:
CHILDREN'S BOOKS.
5 OF THEM.
SHE DOESN'T KNOW WHO HID THEM THERE... MAYBE HER MOTHER, IN SOME FINAL, PATHETIC ATTEMPT AT LOVE. WHO CAN SAY?
BUT IN THOSE BOOKS THE GIRL SAW THINGS. SHE SAW PARENTS. AND FAMILIES. AND CITIES, AND SUNLIGHT, AND AIR AND FOOD AND WATER AND A WORLD, PERHAPS, HIDING SOMEWHERE ABOVE HER CAVE...
SO SHE STARTED DIGGING.
CLICK

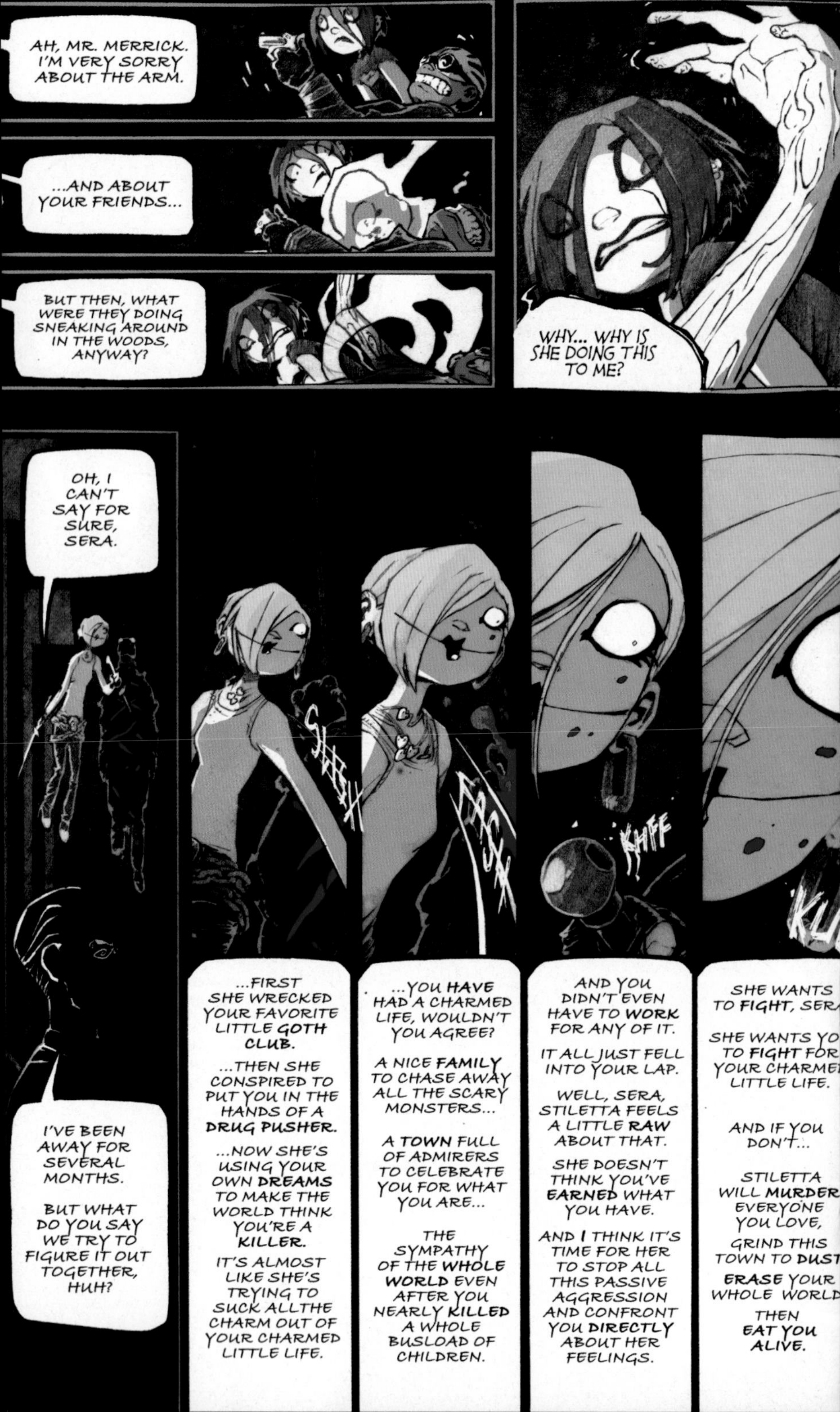
AH, MR. MERRICK. I'M VERY SORRY ABOUT THE ARM.
...AND ABOUT YOUR FRIENDS...
BUT THEN, WHAT WERE THEY DOING SNEAKING AROUND IN THE WOODS, ANYWAY?
WHY... WHY IS SHE DOING THIS TO ME?
OH, I CAN'T SAY FOR SURE, SERA.
I'VE BEEN AWAY FOR SEVERAL MONTHS.
BUT WHAT DO YOU SAY WE TRY TO FIGURE IT OUT TOGETHER, HUH?
...FIRST SHE WRECKED YOUR FAVORITE LITTLE GOTH CLUB.
...THEN SHE CONSPIRED TO PUT YOU IN THE HANDS OF A DRUG PUSHER.
...NOW SHE'S USING YOUR OWN DREAMS TO MAKE THE WORLD THINK YOU'RE A KILLER.
IT'S ALMOST LIKE SHE'S TRYING TO SUCK ALLTHE CHARM OUT OF YOUR CHARMED LITTLE LIFE.
SLISH
...YOU HAVE HAD A CHARMED LIFE, WOULDN'T YOU AGREE?
A NICE FAMILY TO CHASE AWAY ALL THE SCARY MONSTERS...
A TOWN FULL OF ADMIRERS TO CELEBRATE YOU FOR WHAT YOU ARE...
THE SYMPATHY OF THE WHOLE WORLD EVEN AFTER YOU NEARLY KILLED A WHOLE BUSLOAD OF CHILDREN.
KHFF
AND YOU DIDN'T EVEN HAVE TO WORK FOR ANY OF IT.
IT ALL JUST FELL INTO YOUR LAP.
WELL, SERA, STILETTA FEELS A LITTLE RAW ABOUT THAT.
SHE DOESN'T THINK YOU'VE EARNED WHAT YOU HAVE.
AND I THINK IT'S TIME FOR HER TO STOP ALL THIS PASSIVE AGGRESSION AND CONFRONT YOU DIRECTLY ABOUT HER FEELINGS.
SHE WANTS TO FIGHT, SERA
SHE WANTS YO TO FIGHT FOR YOUR CHARME LITTLE LIFE.
AND IF YOU DON'T...
STILETTA WILL MURDER EVERYONE YOU LOVE,
GRIND THIS TOWN TO DUST
ERASE YOUR WHOLE WORLD
THEN EAT YOU ALIVE.

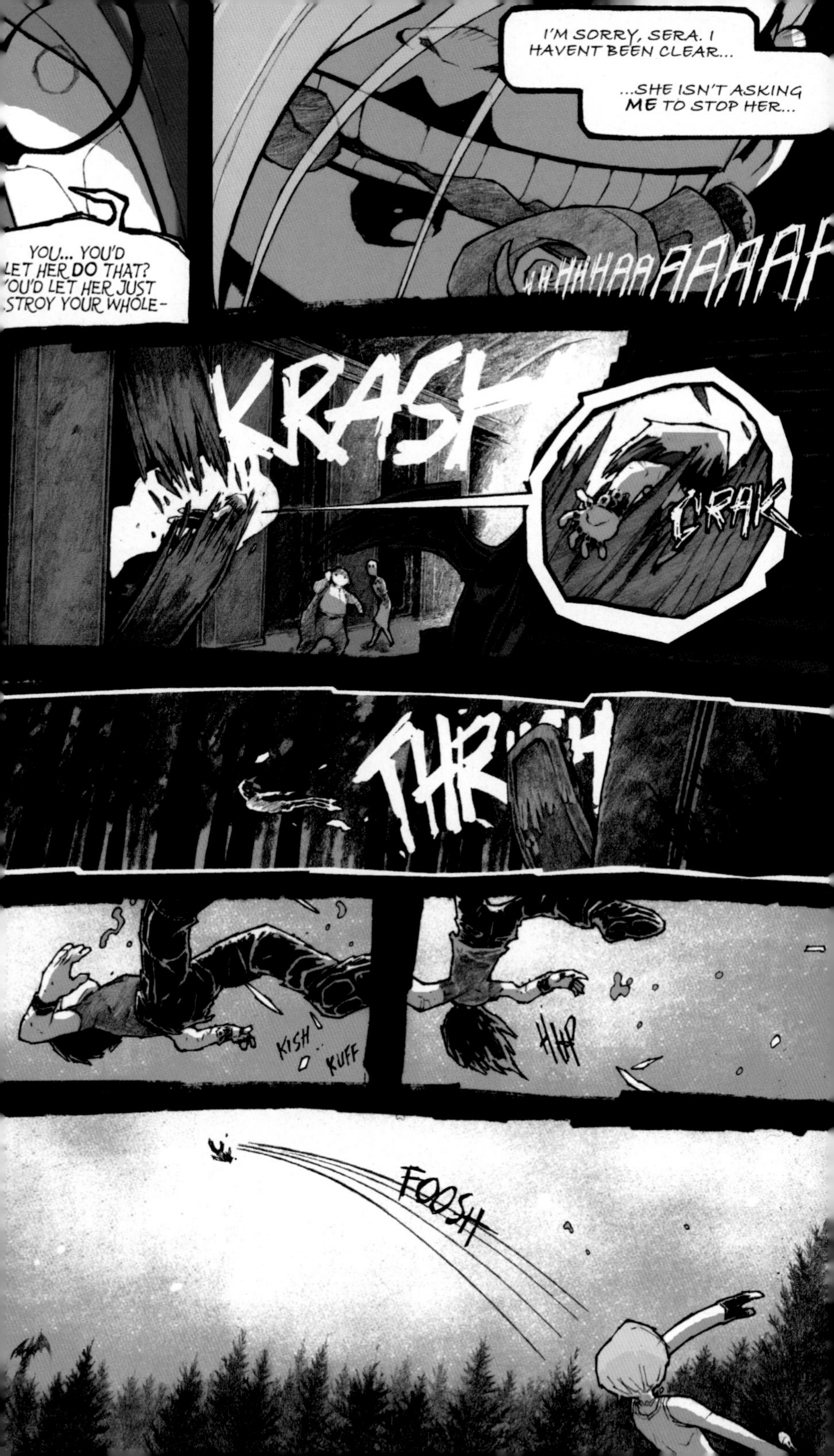

I'M SORRY, SERA. I HAVENT BEEN CLEAR...
...SHE ISN'T ASKING **ME** TO STOP HER...
YOU... YOU'D LET HER **DO** THAT? YOU'D LET HER JUST STROY YOUR WHOLE-
HHHHHAAAAAAAF
KRASH
CRAK
THR
KISH.. KUFF
HUP
FOOSH

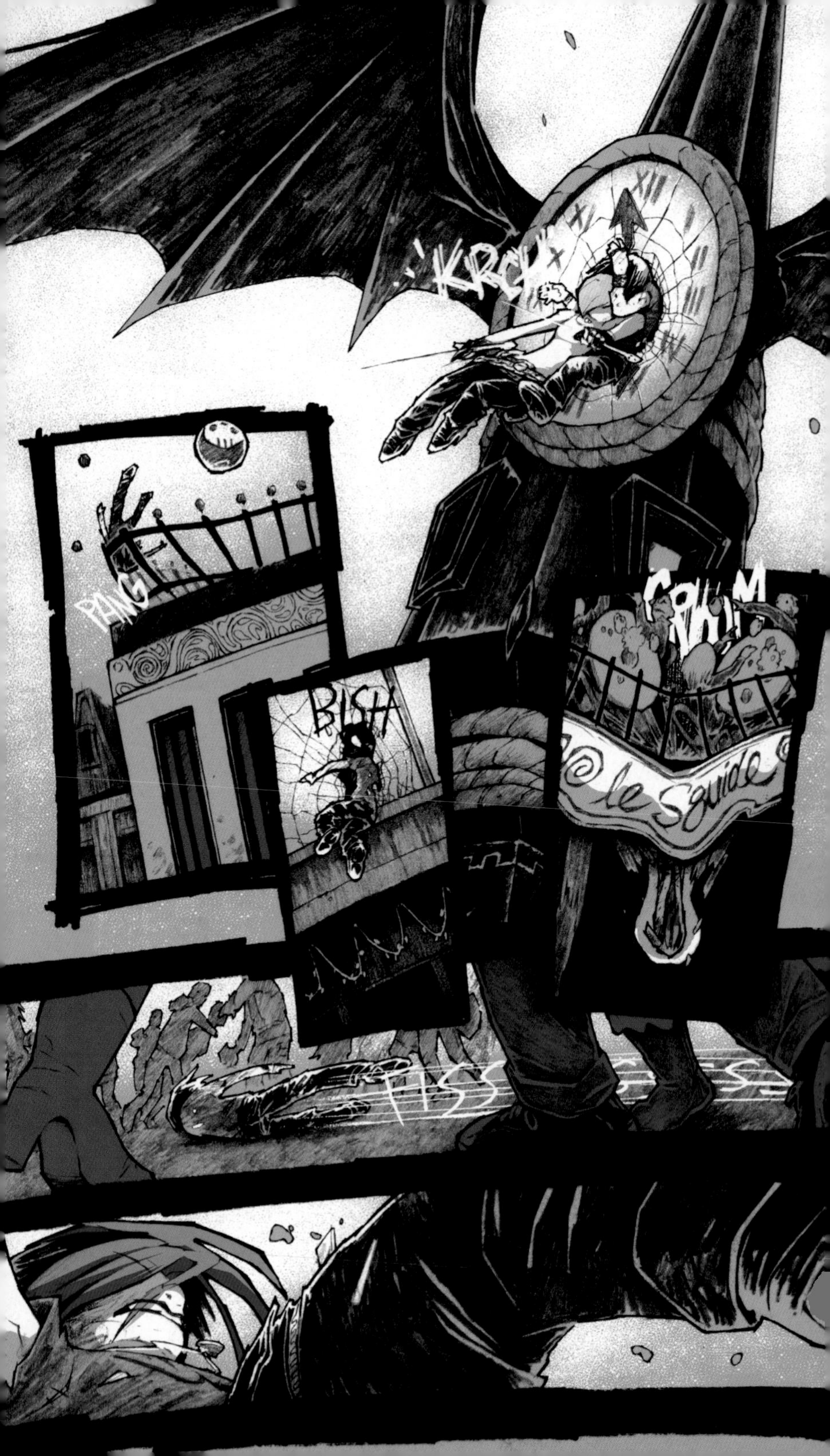
KRCK
PANG
BISH
CRUMM
le Squide
FISSSSS

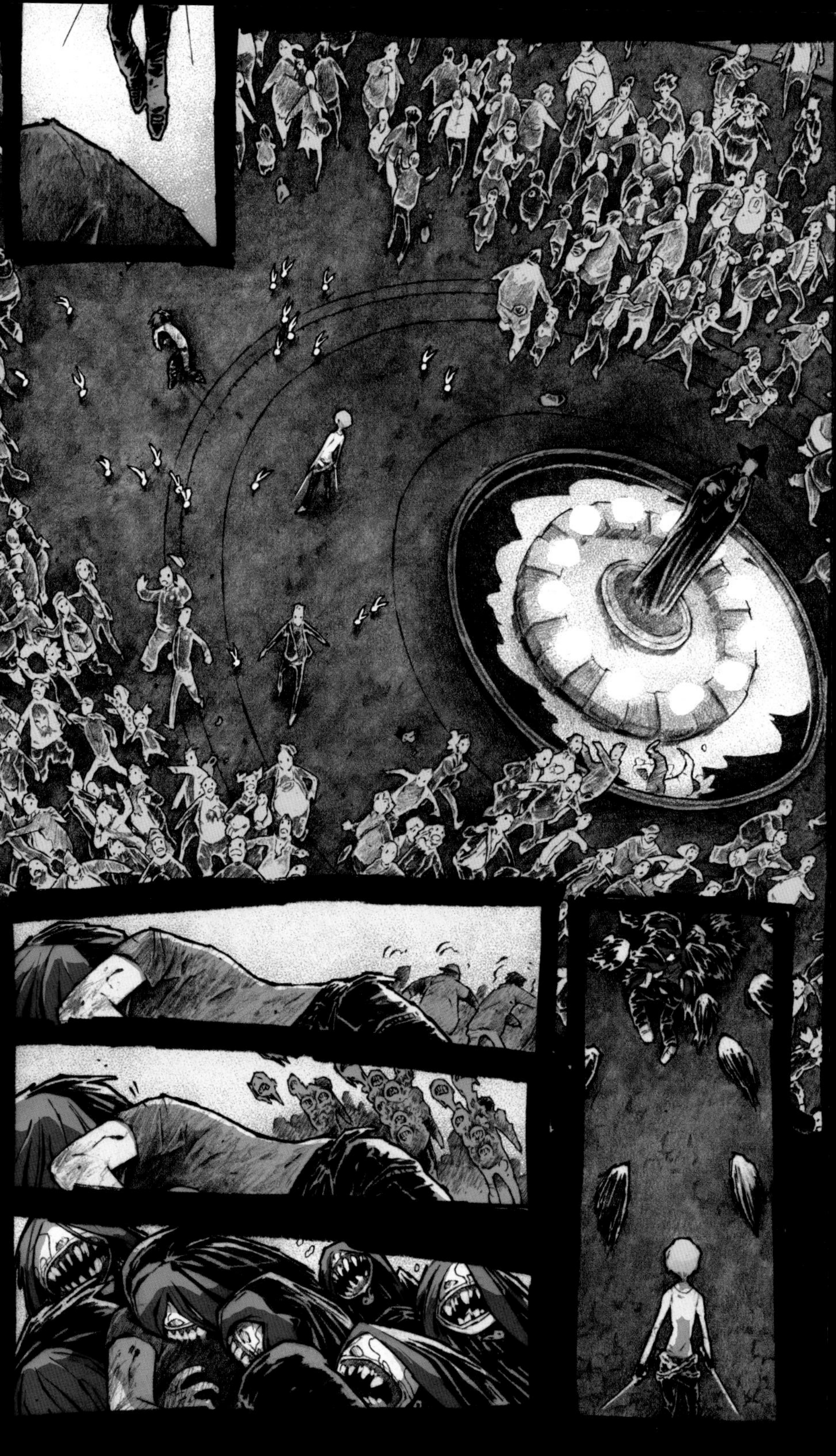

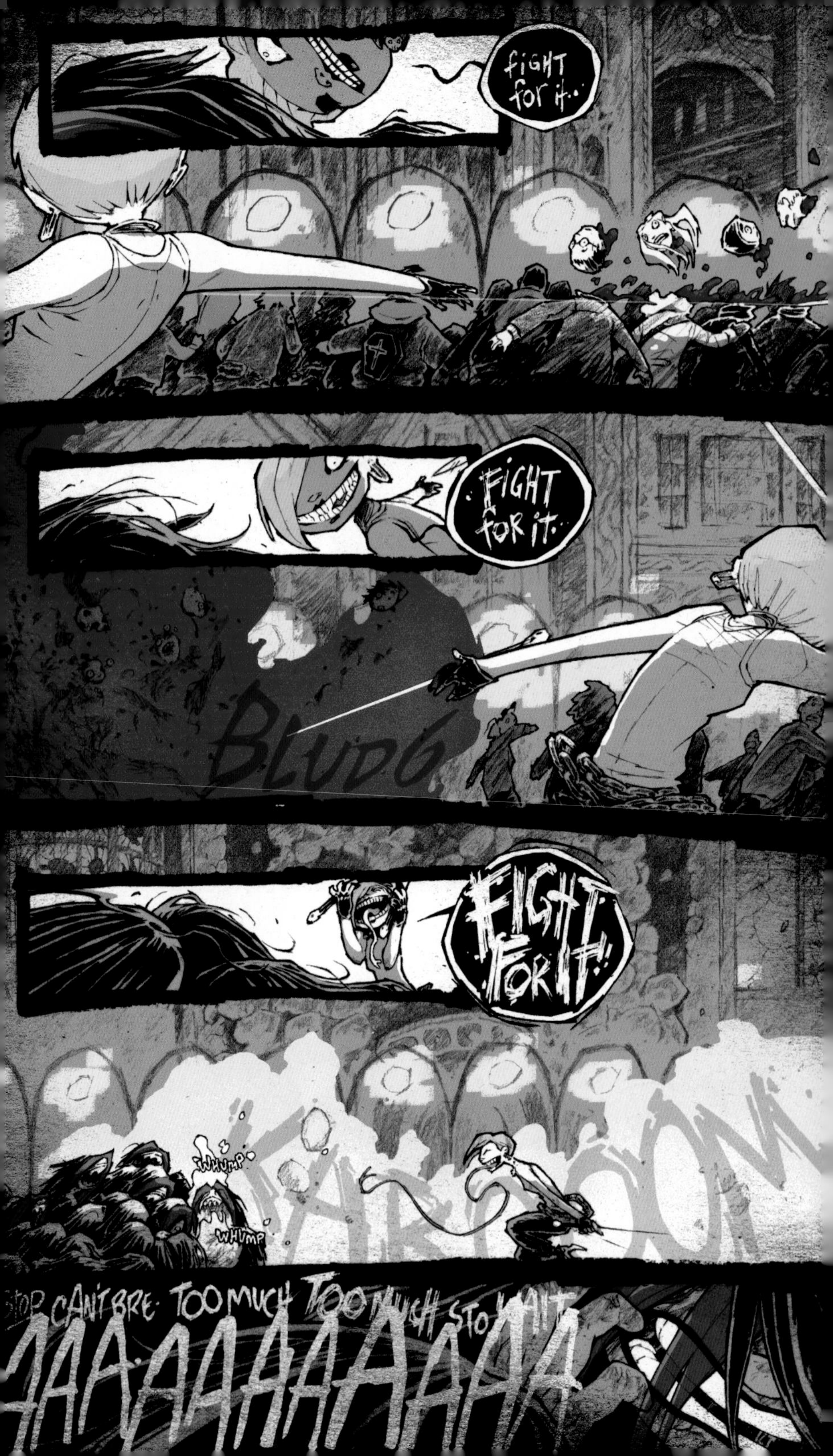
fight for it...
FIGHT for it...
BLUDG
FIGHT FOR IT!
WHUMP
WHUMP
STOP CAN'T BRE- TOO MUCH TOO MUCH STO WAIT
AAAAAAAAAAA

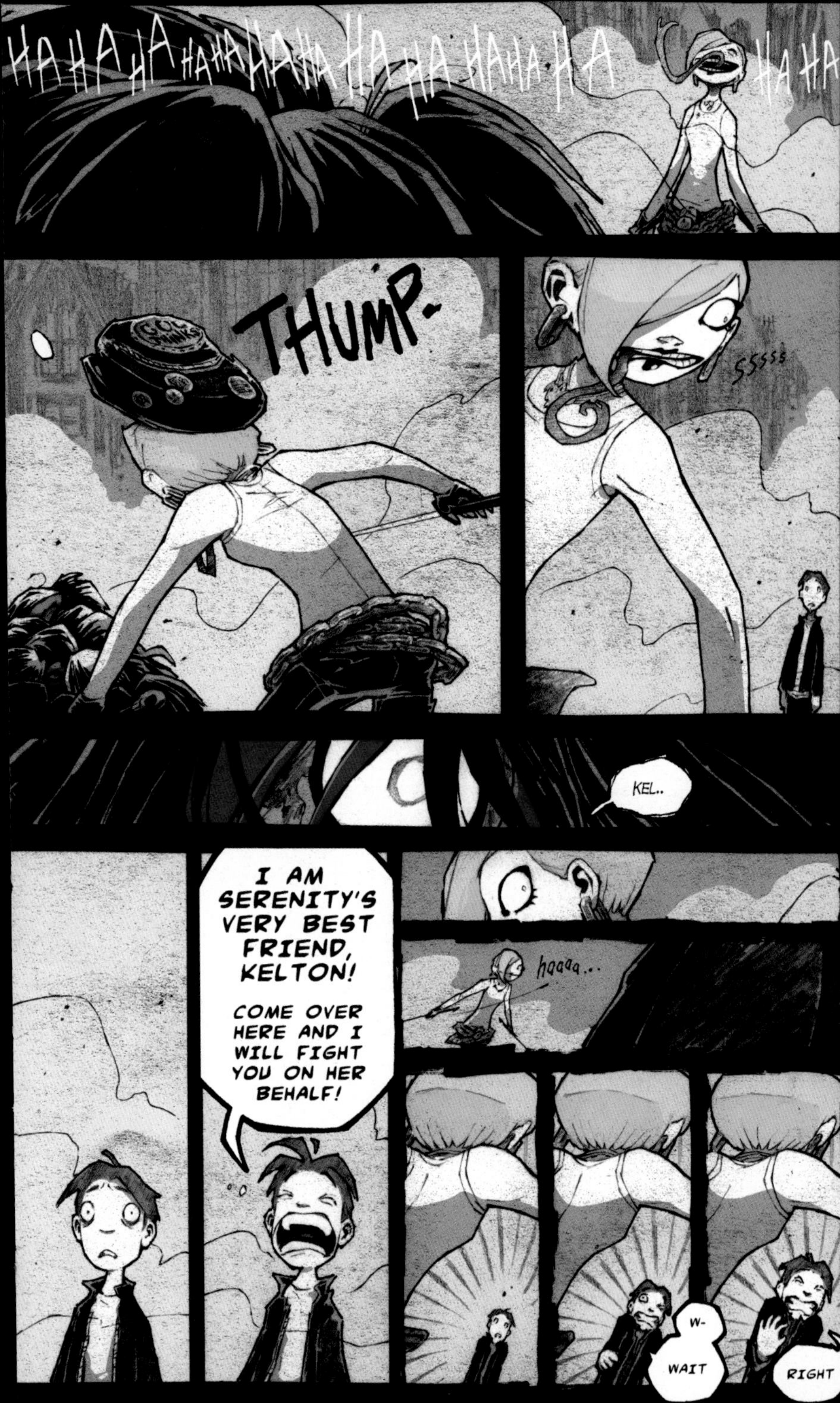
HA HA HA HA HAHAHA HAHA HA HA HAHAHA HA HA HA HA
THUMP.
sssss
KEL..
I AM SERENITY'S VERY BEST FRIEND, KELTON!
COME OVER HERE AND I WILL FIGHT YOU ON HER BEHALF!
haaaa...
W-
WAIT
RIGHT

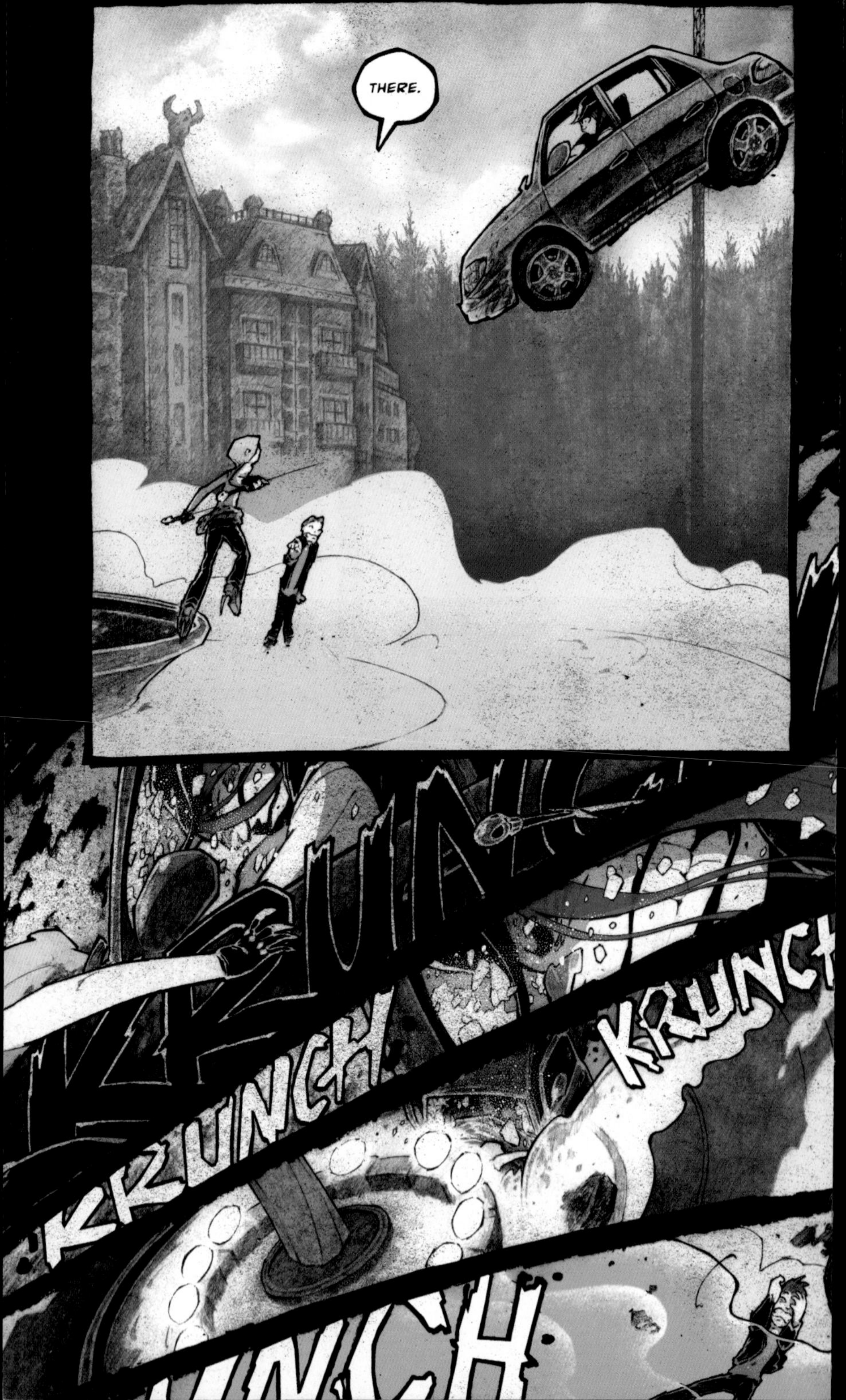
THERE.
KRUNCH
KRUNCH
KRUNCH
KRUNCH

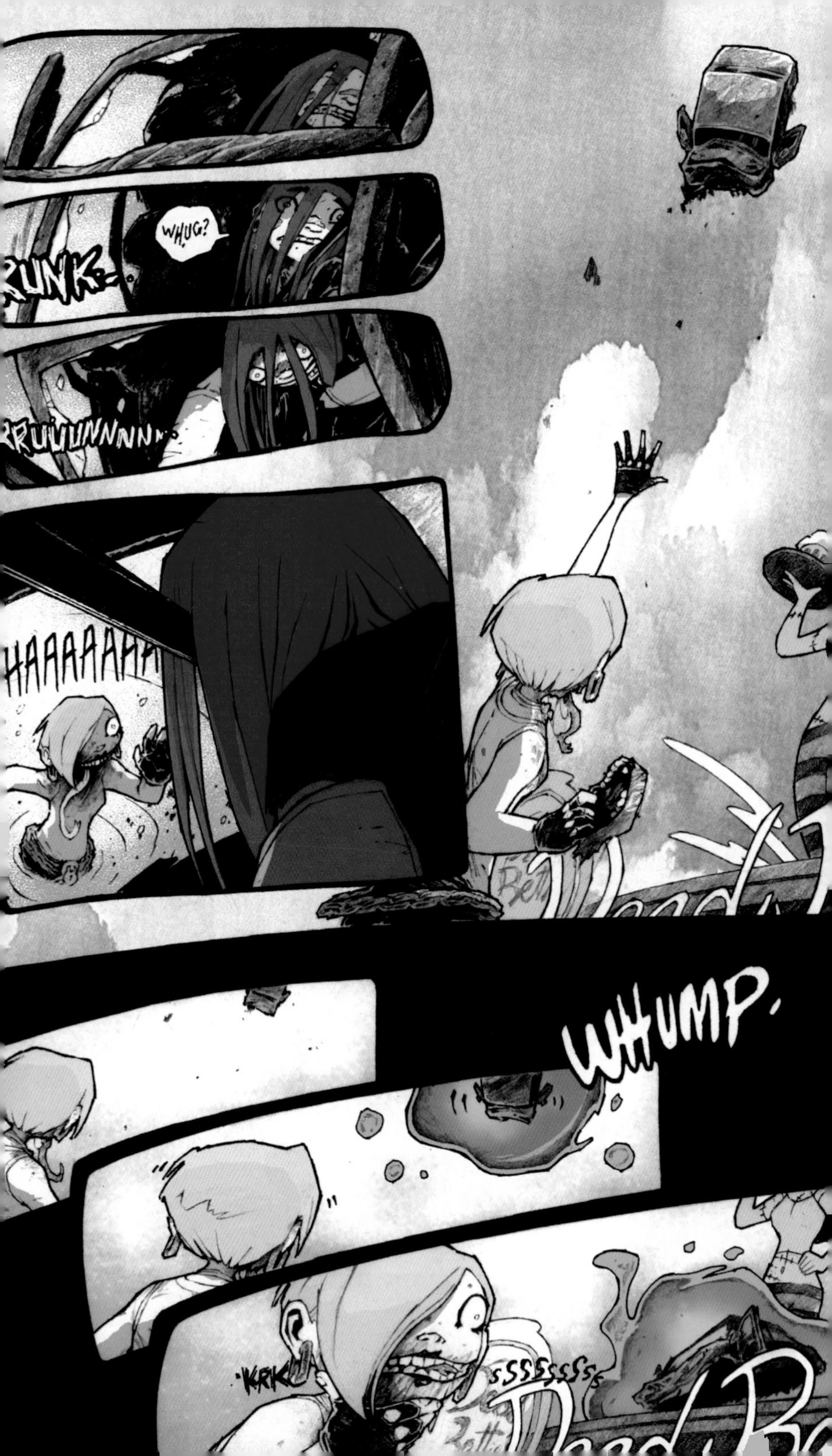

WHUG?
KRUNK-
KRUUUNNNNN-
HAAAAAHH
WHUMP.
KRK
SSSSSSSSS

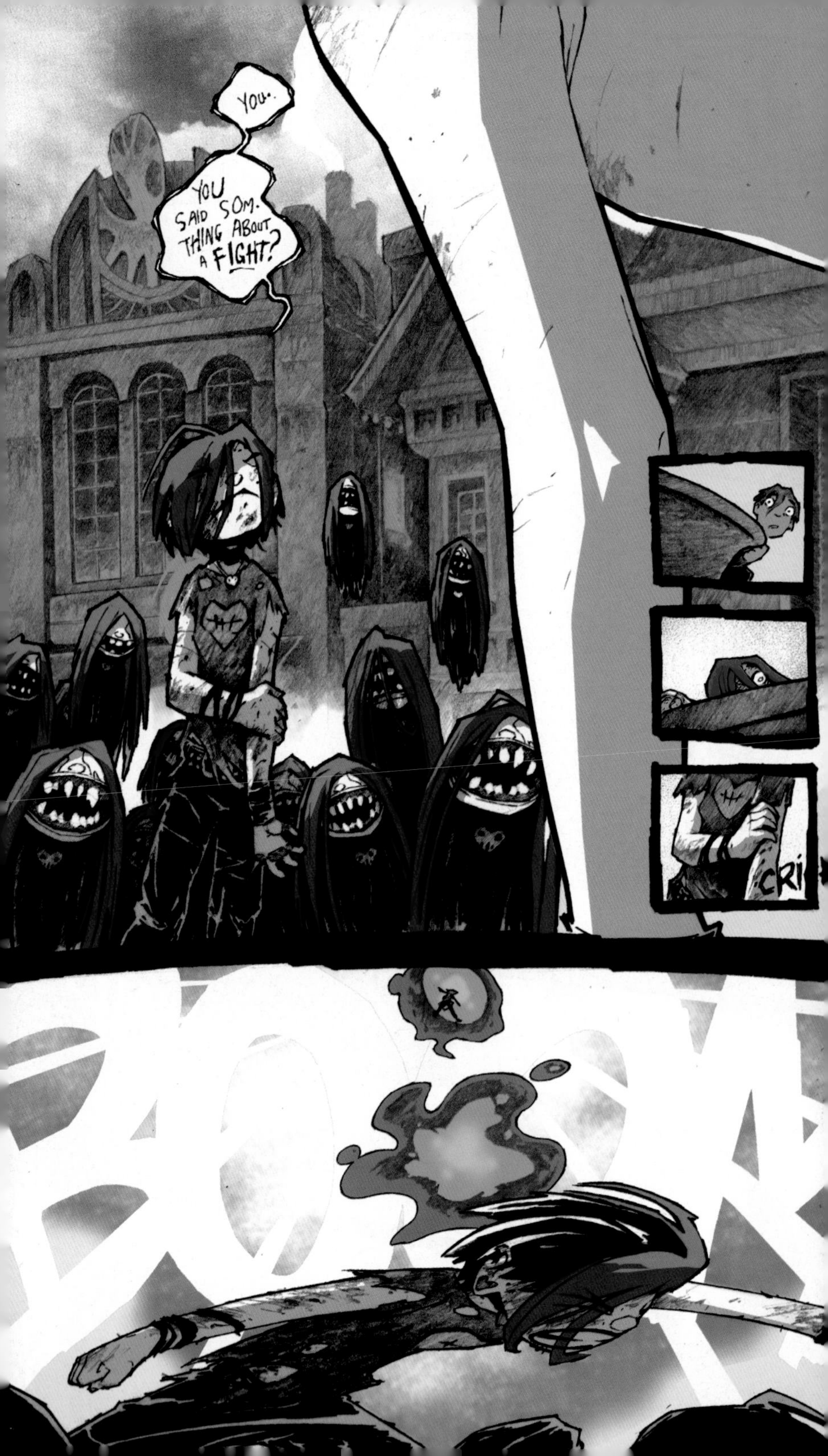
YOU..
YOU SAID SOM. THING ABOUT A FIGHT?
CRI

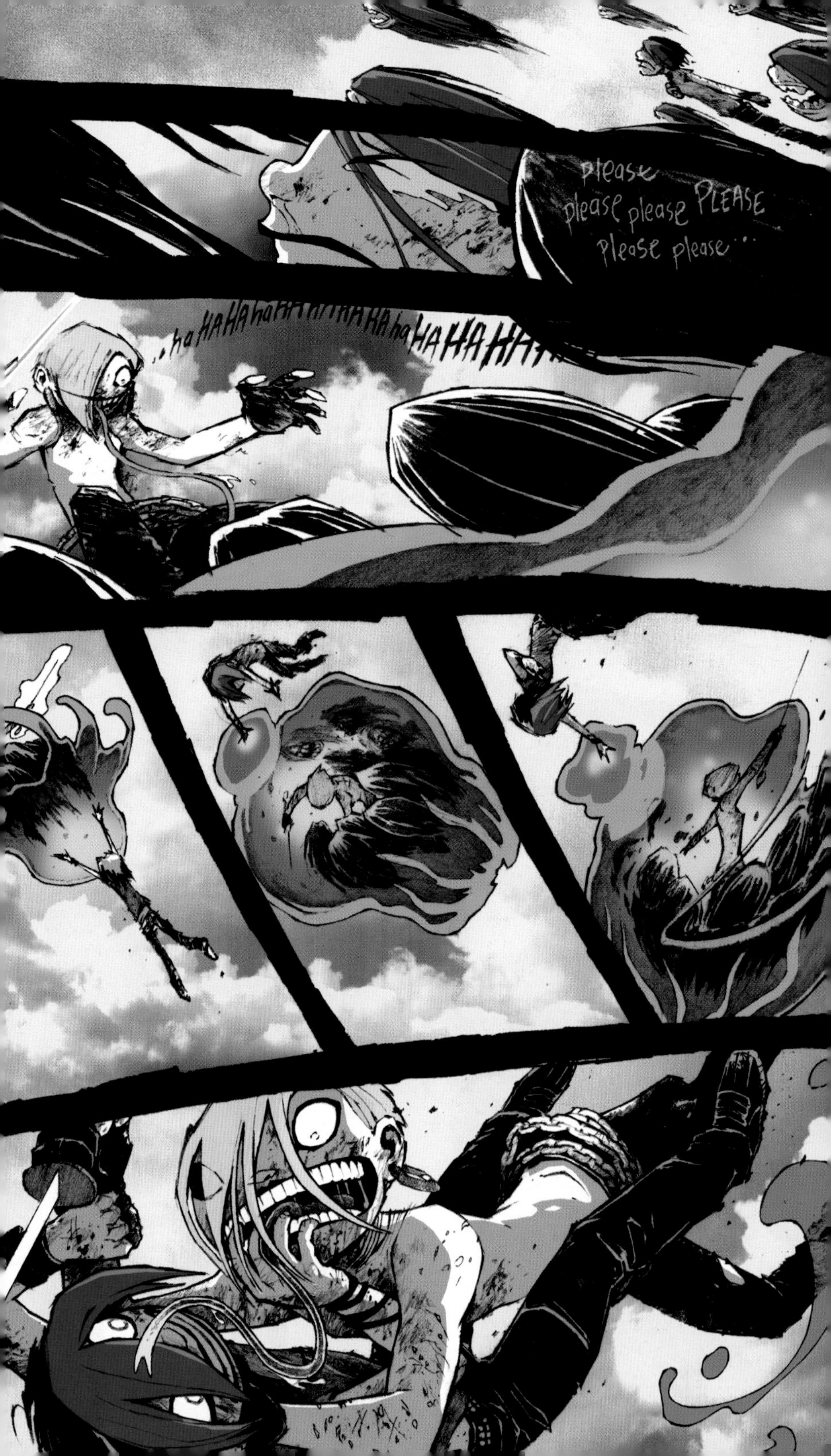

please
please please PLEASE
please please...
..ha HAHAha
ha HAHAHA

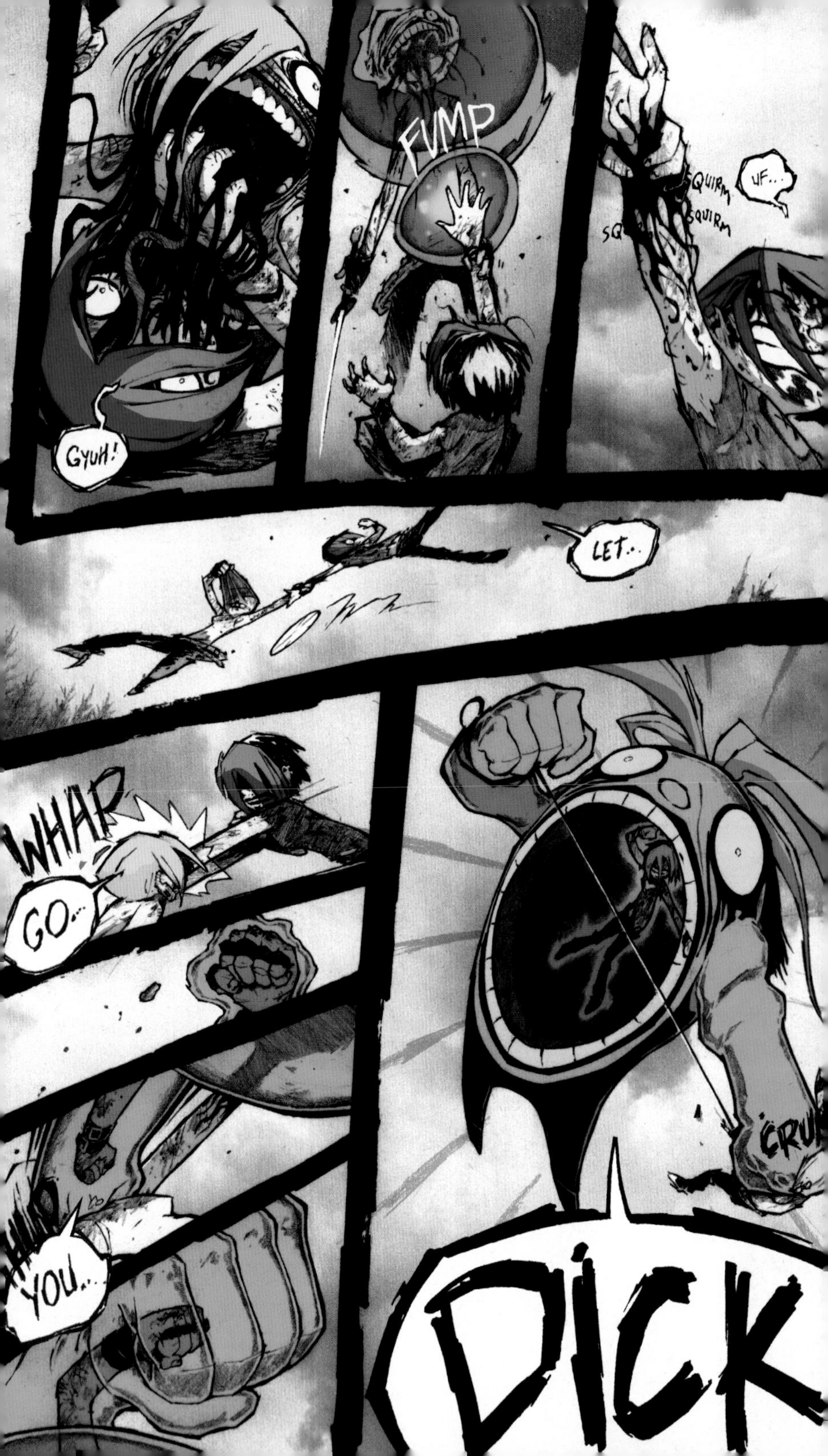
GYUH!
FUMP
SQUIRM
SQUIRM
SQ
UF...
LET...
WHAP
GO...
YOU...
CRU
DICK

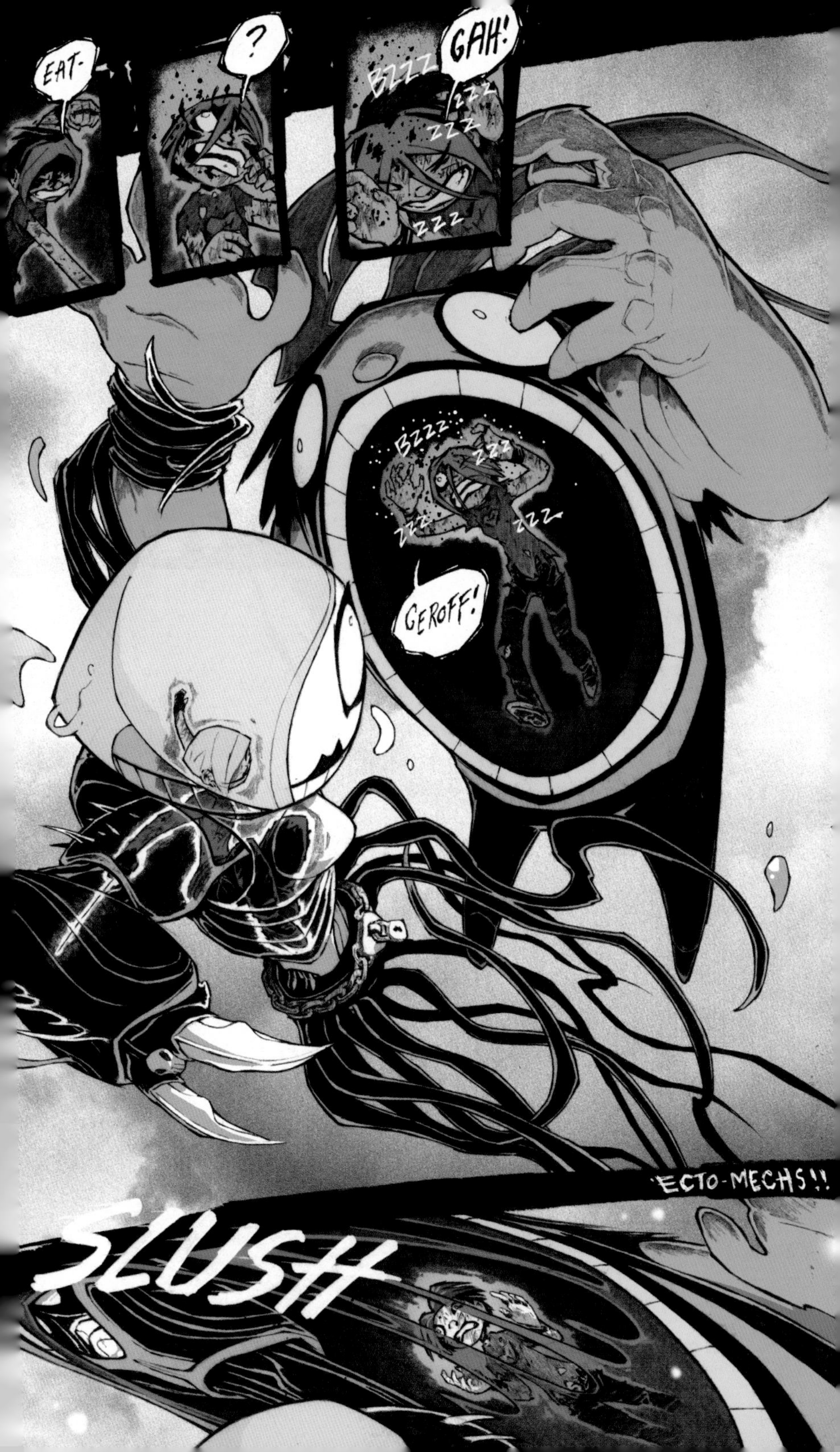
EAT-
?
BZZZ
GAH!
ZZZ
ZZZ
ZZZ
BZZZ
ZZZ
ZZZ
ZZZ
GEROFF!
ECTO-MECHS!!
SLUSH

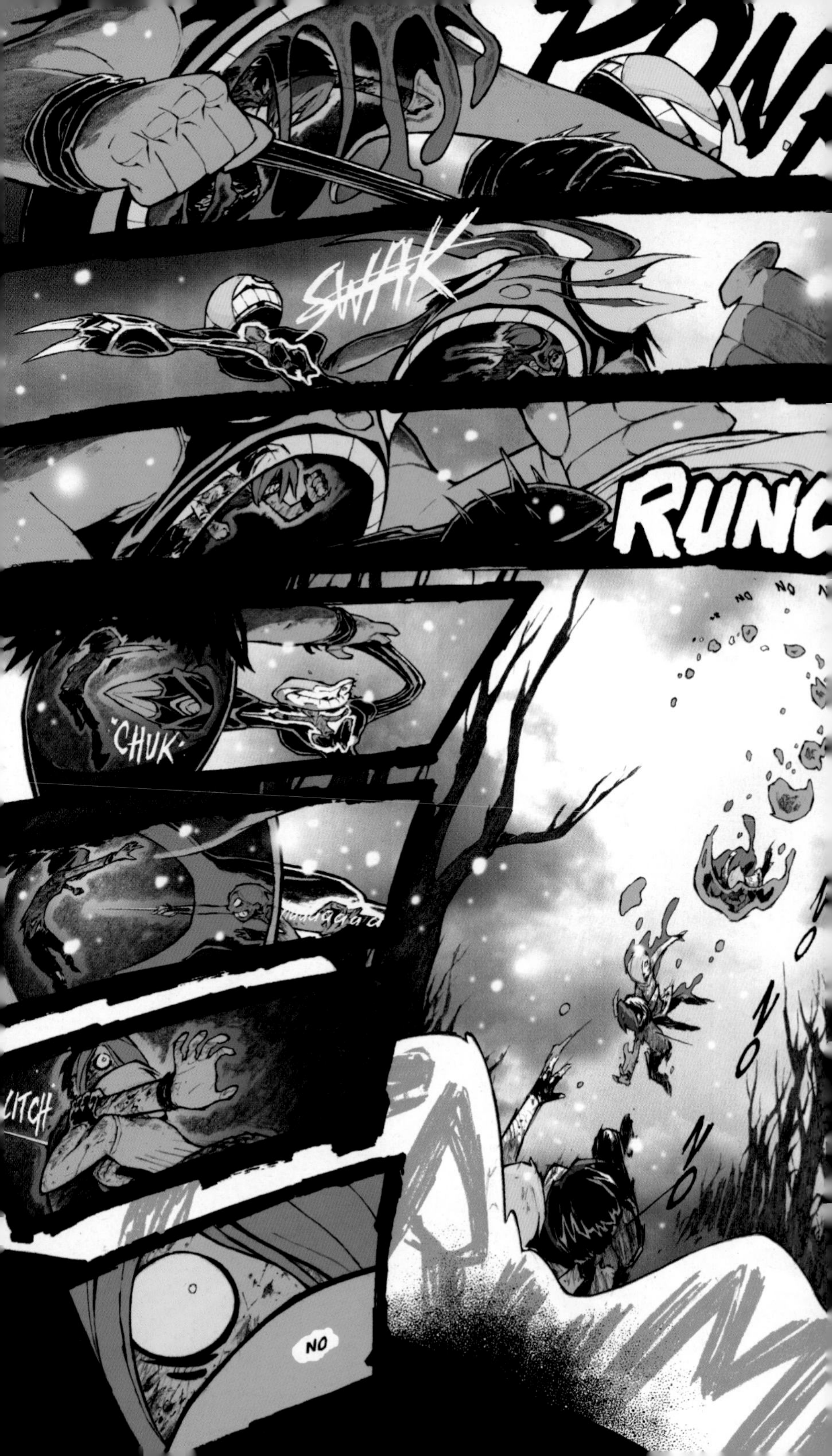
SWAK
RUNC
NO NO
CHUK
nnnnggaa
LITCH
NO
NO
NO
NO

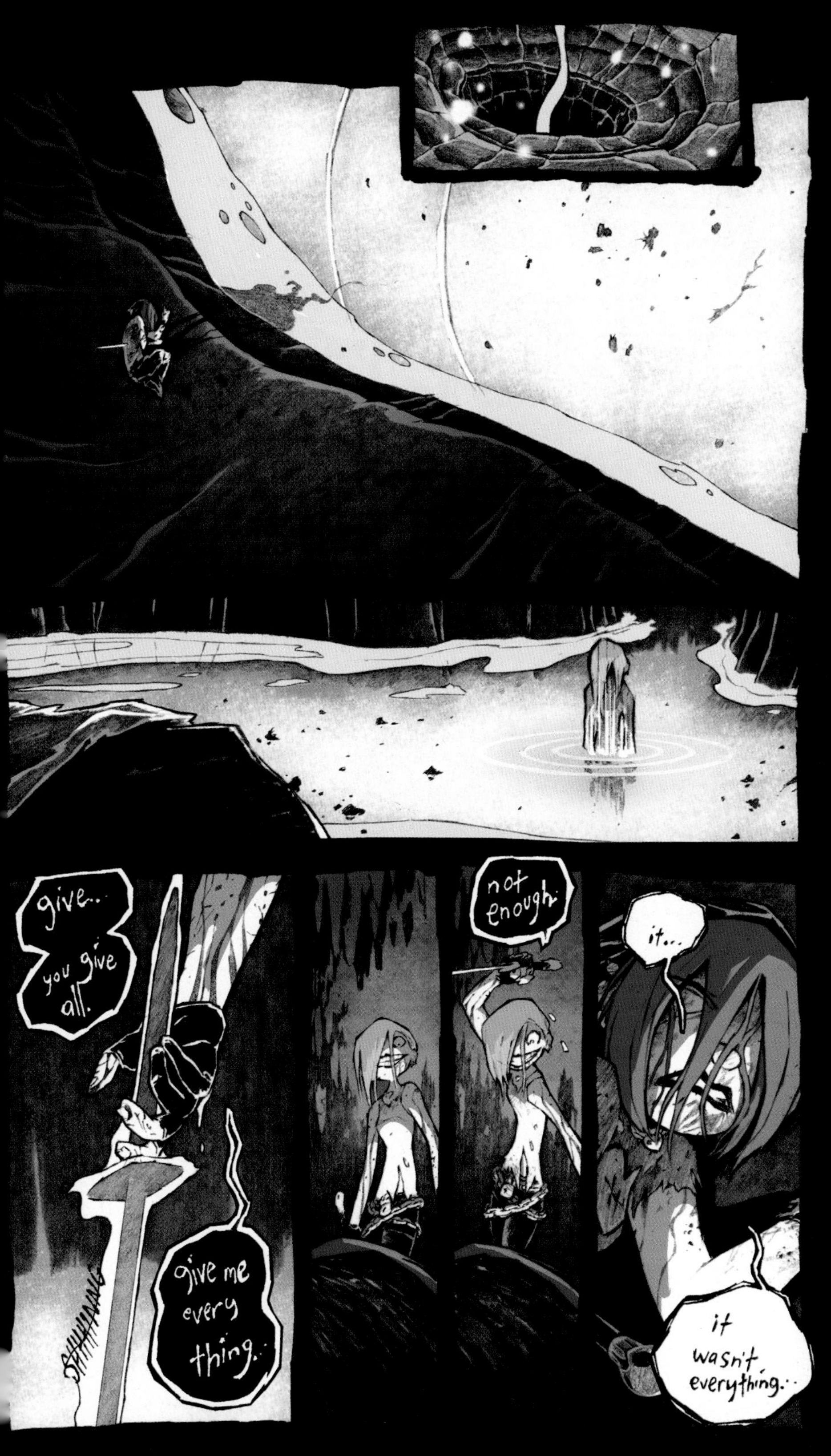
give...
you give all.
give me every thing...
SHHHHNNNG
not enough.
it...
it wasn't everything...

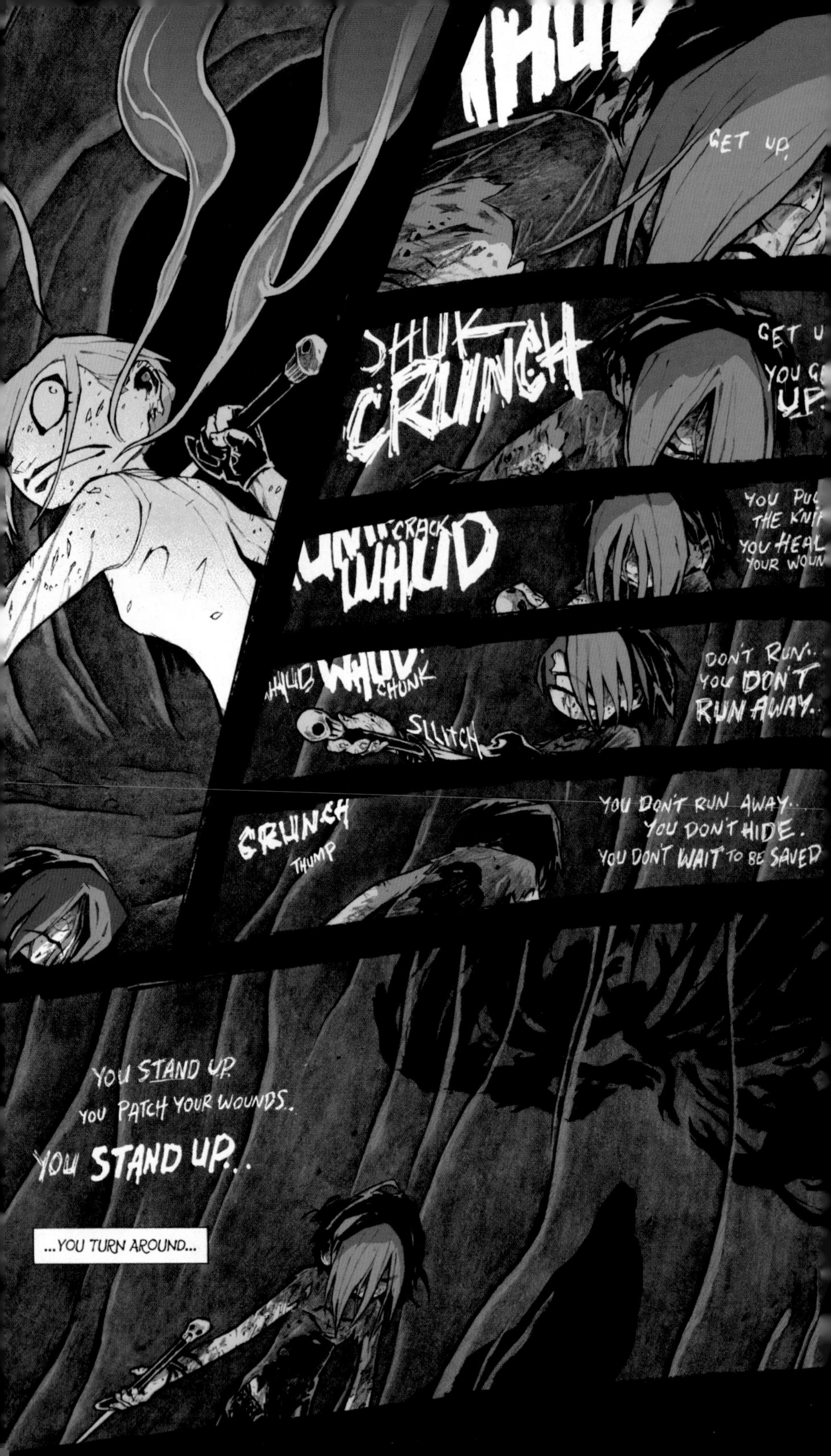

GET UP.
SHUK
CRUNCH
GET U
YOU G
UP.
CRACK
WHUD
YOU PU
THE KNIF
YOU HEAL
YOUR WOUN
WHUD WHUD
CHUNK
SLLITCH
DON'T RUN..
YOU DON'T
RUN AWAY..
CRUNCH
THUMP
YOU DON'T RUN AWAY..
YOU DON'T HIDE.
YOU DON'T WAIT TO BE SAVED
YOU STAND UP.
YOU PATCH YOUR WOUNDS..
YOU STAND UP...
...YOU TURN AROUND...

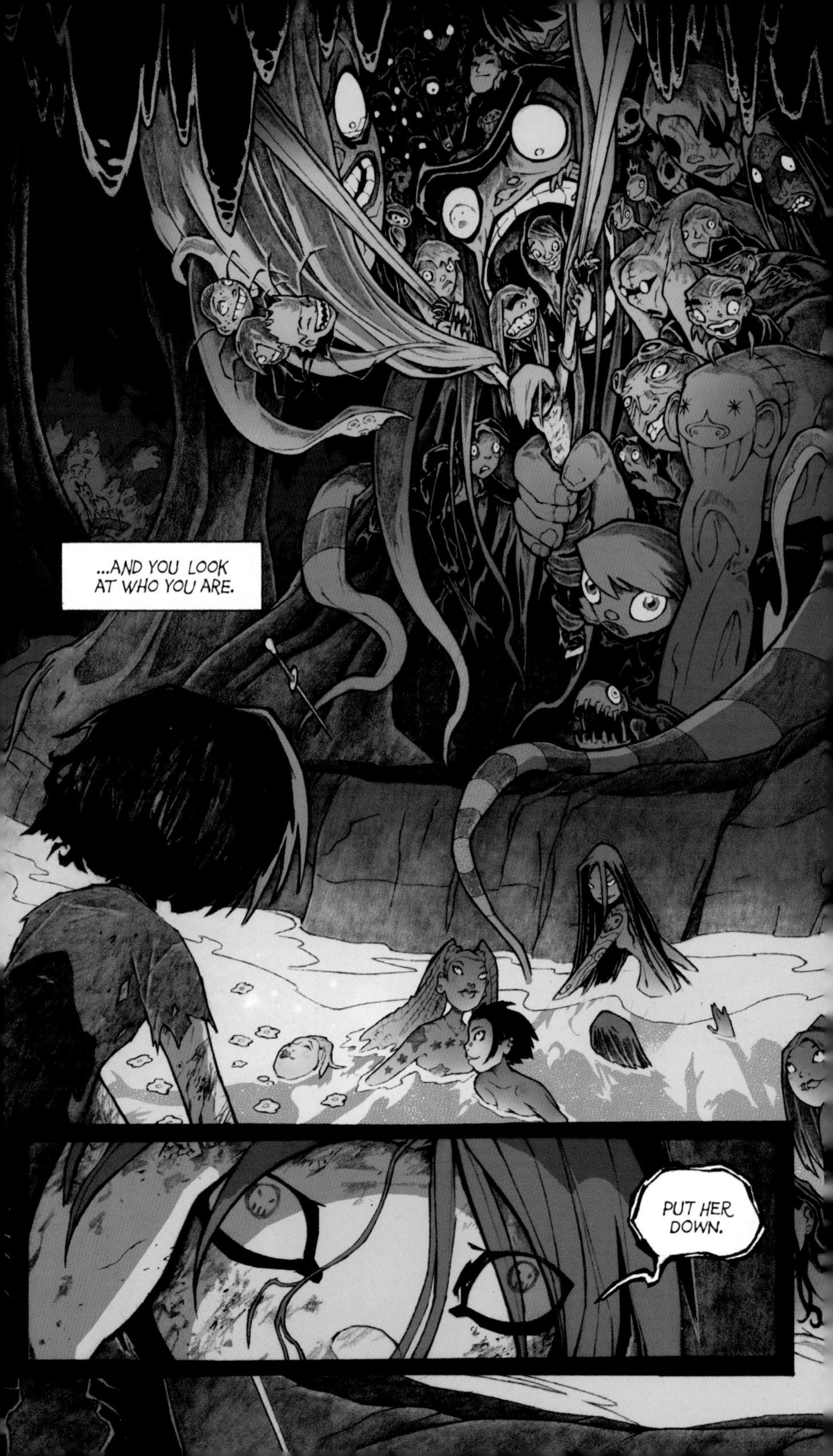
...AND YOU LOOK AT WHO YOU ARE.
PUT HER DOWN.

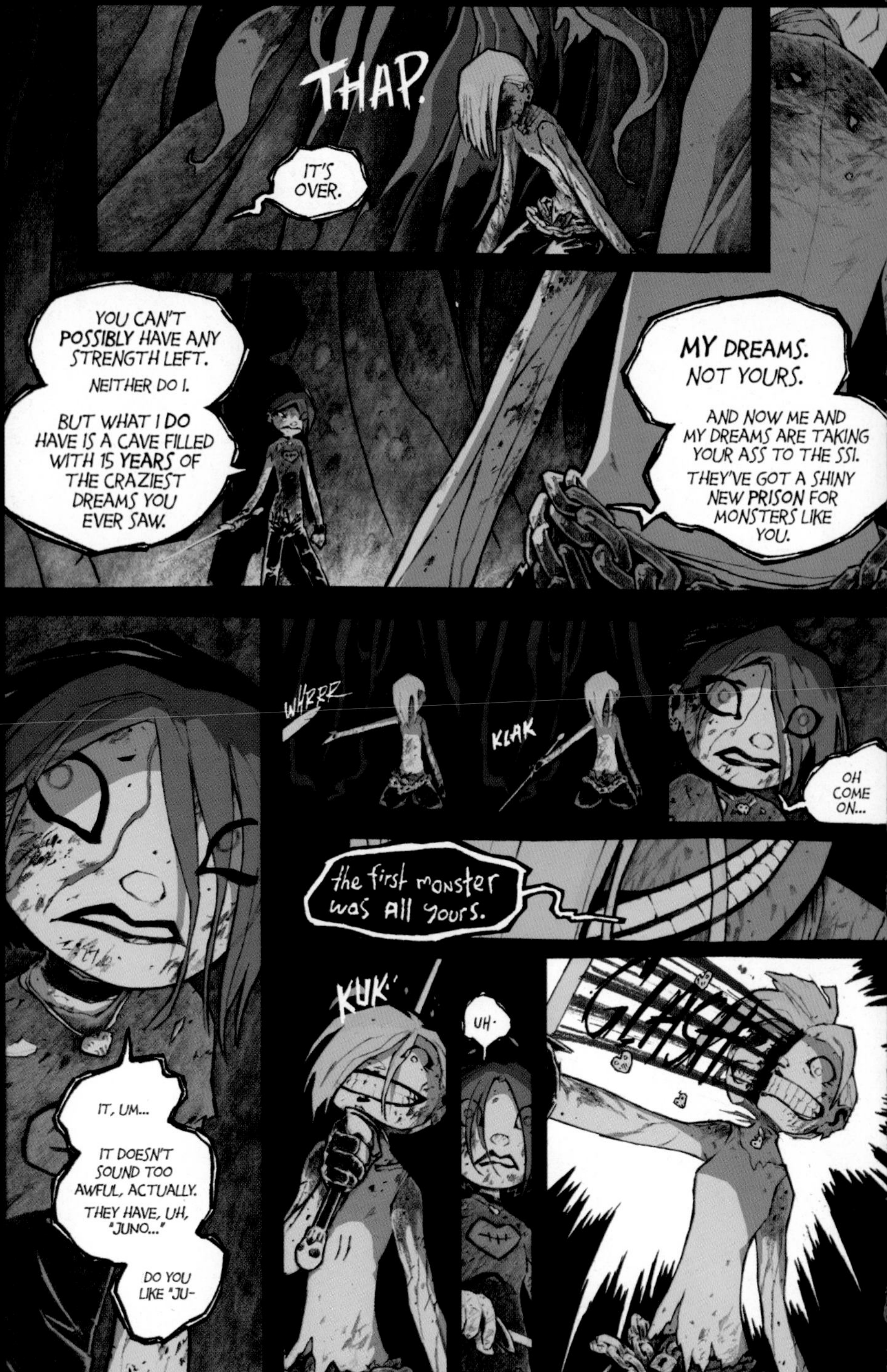
THAP.
IT'S OVER.
YOU CAN'T POSSIBLY HAVE ANY STRENGTH LEFT.
NEITHER DO I.
BUT WHAT I DO HAVE IS A CAVE FILLED WITH 15 YEARS OF THE CRAZIEST DREAMS YOU EVER SAW.
MY DREAMS. NOT YOURS.
AND NOW ME AND MY DREAMS ARE TAKING YOUR ASS TO THE SSI.
THEY'VE GOT A SHINY NEW PRISON FOR MONSTERS LIKE YOU.
WHRRR
KLAK
OH COME ON...
the first monster was all yours.
IT, UM...
IT DOESN'T SOUND TOO AWFUL, ACTUALLY.
THEY HAVE, UH, "JUNO..."
DO YOU LIKE "JU-
KUK
UH.

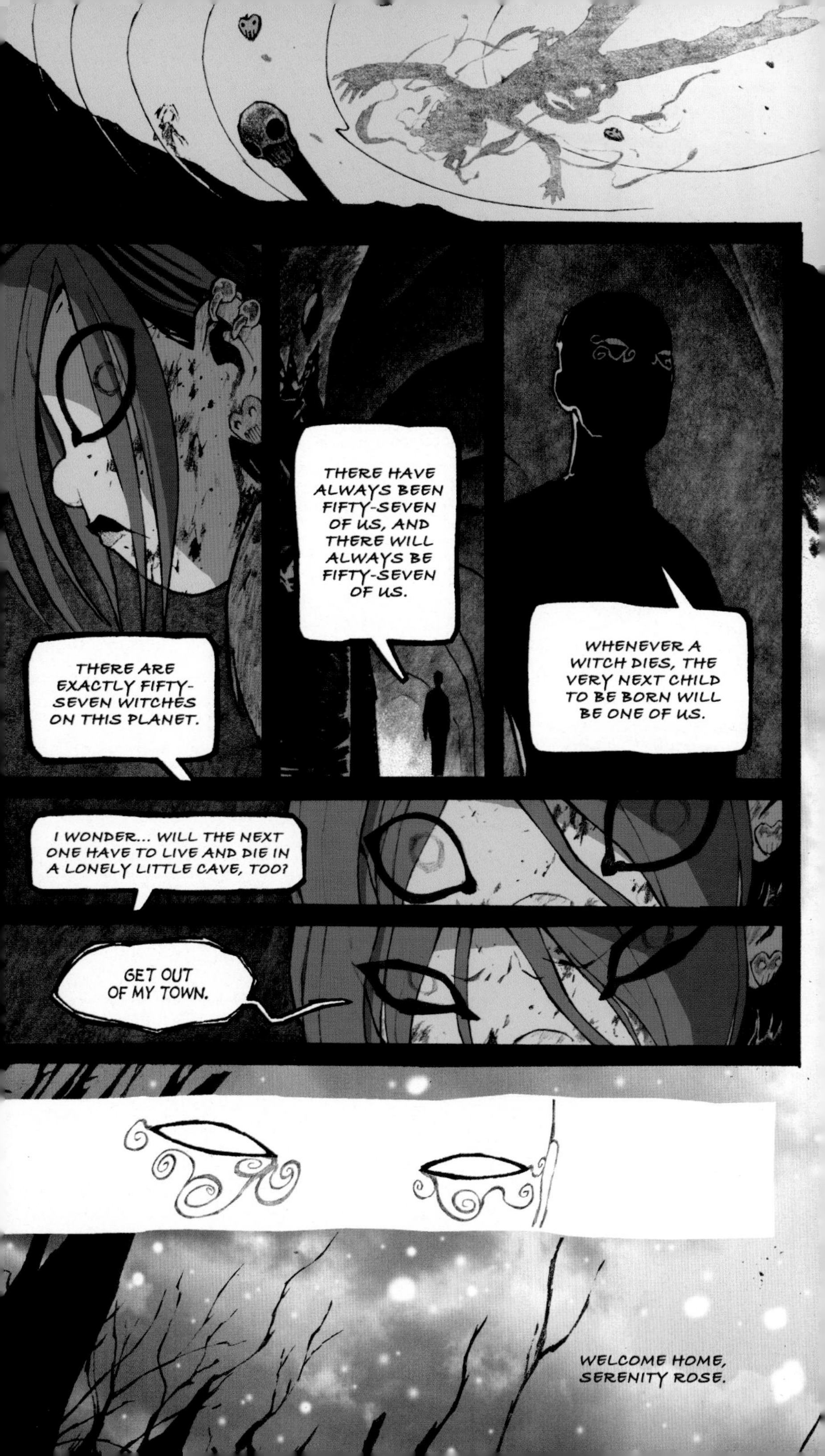
THERE ARE EXACTLY FIFTY-SEVEN WITCHES ON THIS PLANET.
THERE HAVE ALWAYS BEEN FIFTY-SEVEN OF US, AND THERE WILL ALWAYS BE FIFTY-SEVEN OF US.
WHENEVER A WITCH DIES, THE VERY NEXT CHILD TO BE BORN WILL BE ONE OF US.
I WONDER... WILL THE NEXT ONE HAVE TO LIVE AND DIE IN A LONELY LITTLE CAVE, TOO?
GET OUT OF MY TOWN.
WELCOME HOME, SERENITY ROSE.

FOUR DAYS LATER,

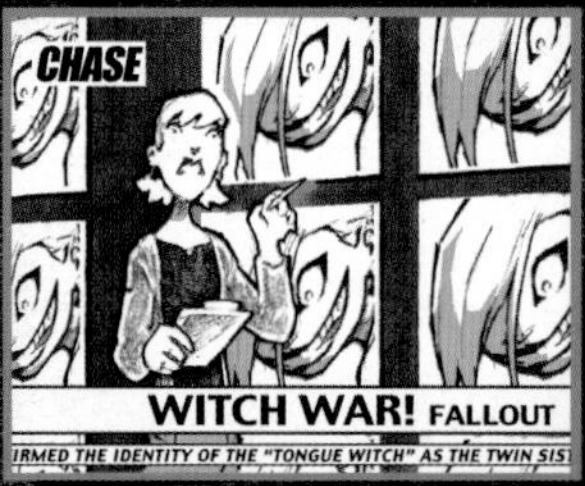
CHASE
WITCH WAR! FALLOUT
IRMED THE IDENTITY OF THE "TONGUE WITCH" AS THE TWIN SIS

"RECAPPING OUR TOP STORIES AT THIS HOUR...

WITCH WAR: THE FALLOUT!

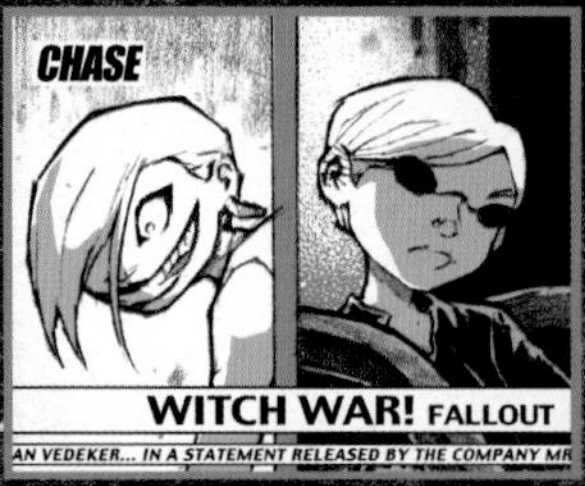
CHASE
WITCH WAR! FALLOUT
AN VEDEKER... IN A STATEMENT RELEASED BY THE COMPANY MR

NEW DNA EVIDENCE RELEASED BY THE SSI HAS **CONFIRMED** THE IDENTITY OF THE BLONDE WITCH AS THE **SISTER** -THE **TWIN** SISTER- OF VAN VEDEKER DIAMOND HEIR **SIMON VAN VEDEKER**.

SSI INTERNATIONAL IS NOW SEARCHING FOR **CONNECTIONS** BETWEEN THE WITCH, THE STILL-**UNSOLVED** DEATHS OF THEO AND CHRISTIANNE VAN VEDEKER, AND OCTOBER'S MATOBO DIAMOND MINE MYSTERY....

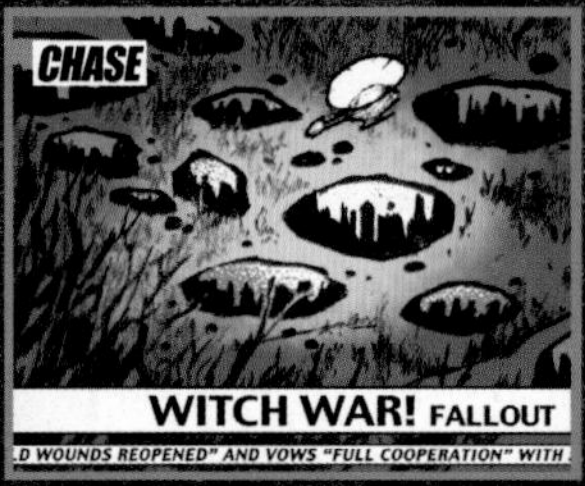
CHASE
WITCH WAR! FALLOUT
D WOUNDS REOPENED" AND VOWS "FULL COOPERATION" WITH

BACK IN CRESTFALLEN, **CHASE NEWS** HAS LEARNED **SSI AND FBI** OFFICIALS ARE NOW **FOCUSING** THEIR CONTINUING INVESTIGATION ON A **CAVE** HIDDEN **DEEP** IN THE **"DOLDRUMS"** REGION OF THE INCONSOLABLE WOOD.

THE CAVE'S **SIGNIFICANCE** HAS YET TO BE REVEALED, BUT SSI CHIEF INVESTIGATOR **CHESTER MERRICK** TOLD US, QUOTE, "WE'RE GOING TO BE HERE A WHILE."

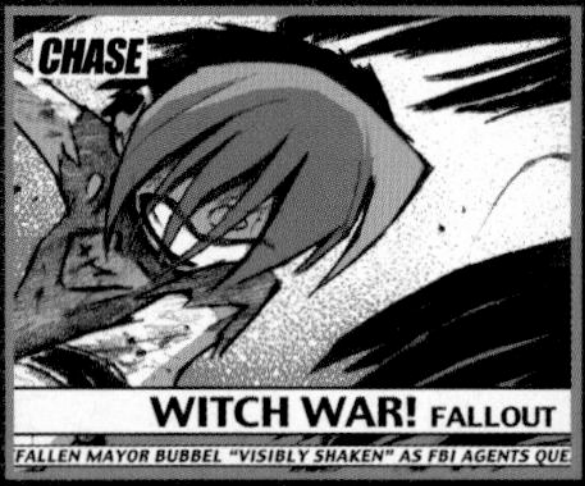
CHASE
WITCH WAR! FALLOUT
FALLEN MAYOR BUBBEL "VISIBLY SHAKEN" AS FBI AGENTS QUE

THAT MEANS BAD NEWS FOR "HERO OF CRESTFALLEN" **SERENITY ROSE**, WHO HAD PLANNED TO BEGIN AN **APPRENTICESHIP** WITH SINGER/SORCERER **VICIOUS WHISPER** THIS MONTH AT HER HOME OUTSIDE OXFORD, ENGLAND.

AUTHORITIES HAVE REQUESTED MS. ROSE **STAY** IN CRESTFALLEN FOR THE **DURATION** OF THEIR OPEN-ENDED INVESTIGATION.

VICIOUS WHISPER, CURRENTLY TRAVELING IN **AFRICA** WTIH **ATLAN SAMUEL**, HAS SO FAR BEEN **UNAVAILABLE** FOR COMMENT.

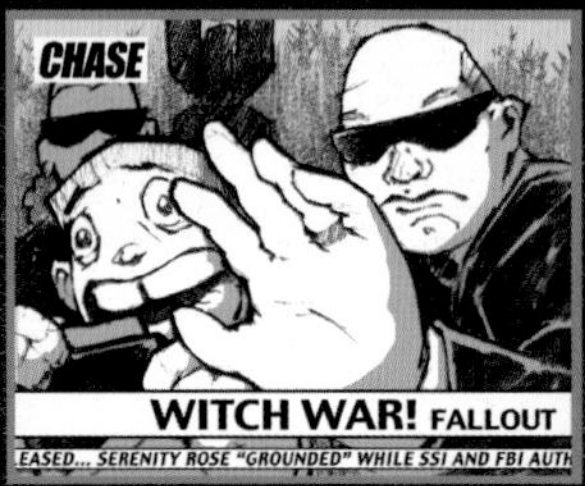
CHASE
WITCH WAR! FALLOUT
EASED... SERENITY ROSE "GROUNDED" WHILE SSI AND FBI AUTH

ALSO UNAVAILABLE FOR COMMENT TODAY: CRESTFALLEN MAYOR ARTHUR J. **"STUBBY"** BUBBEL, WHO WAS **QUESTIONED** BY THE FBI THIS MORNING IN CONNECTION WITH HIS ADMINISTRATION'S HANDLING OF THE EVENTS LEADING **UP** TO LAST WEEK'S MASSACRE.

MAYOR BUBBEL HAS **REPEATEDLY** DENIED RESPONSIBILITY FOR THE DECISION TO KEEP FROZEN CIRCLE PLAZA **OPEN** LAST TUESDAY, BUT THE QUESTION REMAINS: IF MR. BUBBEL **ISN'T** IN CONTROL OF THE "SPOOKIEST LIL TOWN IN AMERICA," WHO **IS?**

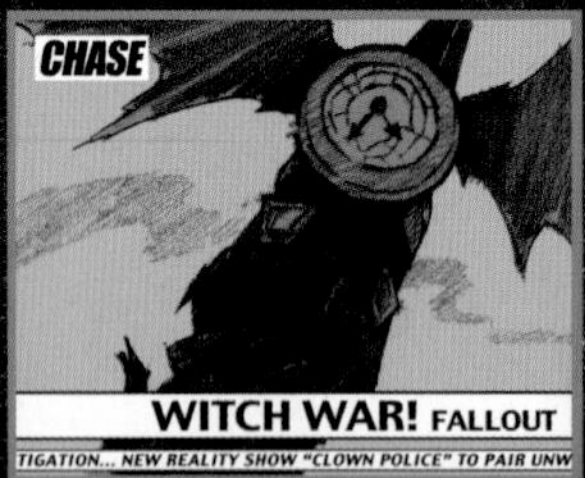
CHASE
WITCH WAR! FALLOUT
TIGATION... NEW REALITY SHOW "CLOWN POLICE" TO PAIR UNW

AND ONE FINAL NOTE...

LAST WEEK WE REPORTED THAT CROW CLOCK, WHICH SINCE JANUARY 5TH, 1857 HAS BEEN STOPPED AT EXACTLY 5 PM, SUDDENLY BEGAN TICKING AGAIN LAST TUESDAY AT 12:45 PM.

TODAY THE SSI RELEASED PHOTOGRAPHIC PROOF.

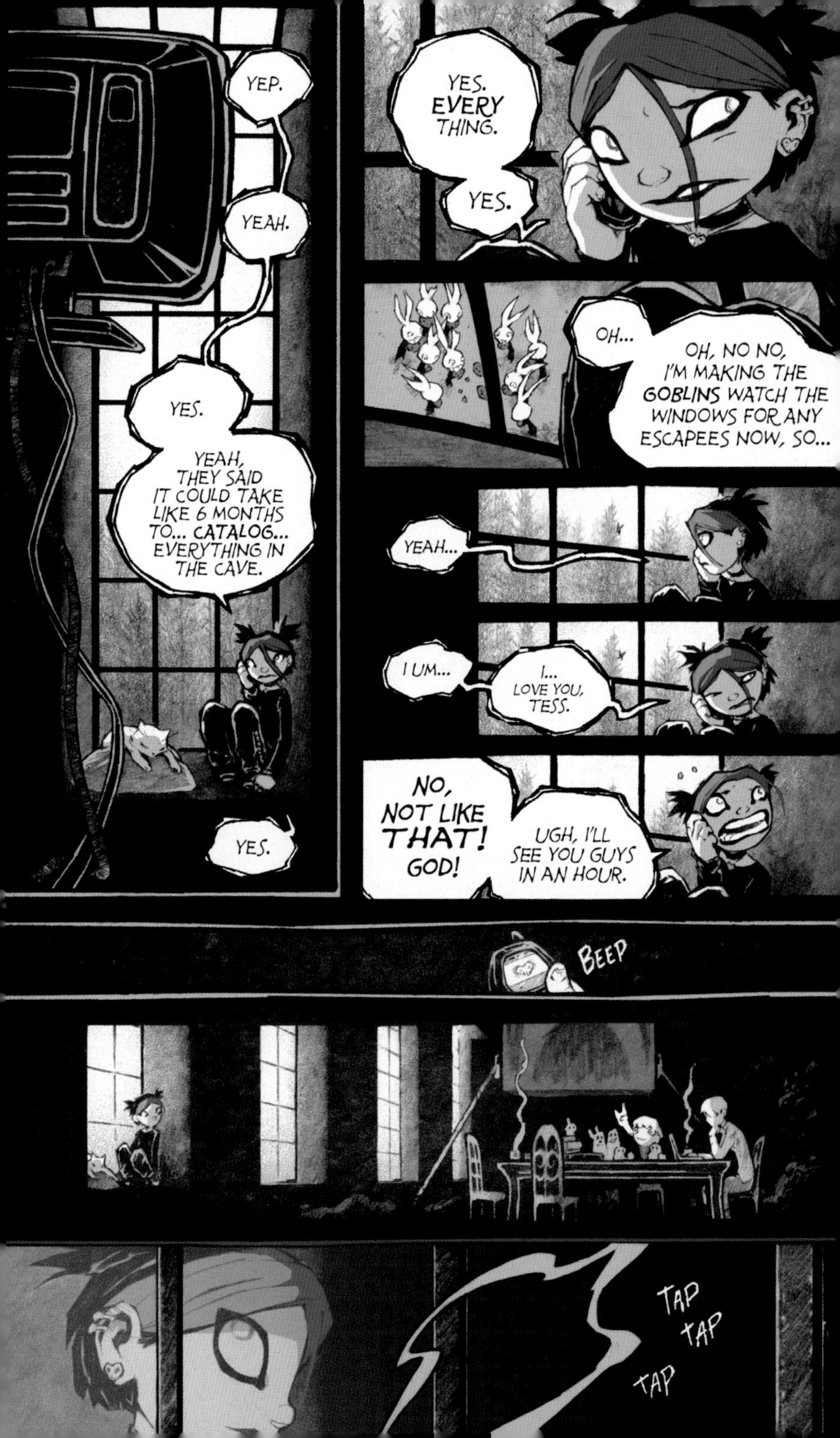
YEP.
YEAH.
YES.
YEAH, THEY SAID IT COULD TAKE LIKE 6 MONTHS TO... CATALOG... EVERYTHING IN THE CAVE.
YES.
YES. EVERY THING.
YES.
OH...
OH, NO NO, I'M MAKING THE GOBLINS WATCH THE WINDOWS FOR ANY ESCAPEES NOW, SO...
YEAH...
I UM...
I... LOVE YOU, TESS.
NO, NOT LIKE THAT! GOD!
UGH, I'LL SEE YOU GUYS IN AN HOUR.
BEEP
TAP
TAP
TAP

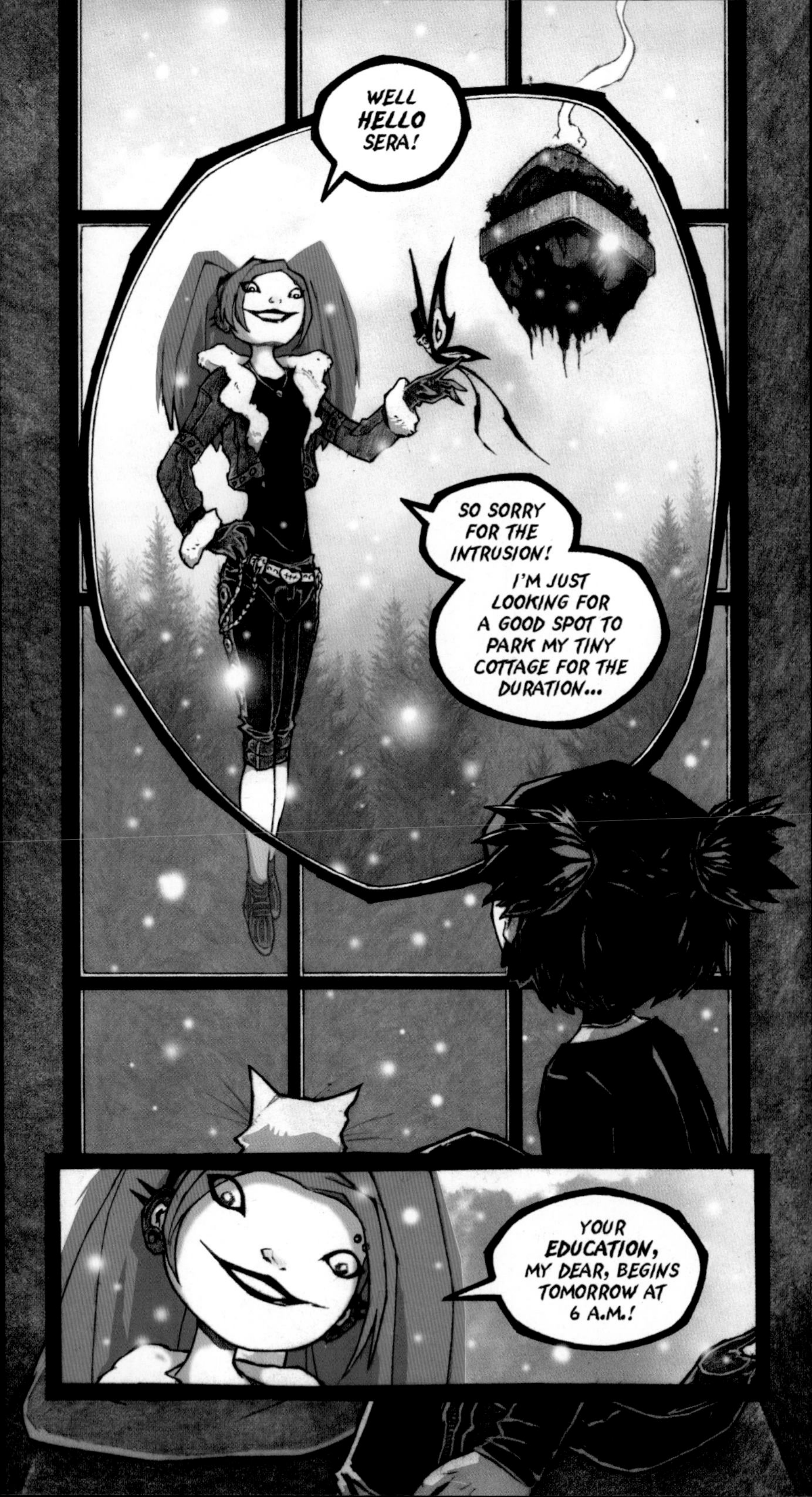
WELL HELLO SERA!
SO SORRY FOR THE INTRUSION!
I'M JUST LOOKING FOR A GOOD SPOT TO PARK MY TINY COTTAGE FOR THE DURATION...
YOUR EDUCATION, MY DEAR, BEGINS TOMORROW AT 6 A.M.!

'VICIOUS WHISPERS'

— SELECTED CARTOONS

IN 2006, WORLD-RENOWNED SINGER/SORCERESS VICTORIA "VICIOUS" WHISPER GAVE HER FANS THE OPPORTUNITY TO SUBMIT QUESTIONS FOR HER TO ANSWER IN A COMIC STRIP CALLED 'VICIOUS WHISPERS' @HEARTSHAPEDSKULL.COM

THE FOLLOWING IS A SELECTION OF THOSE COMICS.

DESPITE THE BEST EFFORTS OF SUPERNATURAL EXPERTS AT OVER 150 PUBLIC AND PRIVATE ORGANIZATIONS SPREAD ACROSS 23 NATIONS AND AT A COMBINED COST OF $1.7 BILLION, NOT ONE OF HER ANSWERS HAS SO FAR BEEN INDEPENDENTLY CORROBORATED.

"WHAT THE HELL ARE 'CORN NUTS?'" SPUTTERS ONE EXPERT.

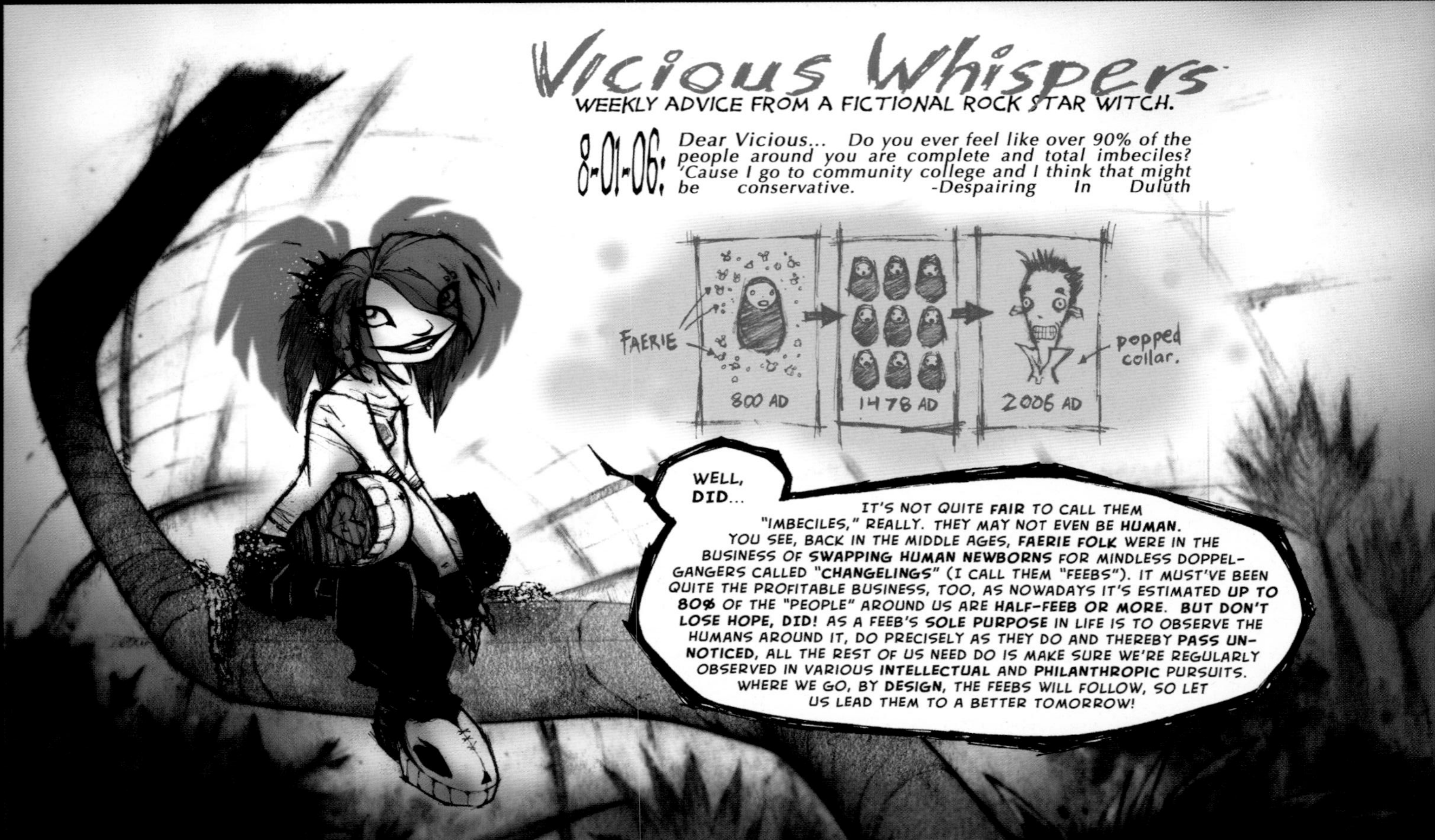
Vicious Whispers
WEEKLY ADVICE FROM A FICTIONAL ROCK STAR WITCH.
8-01-06: Dear Vicious... Do you ever feel like over 90% of the people around you are complete and total imbeciles? 'Cause I go to community college and I think that might be conservative. -Despairing In Duluth
FAERIE
800 AD
1478 AD
2006 AD
popped collar.
WELL, DID...
IT'S NOT QUITE FAIR TO CALL THEM "IMBECILES," REALLY. THEY MAY NOT EVEN BE HUMAN. YOU SEE, BACK IN THE MIDDLE AGES, FAERIE FOLK WERE IN THE BUSINESS OF SWAPPING HUMAN NEWBORNS FOR MINDLESS DOPPELGANGERS CALLED "CHANGELINGS" (I CALL THEM "FEEBS"). IT MUST'VE BEEN QUITE THE PROFITABLE BUSINESS, TOO, AS NOWADAYS IT'S ESTIMATED UP TO 80% OF THE "PEOPLE" AROUND US ARE HALF-FEEB OR MORE. BUT DON'T LOSE HOPE, DID! AS A FEEB'S SOLE PURPOSE IN LIFE IS TO OBSERVE THE HUMANS AROUND IT, DO PRECISELY AS THEY DO AND THEREBY PASS UNNOTICED, ALL THE REST OF US NEED DO IS MAKE SURE WE'RE REGULARLY OBSERVED IN VARIOUS INTELLECTUAL AND PHILANTHROPIC PURSUITS. WHERE WE GO, BY DESIGN, THE FEEBS WILL FOLLOW, SO LET US LEAD THEM TO A BETTER TOMORROW!

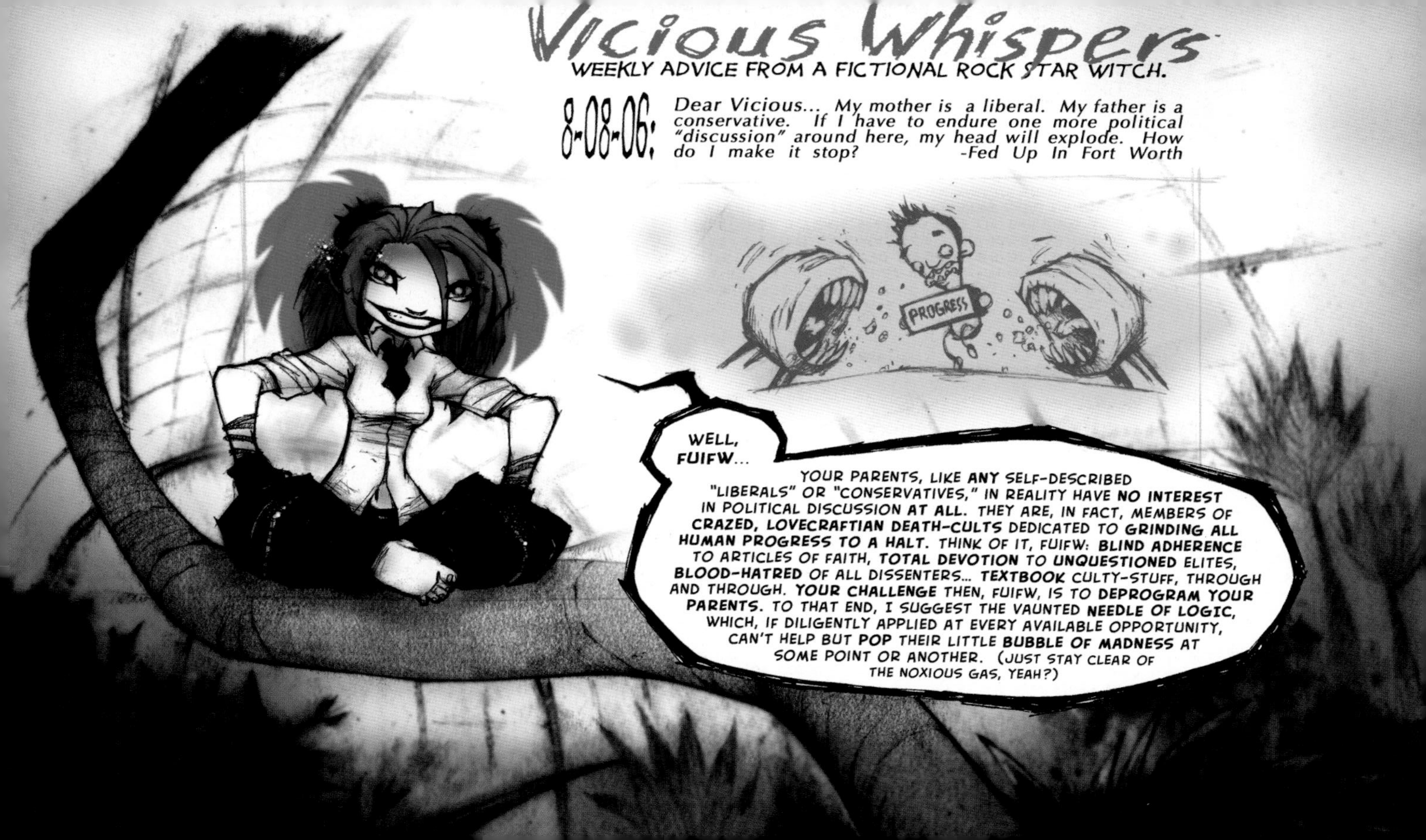

Vicious Whispers
WEEKLY ADVICE FROM A FICTIONAL ROCK STAR WITCH.
8-08-06:
Dear Vicious... My mother is a liberal. My father is a conservative. If I have to endure one more political "discussion" around here, my head will explode. How do I make it stop? -Fed Up In Fort Worth
PROGRESS
WELL, FUIFW...
YOUR PARENTS, LIKE ANY SELF-DESCRIBED "LIBERALS" OR "CONSERVATIVES," IN REALITY HAVE NO INTEREST IN POLITICAL DISCUSSION AT ALL. THEY ARE, IN FACT, MEMBERS OF CRAZED, LOVECRAFTIAN DEATH-CULTS DEDICATED TO GRINDING ALL HUMAN PROGRESS TO A HALT. THINK OF IT, FUIFW: BLIND ADHERENCE TO ARTICLES OF FAITH, TOTAL DEVOTION TO UNQUESTIONED ELITES, BLOOD-HATRED OF ALL DISSENTERS... TEXTBOOK CULTY-STUFF, THROUGH AND THROUGH. YOUR CHALLENGE THEN, FUIFW, IS TO DEPROGRAM YOUR PARENTS. TO THAT END, I SUGGEST THE VAUNTED NEEDLE OF LOGIC, WHICH, IF DILIGENTLY APPLIED AT EVERY AVAILABLE OPPORTUNITY, CAN'T HELP BUT POP THEIR LITTLE BUBBLE OF MADNESS AT SOME POINT OR ANOTHER. (JUST STAY CLEAR OF THE NOXIOUS GAS, YEAH?)

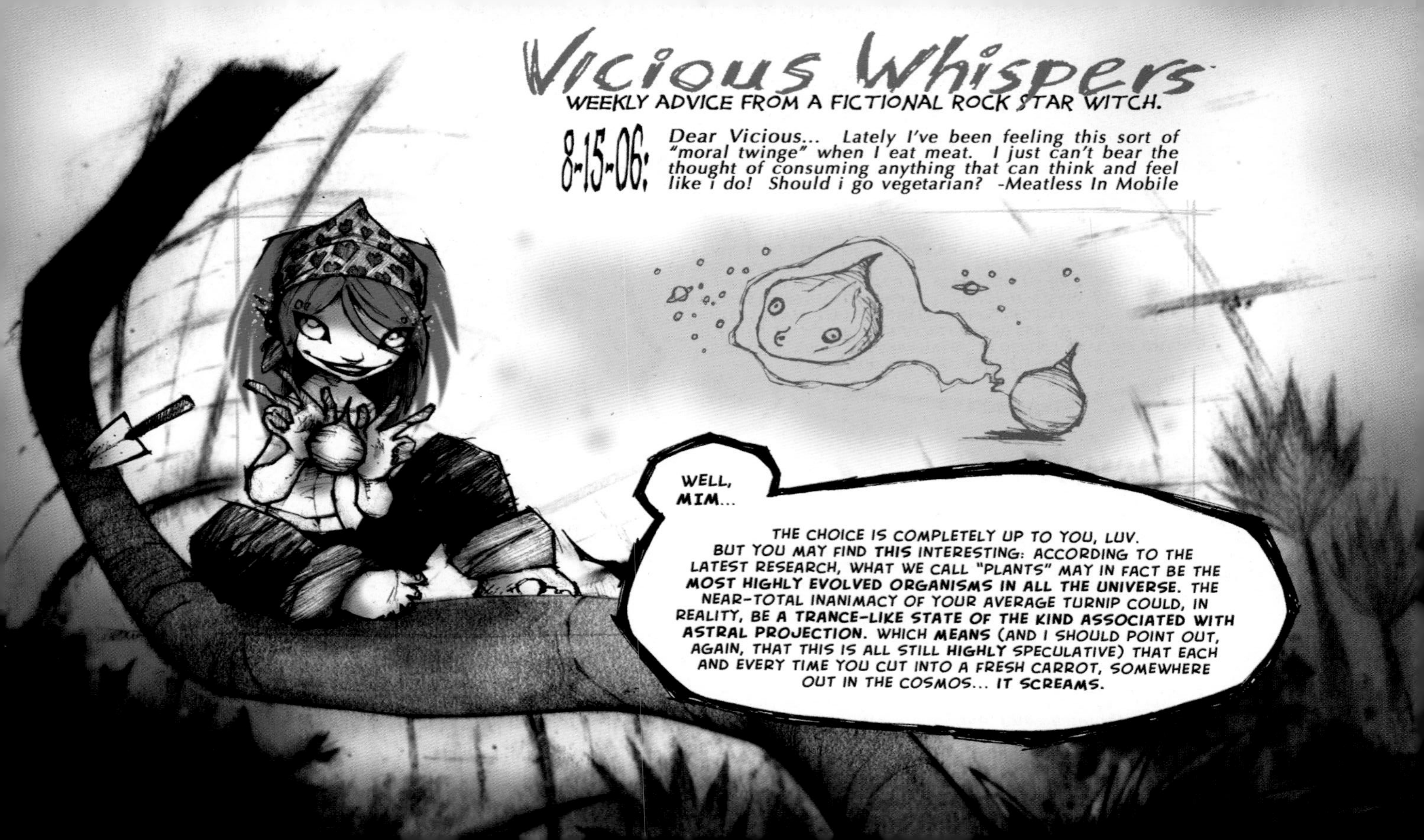
Vicious Whispers
WEEKLY ADVICE FROM A FICTIONAL ROCK STAR WITCH.
8-15-06: Dear Vicious... Lately I've been feeling this sort of "moral twinge" when I eat meat. I just can't bear the thought of consuming anything that can think and feel like i do! Should i go vegetarian? -Meatless In Mobile
WELL, MIM...
THE CHOICE IS COMPLETELY UP TO YOU, LUV. BUT YOU MAY FIND THIS INTERESTING: ACCORDING TO THE LATEST RESEARCH, WHAT WE CALL "PLANTS" MAY IN FACT BE THE MOST HIGHLY EVOLVED ORGANISMS IN ALL THE UNIVERSE. THE NEAR-TOTAL INANIMACY OF YOUR AVERAGE TURNIP COULD, IN REALITY, BE A TRANCE-LIKE STATE OF THE KIND ASSOCIATED WITH ASTRAL PROJECTION. WHICH MEANS (AND I SHOULD POINT OUT, AGAIN, THAT THIS IS ALL STILL HIGHLY SPECULATIVE) THAT EACH AND EVERY TIME YOU CUT INTO A FRESH CARROT, SOMEWHERE OUT IN THE COSMOS... IT SCREAMS.

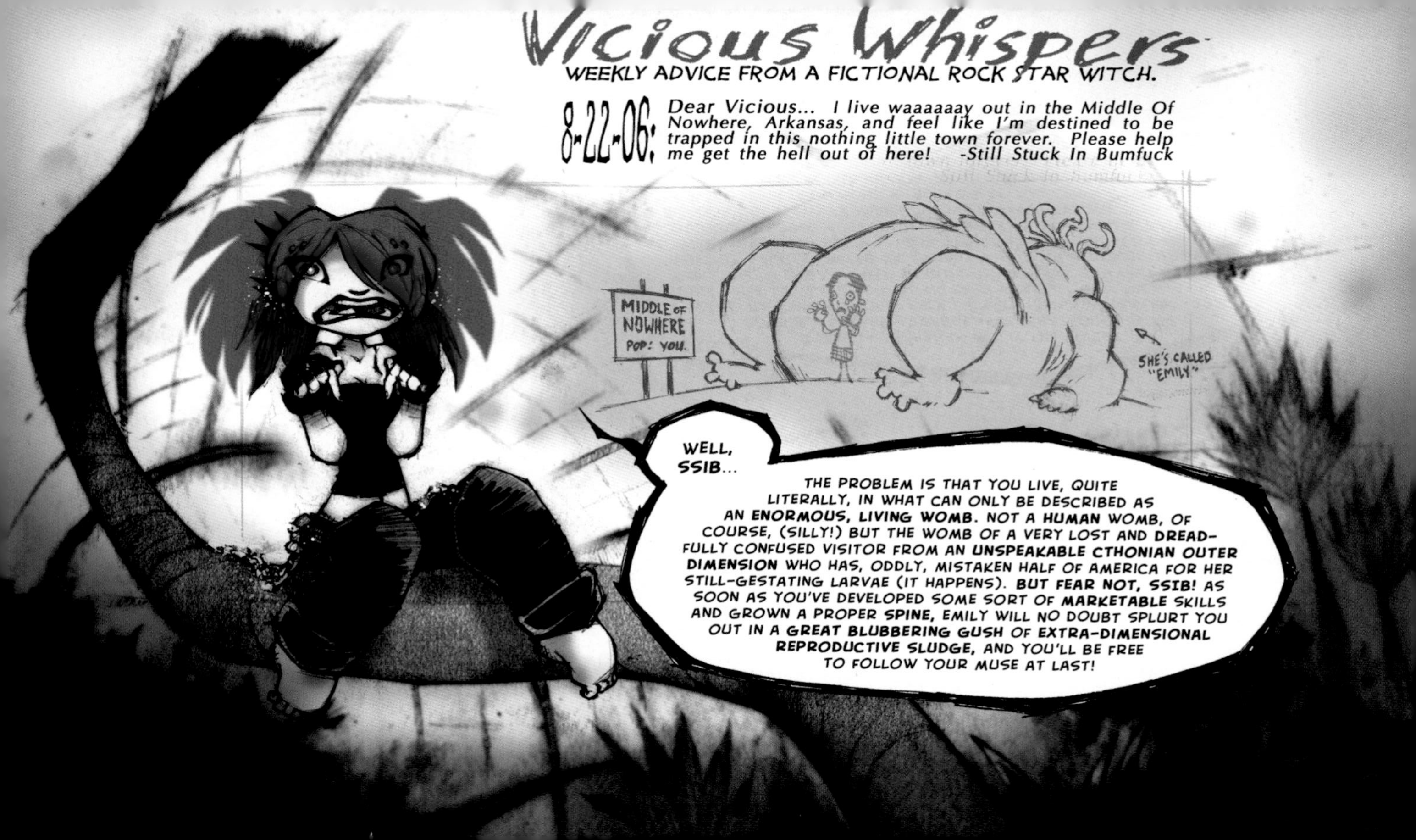
Vicious Whispers
WEEKLY ADVICE FROM A FICTIONAL ROCK STAR WITCH.
8-22-06:
Dear Vicious... I live waaaaaay out in the Middle Of Nowhere, Arkansas, and feel like I'm destined to be trapped in this nothing little town forever. Please help me get the hell out of here! -Still Stuck In Bumfuck
MIDDLE OF NOWHERE POP: YOU.
SHE'S CALLED "EMILY"
WELL, SSIB...
THE PROBLEM IS THAT YOU LIVE, QUITE LITERALLY, IN WHAT CAN ONLY BE DESCRIBED AS AN ENORMOUS, LIVING WOMB. NOT A HUMAN WOMB, OF COURSE, (SILLY!) BUT THE WOMB OF A VERY LOST AND DREADFULLY CONFUSED VISITOR FROM AN UNSPEAKABLE CTHONIAN OUTER DIMENSION WHO HAS, ODDLY, MISTAKEN HALF OF AMERICA FOR HER STILL-GESTATING LARVAE (IT HAPPENS). BUT FEAR NOT, SSIB! AS SOON AS YOU'VE DEVELOPED SOME SORT OF MARKETABLE SKILLS AND GROWN A PROPER SPINE, EMILY WILL NO DOUBT SPLURT YOU OUT IN A GREAT BLUBBERING GUSH OF EXTRA-DIMENSIONAL REPRODUCTIVE SLUDGE, AND YOU'LL BE FREE TO FOLLOW YOUR MUSE AT LAST!

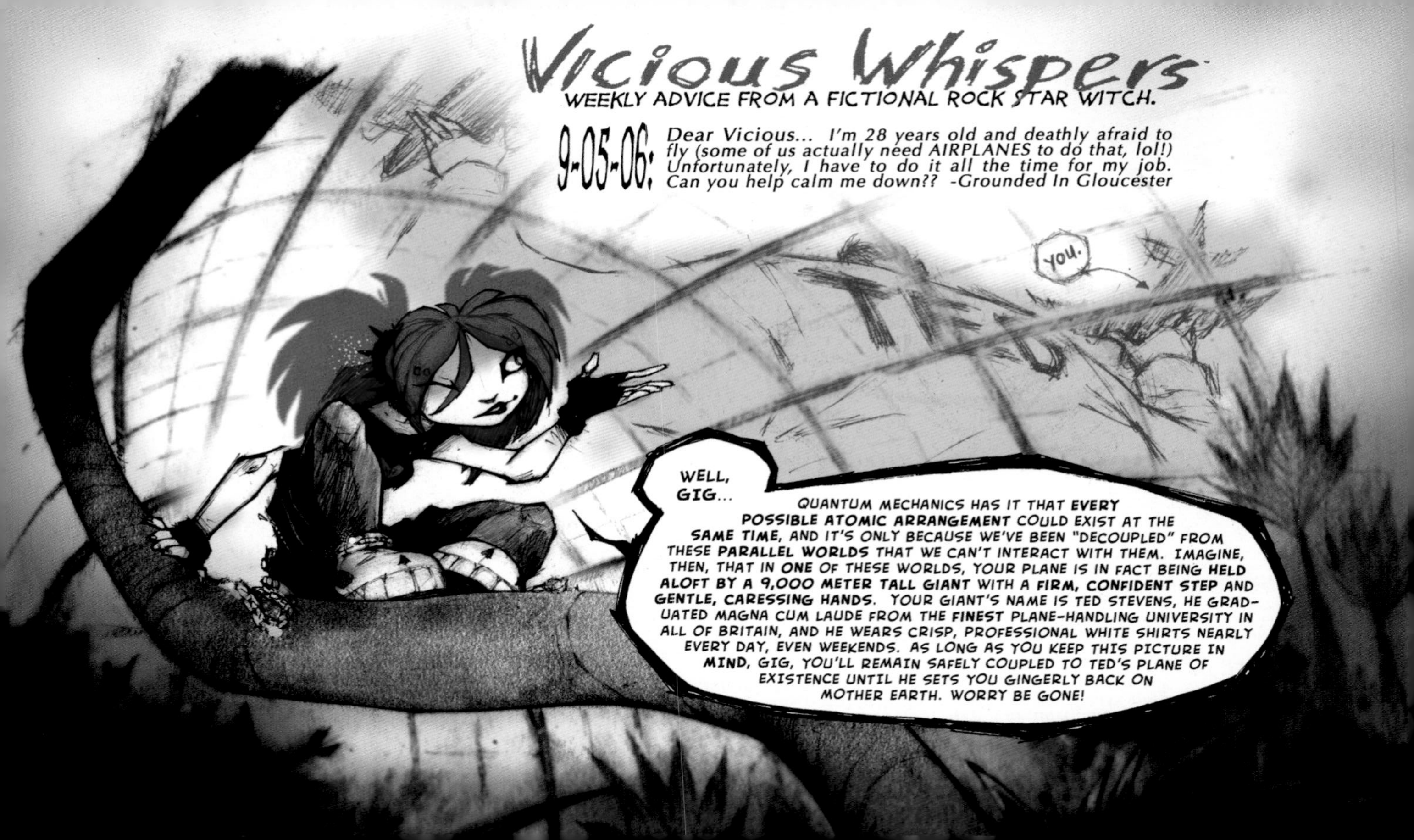
Vicious Whispers
WEEKLY ADVICE FROM A FICTIONAL ROCK STAR WITCH.
9-05-06:
Dear Vicious... I'm 28 years old and deathly afraid to fly (some of us actually need AIRPLANES to do that, lol!) Unfortunately, I have to do it all the time for my job. Can you help calm me down?? -Grounded In Gloucester
YOU.
WELL, GIG...
QUANTUM MECHANICS HAS IT THAT EVERY POSSIBLE ATOMIC ARRANGEMENT COULD EXIST AT THE SAME TIME, AND IT'S ONLY BECAUSE WE'VE BEEN "DECOUPLED" FROM THESE PARALLEL WORLDS THAT WE CAN'T INTERACT WITH THEM. IMAGINE, THEN, THAT IN ONE OF THESE WORLDS, YOUR PLANE IS IN FACT BEING HELD ALOFT BY A 9,000 METER TALL GIANT WITH A FIRM, CONFIDENT STEP AND GENTLE, CARESSING HANDS. YOUR GIANT'S NAME IS TED STEVENS, HE GRADUATED MAGNA CUM LAUDE FROM THE FINEST PLANE-HANDLING UNIVERSITY IN ALL OF BRITAIN, AND HE WEARS CRISP, PROFESSIONAL WHITE SHIRTS NEARLY EVERY DAY, EVEN WEEKENDS. AS LONG AS YOU KEEP THIS PICTURE IN MIND, GIG, YOU'LL REMAIN SAFELY COUPLED TO TED'S PLANE OF EXISTENCE UNTIL HE SETS YOU GINGERLY BACK ON MOTHER EARTH. WORRY BE GONE!

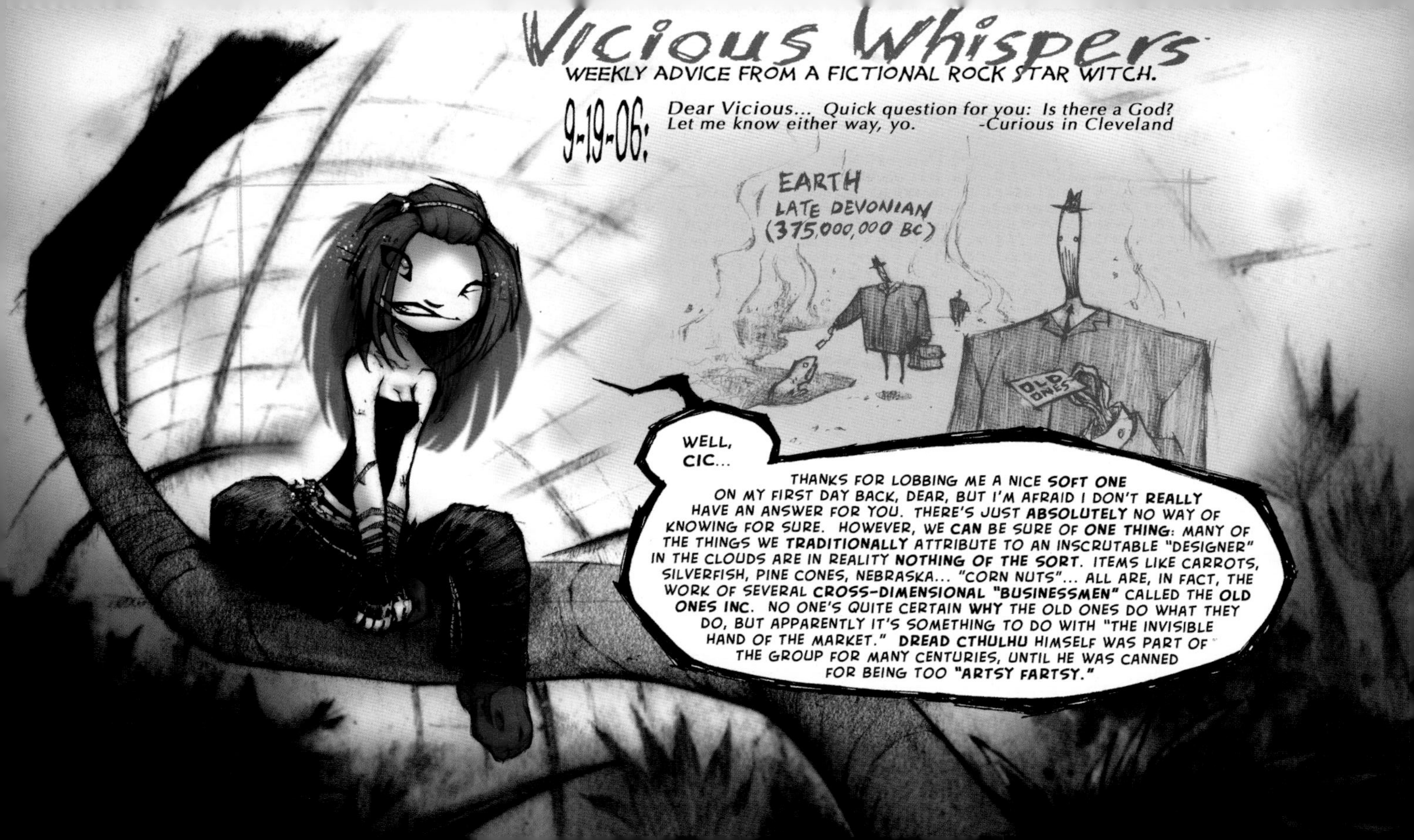
Vicious Whispers
WEEKLY ADVICE FROM A FICTIONAL ROCK STAR WITCH.
9-19-06:
Dear Vicious... Quick question for you: Is there a God? Let me know either way, yo. -Curious in Cleveland
EARTH LATE DEVONIAN (375,000,000 BC)
OLD ONES
WELL, CIC...
THANKS FOR LOBBING ME A NICE SOFT ONE ON MY FIRST DAY BACK, DEAR, BUT I'M AFRAID I DON'T REALLY HAVE AN ANSWER FOR YOU. THERE'S JUST ABSOLUTELY NO WAY OF KNOWING FOR SURE. HOWEVER, WE CAN BE SURE OF ONE THING: MANY OF THE THINGS WE TRADITIONALLY ATTRIBUTE TO AN INSCRUTABLE "DESIGNER" IN THE CLOUDS ARE IN REALITY NOTHING OF THE SORT. ITEMS LIKE CARROTS, SILVERFISH, PINE CONES, NEBRASKA... "CORN NUTS"... ALL ARE, IN FACT, THE WORK OF SEVERAL CROSS-DIMENSIONAL "BUSINESSMEN" CALLED THE OLD ONES INC. NO ONE'S QUITE CERTAIN WHY THE OLD ONES DO WHAT THEY DO, BUT APPARENTLY IT'S SOMETHING TO DO WITH "THE INVISIBLE HAND OF THE MARKET." DREAD CTHULHU HIMSELF WAS PART OF THE GROUP FOR MANY CENTURIES, UNTIL HE WAS CANNED FOR BEING TOO "ARTSY FARTSY."

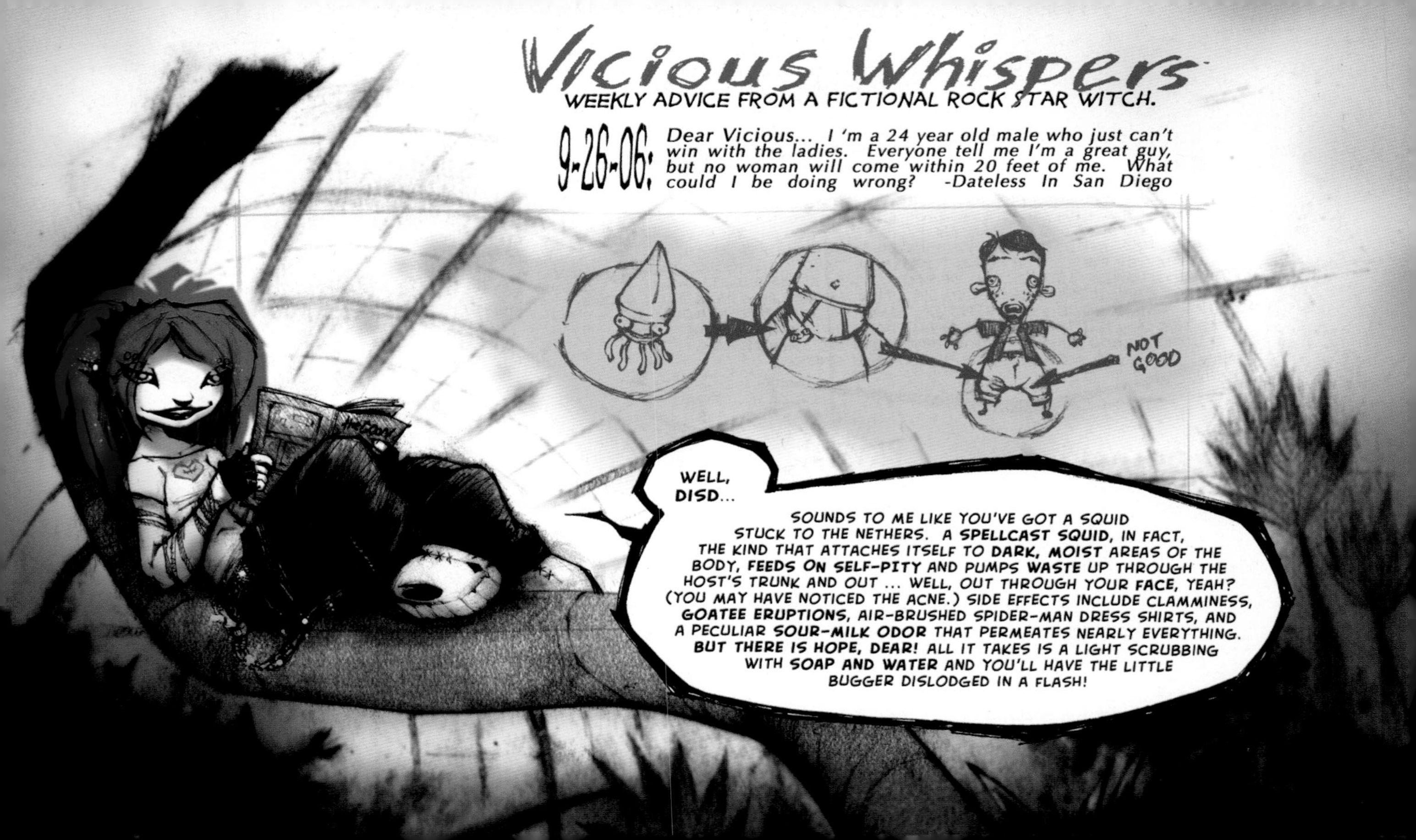
Vicious Whispers
WEEKLY ADVICE FROM A FICTIONAL ROCK STAR WITCH.
9-26-06: Dear Vicious... I 'm a 24 year old male who just can't win with the ladies. Everyone tell me I'm a great guy, but no woman will come within 20 feet of me. What could I be doing wrong? -Dateless In San Diego
NOT GOOD
WELL, DISD...
SOUNDS TO ME LIKE YOU'VE GOT A SQUID STUCK TO THE NETHERS. A **SPELLCAST SQUID**, IN FACT, THE KIND THAT ATTACHES ITSELF TO **DARK, MOIST** AREAS OF THE BODY, **FEEDS ON SELF-PITY** AND PUMPS **WASTE** UP THROUGH THE HOST'S TRUNK AND OUT ... WELL, OUT THROUGH YOUR **FACE**, YEAH? (YOU MAY HAVE NOTICED THE ACNE.) SIDE EFFECTS INCLUDE CLAMMINESS, **GOATEE ERUPTIONS**, AIR-BRUSHED SPIDER-MAN DRESS SHIRTS, AND A PECULIAR **SOUR-MILK ODOR** THAT PERMEATES NEARLY EVERYTHING. **BUT THERE IS HOPE, DEAR!** ALL IT TAKES IS A LIGHT SCRUBBING WITH **SOAP AND WATER** AND YOU'LL HAVE THE LITTLE BUGGER DISLODGED IN A FLASH!

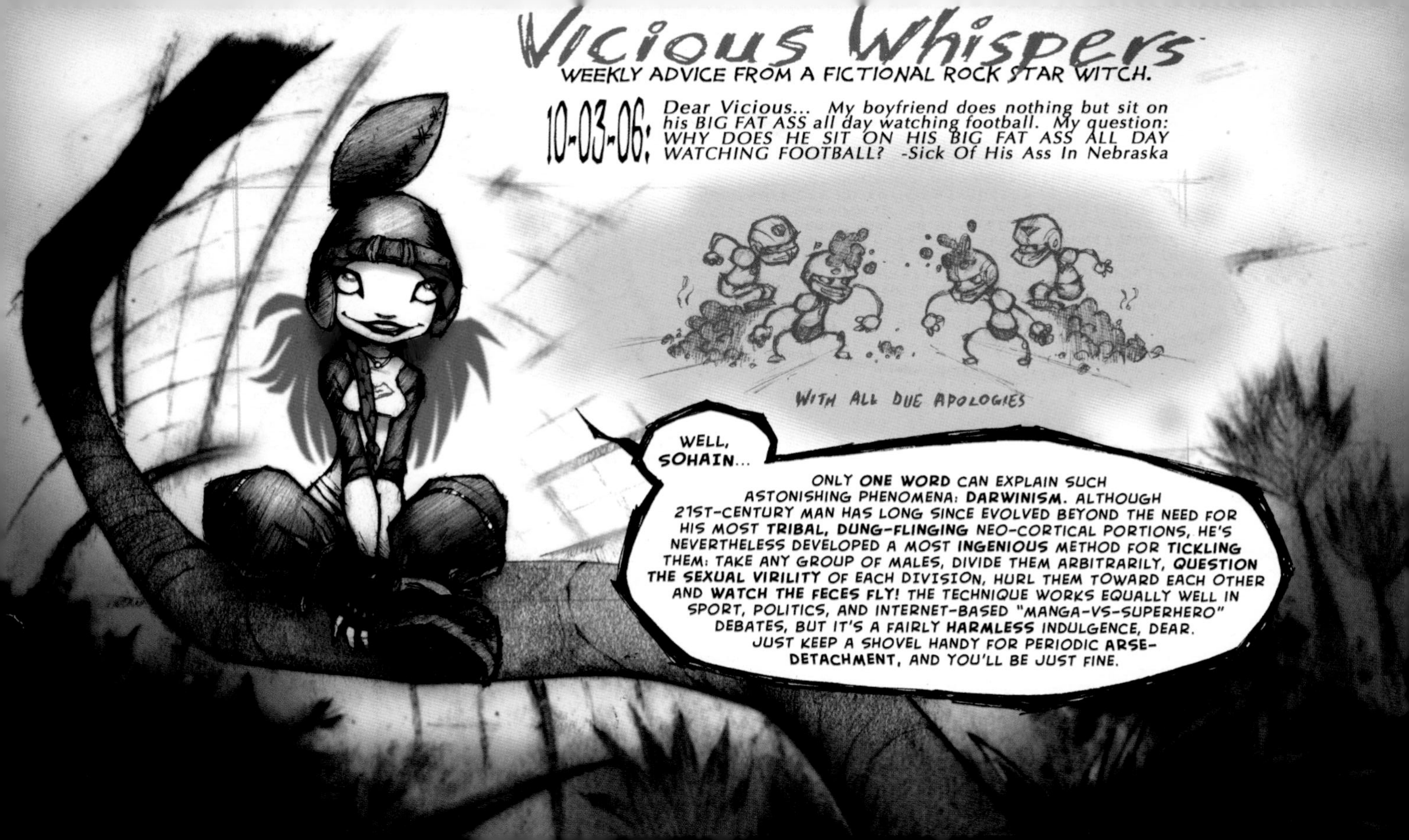
Vicious Whispers
WEEKLY ADVICE FROM A FICTIONAL ROCK STAR WITCH.
10-03-06:
Dear Vicious... My boyfriend does nothing but sit on his BIG FAT ASS all day watching football. My question: WHY DOES HE SIT ON HIS BIG FAT ASS ALL DAY WATCHING FOOTBALL? -Sick Of His Ass In Nebraska
WITH ALL DUE APOLOGIES
WELL, SOHAIN...
ONLY ONE WORD CAN EXPLAIN SUCH ASTONISHING PHENOMENA: DARWINISM. ALTHOUGH 21ST-CENTURY MAN HAS LONG SINCE EVOLVED BEYOND THE NEED FOR HIS MOST TRIBAL, DUNG-FLINGING NEO-CORTICAL PORTIONS, HE'S NEVERTHELESS DEVELOPED A MOST INGENIOUS METHOD FOR TICKLING THEM: TAKE ANY GROUP OF MALES, DIVIDE THEM ARBITRARILY, QUESTION THE SEXUAL VIRILITY OF EACH DIVISION, HURL THEM TOWARD EACH OTHER AND WATCH THE FECES FLY! THE TECHNIQUE WORKS EQUALLY WELL IN SPORT, POLITICS, AND INTERNET-BASED "MANGA-VS-SUPERHERO" DEBATES, BUT IT'S A FAIRLY HARMLESS INDULGENCE, DEAR. JUST KEEP A SHOVEL HANDY FOR PERIODIC ARSE-DETACHMENT, AND YOU'LL BE JUST FINE.

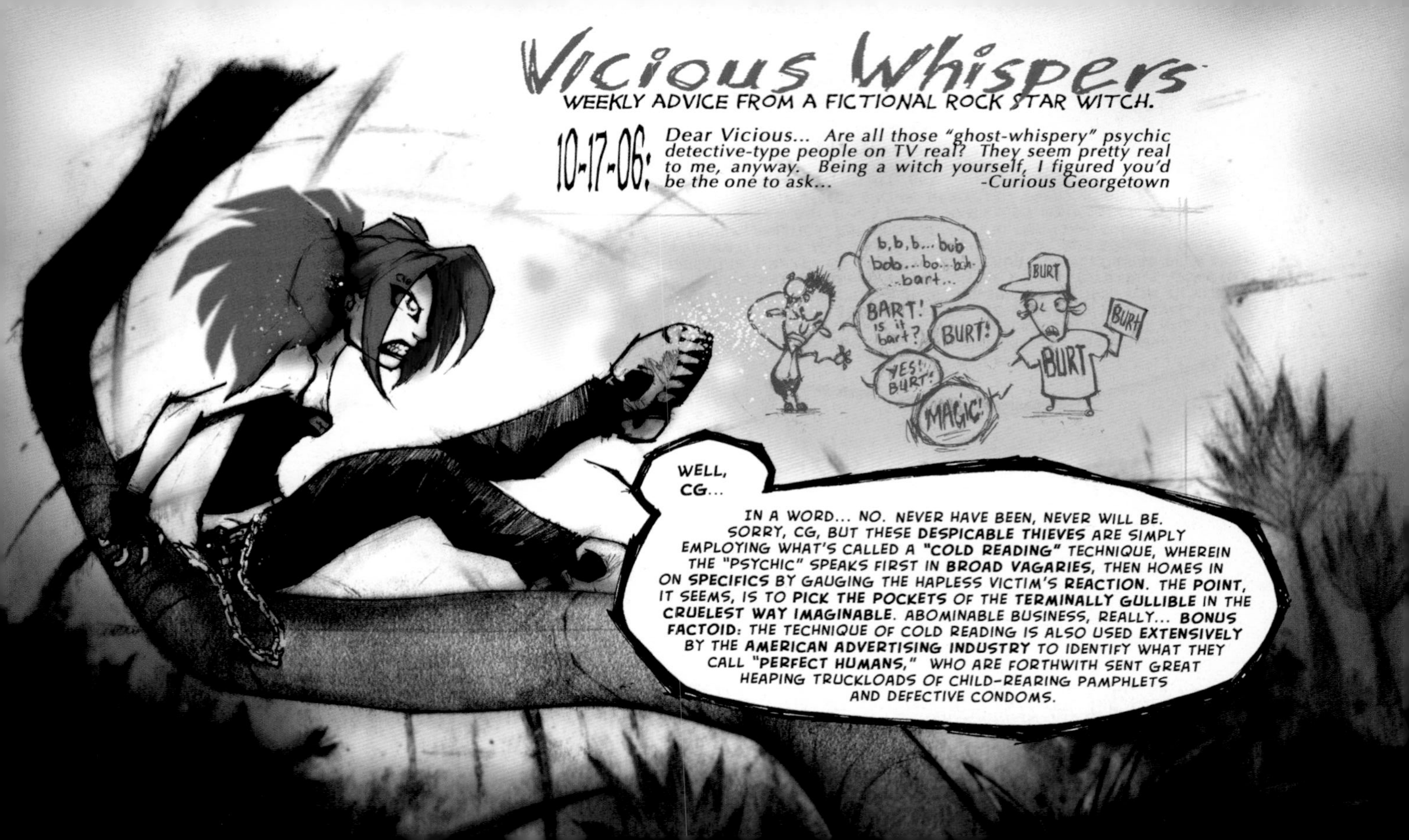
Vicious Whispers
WEEKLY ADVICE FROM A FICTIONAL ROCK STAR WITCH.
10-17-06:
Dear Vicious... Are all those "ghost-whispery" psychic detective-type people on TV real? They seem pretty real to me, anyway. Being a witch yourself, I figured you'd be the one to ask...
-Curious Georgetown
b, b, b... bub bob... bo... boh... bart...
BART! is it bart?
BURT!
YES! BURT!
MAGIC!
BURT
BURT
BURT
WELL, CG...
IN A WORD... NO. NEVER HAVE BEEN, NEVER WILL BE. SORRY, CG, BUT THESE DESPICABLE THIEVES ARE SIMPLY EMPLOYING WHAT'S CALLED A "COLD READING" TECHNIQUE, WHEREIN THE "PSYCHIC" SPEAKS FIRST IN BROAD VAGARIES, THEN HOMES IN ON SPECIFICS BY GAUGING THE HAPLESS VICTIM'S REACTION. THE POINT, IT SEEMS, IS TO PICK THE POCKETS OF THE TERMINALLY GULLIBLE IN THE CRUELEST WAY IMAGINABLE. ABOMINABLE BUSINESS, REALLY... BONUS FACTOID: THE TECHNIQUE OF COLD READING IS ALSO USED EXTENSIVELY BY THE AMERICAN ADVERTISING INDUSTRY TO IDENTIFY WHAT THEY CALL "PERFECT HUMANS," WHO ARE FORTHWITH SENT GREAT HEAPING TRUCKLOADS OF CHILD-REARING PAMPHLETS AND DEFECTIVE CONDOMS.

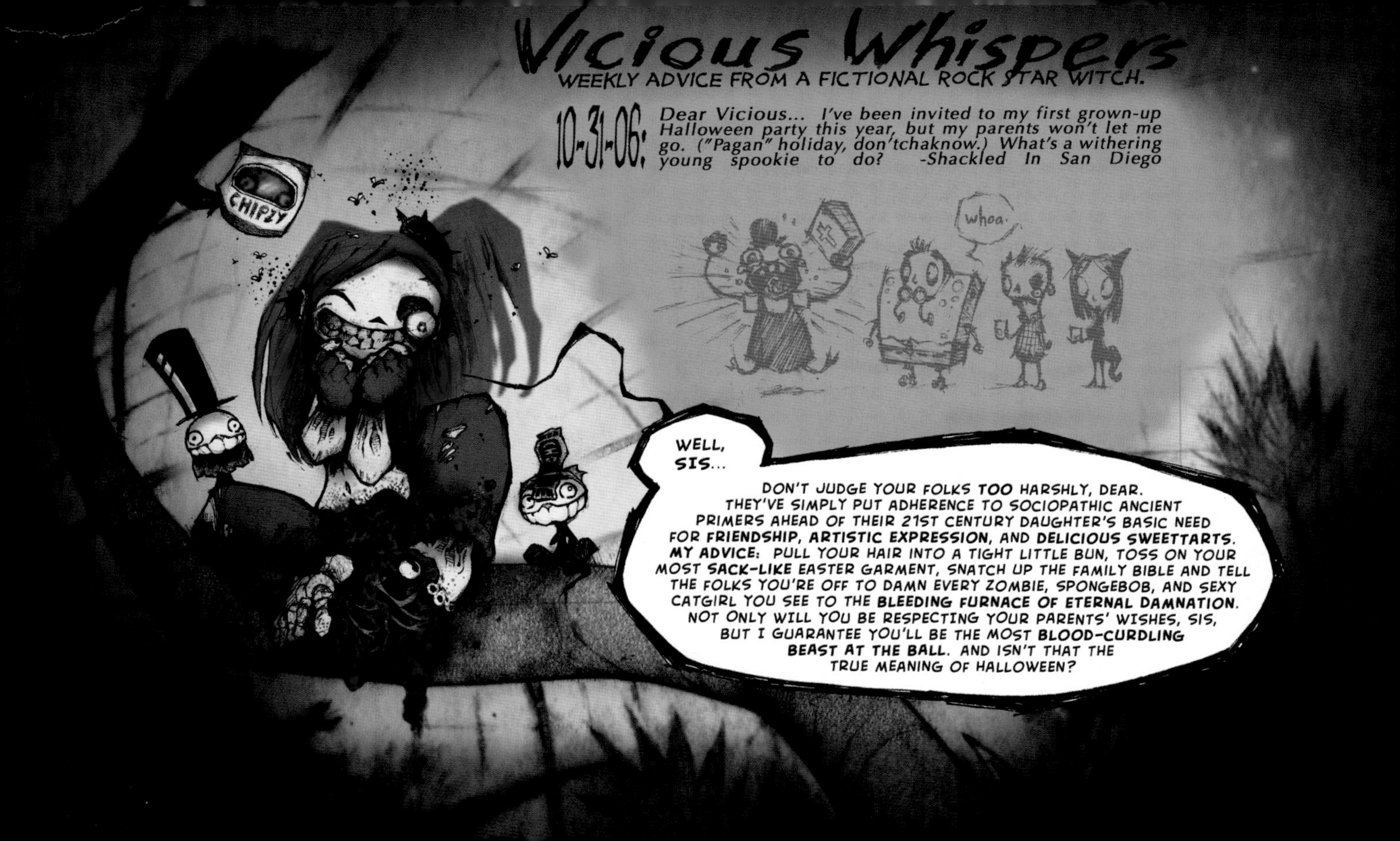
Vicious Whispers
WEEKLY ADVICE FROM A FICTIONAL ROCK STAR WITCH.
10-31-06:
Dear Vicious... I've been invited to my first grown-up Halloween party this year, but my parents won't let me go. ("Pagan" holiday, don'tchaknow.) What's a withering young spookie to do? -Shackled In San Diego
CHIPZY
whoa.
WELL, SIS...
DON'T JUDGE YOUR FOLKS **TOO** HARSHLY, DEAR. THEY'VE SIMPLY PUT ADHERENCE TO SOCIOPATHIC ANCIENT PRIMERS AHEAD OF THEIR 21ST CENTURY DAUGHTER'S BASIC NEED FOR **FRIENDSHIP, ARTISTIC EXPRESSION,** AND **DELICIOUS SWEETTARTS. MY ADVICE:** PULL YOUR HAIR INTO A TIGHT LITTLE BUN, TOSS ON YOUR MOST **SACK-LIKE** EASTER GARMENT, SNATCH UP THE FAMILY BIBLE AND TELL THE FOLKS YOU'RE OFF TO DAMN EVERY ZOMBIE, SPONGEBOB, AND SEXY CATGIRL YOU SEE TO THE **BLEEDING FURNACE OF ETERNAL DAMNATION.** NOT ONLY WILL YOU BE RESPECTING YOUR PARENTS' WISHES, SIS, BUT I GUARANTEE YOU'LL BE THE MOST **BLOOD-CURDLING BEAST AT THE BALL.** AND ISN'T THAT THE TRUE MEANING OF HALLOWEEN?

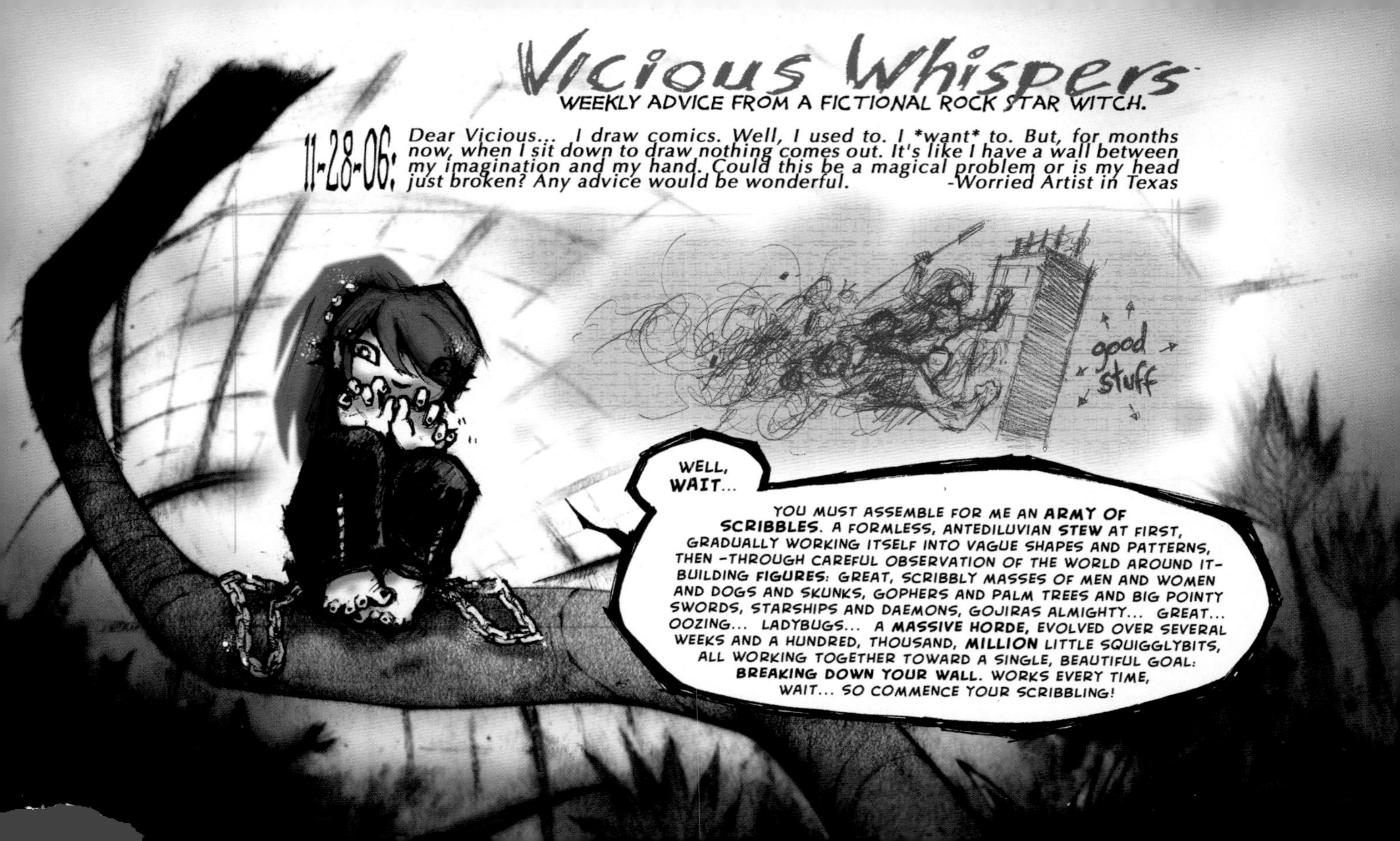
Vicious Whispers
WEEKLY ADVICE FROM A FICTIONAL ROCK STAR WITCH.
11-28-06:
Dear Vicious... I draw comics. Well, I used to. I *want* to. But, for months now, when I sit down to draw nothing comes out. It's like I have a wall between my imagination and my hand. Could this be a magical problem or is my head just broken? Any advice would be wonderful. -Worried Artist in Texas
good stuff
WELL, WAIT...
YOU MUST ASSEMBLE FOR ME AN ARMY OF SCRIBBLES. A FORMLESS, ANTEDILUVIAN STEW AT FIRST, GRADUALLY WORKING ITSELF INTO VAGUE SHAPES AND PATTERNS, THEN -THROUGH CAREFUL OBSERVATION OF THE WORLD AROUND IT- BUILDING FIGURES: GREAT, SCRIBBLY MASSES OF MEN AND WOMEN AND DOGS AND SKUNKS, GOPHERS AND PALM TREES AND BIG POINTY SWORDS, STARSHIPS AND DAEMONS, GOJIRAS ALMIGHTY... GREAT... OOZING... LADYBUGS... A MASSIVE HORDE, EVOLVED OVER SEVERAL WEEKS AND A HUNDRED, THOUSAND, MILLION LITTLE SQUIGGLYBITS, ALL WORKING TOGETHER TOWARD A SINGLE, BEAUTIFUL GOAL: BREAKING DOWN YOUR WALL. WORKS EVERY TIME, WAIT... SO COMMENCE YOUR SCRIBBLING!